TRADITIONAL OKINAWAN KARATE THE TRANSFORMATION OF TIY (手)

First Volume

Without knowing about *tiy*, one cannot talk about karate.

Koei Nohara

Translated from Japanese by
Wesley Ueunten and Naoki Namihira

Contents 第一巻 First volume

Introduction

Emerging during the historical formation of the Ryukyuan Kingdom, *tiy* developed over many years before it reached the Japanese mainland, where it became known as karate. From Japan, karate spread to 150 countries around the world and is now practiced by 50 million *karateka*. Karate will likely continue to flourish. However, during its rapid internationalization, the meaning associated with karate has changed drastically from its original intent. Karate began as a killing method on the battlefield and later transformed into a "living technique" or a *budo* (martial art for the cultivation of mind, body, and spirit. But as karate expanded globally after World War II, it has been reduced to a sport where the focus is on winning and losing.

From an anthropological perspective, the phenomenon where a cultural tradition is disseminated from one society to another is very interesting. We cannot only note how the traditional techniques themselves change in the receiving society, whose value system and concept of competition are different, but we can also observe how the meanings associated with those techniques as well as the philosophical approach also change. This may be best symbolized in the current debate over making karate an Olympic sport. Similar to karate, judo developed as an ancient martial technique before spreading throughout Japan and internationally. When judo became an Olympic sport, there was a gradual deviation from the original standards of judging victory, proficiency, and *gi* (technique that is rooted in Japanese tradition. The Western tendency toward quantitative measurement (as seen in the point system for determining the winner had a subtle influence on the very character of judo *gi*, which is based in Eastern thought as expressed by such sayings as *go no sen* (wait and see before attacking and *niku wo kirashite hone wo kiru* (take a flesh wound from your opponent before cutting him/her to the bone.

—

4

One may argue that this state of affairs merely represents the conflict between old and new. From this perspective, it would seem inevitable that Japan's ancient traditional martial arts would become a global modern sport. On the other hand, however, Okinawan and Japanese practitioners feel a sense of crisis as the cultivation of self through training both mind and body gives way to the emphasis on entertainment and competitiveness in sports. This phenomenon is not limited to karate, but can also be seen in the conflict between tradition and modernity and between cultural nationalism and internationalism in Japan.

The current debate over karate as an Olympic sport has reached intense levels not only in Japan, but in the international karate community as well. However, because the divisions in the debate are related to the different understandings of *karatedo*, the more fruitful discussion would be over the more fundamentally essential question of "What is karatedo?" In fact, when we look back through the history of karate, we see that the philosophical differences over karatedo have been around longer than it may seem. Many karateka in Okinawa were already feeling a sense of crises over the changes in the late 1950s and early 1960s when karate evolved as a competitive sport after being adopted in the Japanese mainland. The discussion over the essential character of karate, however, happened only after the global spread of karate had reached a critical mass. Consequently, from the perspective of Okinawan karateka, the discussion over "What is karate?" is both old and new.

I began learning the Shuri-te style of *Okinawa karate* with its 1,000 year tradition as a child and am writing from the perspective of a teacher of this style. One could say that I take a traditional conservative position toward the internationalization of karate and the question of the essential nature of karate. To begin with, the motivation for this book was the irresistible desire to pursue the true essence of karate. However, in an attempt to control my own personal feelings and subjectivity, I hope to objectively explore anthropological issues of cultural propagation and cultural transformation, or as expressed in a more recent term, transculturation. I focus on how Okinawa karate, whose name originated as *"Tiy"* (before becoming *"Tūdiy"* and traveling to mainland Japan where it became known as "Karate" and then spread throughout the world), has been accepted globally and the changes it has undergone. I also look at how karate is understood by its teachers and students in foreign countries as well as the expectations for karate in the future, especially the international controversies surrounding the entry of competitive karate to the Olympics.

While looking for keys to understand karate through the study of the precious work of earlier researchers, I take a global perspective and gather the opinions of karate enthusiasts and practitioners in foreign countries to find out what kind of actual changes karate has undergone and what are the characteristics of karate in foreign countries as seen in the judging standards of *kata* and *waza*. In shedding light on the present realities of karate, I seek to deal with the questions of what karate is and what it should be in the future. I believe that this kind of research has been rare up to now.

As I have pointed out, we are at a point in time where it is crucial to seriously think about the essence of karate. I believe that without telling the history of Okinawa karate as the origin of karate, it is not possible to talk about the essence of karate. Therefore, I begin this book by identifying karate's essential characteristics by following the history of Okinawa karate's origins and developmental changes. I then observe the changes in karate in the process of its absorption in the present age of globalization from different perspectives. Finally, I express my ideas about the tasks and hopes by addressing the question of what karate should be in its ideal form. I narrow down my approach as follows:

1) I look at the cultural, martial arts, and global aspects of Okinawa karate, which is the original form of karate. That is, by observing the changes in the original *tiy*, I attempt to shed light on the essence of karate by addressing the question, "What is karate?"

2) While tracing the changes of *tiy* as the original karate, I clarify the difference between traditional karate and competitive karate and between martial arts karate and sports karate. In doing so, I discuss the ideal form of karate.

Based on the above, I conclude the book by presenting my opinions on the role of Okinawa karate and what the responsibility of Okinawa karateka should be.

Although karate has spread widely throughout the world, the understanding of its techniques, forms, and purpose have changed slightly in the countries it has spread to based on differences in culture. In Okinawa and Japan, we have seen the move from "karate as a martial art" to "karate as a sport." Consequently, the understanding of *kata* has changed as well as the motivation and goals of training. Instead of self-discipline, the emphasis is on competitiveness and winning or losing.

The essence of Okinawa karate is rooted in exacting a mortal blow. Okinawa karate originated in Okinawa's *gusuku* period as a method for bringing down an opponent with one strike. The techniques of karate in their formal state were born in the process of polishing such skills. A consciousness for determining the form of such techniques was also born simultaneously. It follows that the essence of karate is in the mortal blow techniques, which developed both mind and body training. The single blow that determines life or death has to be the essence of karate. However, in competitive karate, dangerous punches to the head, kicks to the groin, and other tactics are prohibited. This priority for safety has resulted in the unavoidable deviation of karate from its original essence. In its present competitive form, karate has strayed from its essence because it can only be performed as hypothetical punches or kicks.

Upon looking back at the history of karate's development and understanding the original nature of karate by clearly identifying the changes it has undergone, I cannot help but feel strongly that the estrangement of karate from its essence grows in proportion to its spread to the rest of the world.

However, this phenomenon can perhaps be examined by again asking the question "What is karate?" as part of the discussion over karate's true nature.

In traditional karate, unlike in sports, victory is not the primary goal. In other words, matches were not held to determine a winner. Karate is a means and method for lifelong self-discipline. However, the goal of present-day competitive karate is to win matches, which leads to situations where practitioners quit when their competitive careers end. In traditional martial arts karate, karate is for life.

However, among the foreign Okinawan karate enthusiasts I have come in contact with, I have met those who actually emphasize the significance of traditional Okinawan karate and oppose or question the making of karate into a competitive Olympic sport. Such sentiments were manifested more frequently than I expected in the results of a survey I conducted (on Westerners) and in interviews with three internationally prominent karateka.

What do the above findings suggest? Despite the mainstream flow toward the internationalization of karate, or perhaps because of it, it seems to me that interest in traditional karate has been heightened and that "Okinawan karate" is a brand name that has attracted attention throughout the world. It is notable that the more karate becomes internationalized, the higher the brand value of Okinawan karate is. The questions of how to protect traditional Ryukyuan *tiy* from the effects of present-day sports karate and how to preserve the pure martial arts culture are certain to profoundly influence the historical course of karate from now into the future.

Chapter 1 Cultural Aspects of Okinawan Karate Part 1

The Transformation of Okinawa Traditional Karate *Tiy* (手)

Section 1 Background of The Emergence of *Tiy*

Karatedō has its origins in Ryūkyū, more commonly known as Okinawa. Starting from the 7th century, Ryūkyū underwent a long period of history that was characterized by numerous *gusuku* or fortresses from which warlords called *aji* (or *anji*) competed for supremacy. The fighting techniques that were used during that period are unique to Ryūkyū and are called *Tiy*. *Karate* is firmly rooted in *Tiy*. Why did *Tiy* emerge and develop in Ryūkyū? The key to answering this question requires looking at the historical context that includes the aforementioned *gusuku* period as well as the formation of the Ryūkyū Kingdom, tributary relations with the Ming Dynasty, King Shō Shin's sword confiscation, a golden era of Ryukyuan trade, and Satsuma's invasion and subsequent prohibition of weapons. It would be difficult, if not impossible, to talk about Okinawan *Tiy* without examining it in the context of Ryukyuan history. To understand Okinawan karate, we must look at Ryukyuan history as backdrop for the development of *Tiy*.

The people of the Ryukyu

What is now known as the Ryukyuan Archipelago was connected to continental China until about 1.5 million years ago. The formation of three island groups the archipelago happened about 20,000 years ago during the Last Glacial Maximum. The islands were much larger than what they are now and the Ryukyuan Archipelago only took its present shape when ocean levels rose by about 100 meters after the end of the ice age.

Humans first appeared on Earth around 3 million years ago during the Pleistocene Period. It is believed that human evolution went through the primate, primitive man, paleoanthropic man, and homo sapien stages. Nakahashi Takahiro claims in his book *The Origins of Japanese* (日本人の起源 that all modern humans can be traced back about 200,000 years to a single female in Africa. Further, Hōrai Satoshi makes the following highly interesting hypothesis in *DNA Human Evolution Studies* (DNA 人類進化学). Using nucleotide diversity net value DA to assess the association between eight groups (Africans, Europeans, indigenous Americans, Ainu, Chinese, Ryukyuans, Koreans, and mainland Japanese), he concludes that Africans are the most genetically distant from the other groups. Conversely, the five East Asian groups have very small genetic differences from each other. This is especially true for Koreans and mainland Japanese who have a genetic distance of zero. This confirms the fact that Koreans and Japanese share a very close relationship to each other.

Using the genetic distance between groups, we can locate the origins of humans as Africans from whom Europeans and indigenous Americans branched off from. The five East Asian groups are part a single branch in this lineage that emerged most recently. Among the five groups, the Ainu formed a sub-branch the earliest, followed by the Chinese. Next to branch off were the Ryukyuans and the last to branch off were Koreans and Japanese mainlanders who remain closely related. Consequently, it is argued that Ainu and Ryukyuans are Jomon people while mainland Japanese are Yayoi people. However, one must point out that although there is a close genetic relationship between Ainu and Ryukyuans, with the influx of new groups during the Yayoi period, the two groups developed into separate groups.

In other words, it has been Ryukyuans, descendants of Jomon people, who first created *Tiy* and it has been the Japanese, descendants of Yayoi people, who have developed *Tiy* into *karate*. There have been various discoveries of the remains of Paleolithic people in the Ryūkyū Archipelago including: the 32,000-year-old Yamashita Cave Man (discovered in Naha City in 1962), the 30,000-year-old Yonehara Man (Ishigaki City, 1966), the 25,000-year-old Pinzaabu Man (Ueno Village, Miyako, 1979), the 20,000-year-old Iegohezu Man (Ie Village, 1977), the 18,000-year-old Minatogawa Man (Gushikawa Village, 1967), the 18,000-year-old Ōyama Man (Ginowan City, 1966), and the 15,000-year-old Shimojibaru Cave Man (Gushikawa Village, Kume Island, 1983). The aforementioned Yamashita Cave Man discovery, which included fragments of the thigh and shin bones of an approximately 7-year-old child, are the oldest human bones to have been found anywhere in Japan.

"Ryūkyū" and "Okinawa"

The Ryukyuan descendants of the Jomon have believed from ancient times in Nirai Kanai. Nirai Kanai is a paradise that exists across the ocean and beyond the horizon of the world that we presently live in. As if to symbolize the yearning to go to Nirai Kanai, since before World War II, Okinawa has had the highest proportion of overseas emigrants among all prefectures in Japan. There are about 360,000 *Uchinanchu* in Brazil, Argentina, Peru, Hawai'i, the U.S. mainland, and Canada.

Every five years, a large five-day World Uchinanchu Festival is held in Okinawa to welcome first, second, third, and fourth generation overseas Okinawans. Okinawa is the only prefecture in Japan to hold such an event for its overseas emigrants. In the years leading up to each Festival, teachers, artists, and performers from Okinawa go overseas to share Okinawan culture in regions where there are sizable populations of Okinawans. These overseas cultural performances always include Ryukyuan dance, music, and karate. Among these, it is obvious that karate is the most widely spread aspect of Okinawan culture in the world. For overseas Okinawans, these Okinawa cultural performances revive memories of a faraway homeland and confirm and bolster their Okinawa identity.

Here it is necessary to contextualize the terms "Ryūkyū," "Okinawa," "Ryukyuan," and "Okinawan." Although the name "Ryūkyū" (琉球) is has been most commonly used in history, there have been other names used such as "Ryūkyū (流求 [note difference in second character])," "Ryūgu (龍宮)," "Uruma (石流間)," and "Kyūyou (球陽)." The characters for "Ryūkyū" (琉求) first appear in *Ryūkyū Koku Den* (流求国伝) of the *Sui Sho* (隋書), the official history of the Sui Dynasty (605 AD). The *Shinkō Okinawa Issennen Shi* writes that, "Because the islands looked like a long serpentine dinosaur floating on the faraway ocean, they were first named Ryūkyū using the characters 流礼 and later 琉球." Other characters used for "Ryūkyū" included 流求, 瑠求, 留求, 流礼, 竜礼, 流鬼, 瑠球, and 留仇. During the Chinese Sui Dynasty the characters 琉球 were used. In the Yuan Dynasty 流礼 were the preferred characters, but in the Ming Dynasty, 琉球 were used again. In China, Okinawa was called "Greater Ryūkyū (大琉球)," while Taiwan was called "Lesser Ryūkyū (小琉球)."

The name "Okinawa" first appears in *Tōdaiwajōtōseiden* and Shoku *Nihongi* that both wrote about Ganjin who had come from Tang China during the Nara Period. According to these accounts, the fleet of ships that carried envoys to T'ang China along with Ganjin and others left the Chinese port of Suzhou on November 16, 753. On November 20, the third ship in the fleet landed at "Akinawa (Okinawa)." The first and second ships landed there on November 21. Ganjin then passed through Ekkyu (Yaku) Island and Ata-Gun in Satsuma-*kuni* before reaching the capital city of Nara in 754. According to these accounts, Ganjin spent about 14 days on Okinawa after landing there.

Subsequently, the characters used for Okinawa included 於幾奈波, 悪鬼納, and 倭寇奈. It is believed that the present characters 沖縄 were first used by Arai Hakuseki (1657-1752) in his Nanto Shi (South Island Journal) because the islands stretched north to south like a long, thin rope (縄) in the offing (沖). These characters became standard from 1872.

One could say that Okinawa is the islands' Japanese name and Ryūkyū is their Chinese name. Similarly, until Ryūkyū became part of Japan, Ryukyuans had both "Japanese" and "Chinese" names. For example, the Japanese name of the founder of *Shui-tiy* (Shuri-te), Bushi Matsumura Pēchin, was Matsumura Sōkon. His Chinese name was Wu Cheng Da (武成達). Because the names of many Ryukyuan *karate* masters of the past were written in Chinese, people have been quick to believe that *karate* was simply of Chinese origin. This assumption that *karate* is Chinese merely because the names of *karate* masters and *kata* were Chinese must be examined more closely.

Further, in historical records, the name "Ryūkyū" appeared 148 years before "Okinawa" does. The name "Ryūkyū" testifies to the islands' closer relationship to China than to Japan. Although "Okinawa" is most commonly used, "Ryūkyū" was used historically for over a millennium. The common use of "Okinawa" has only a 130-year history and did not begin until after the abolishment of the Ryukyuan Kingdom in 1879. In fact, many Chinese still fondly refer to Okinawa as "Ryūkyū." Many Japanese may be in for a surprise when they fly from Taipei to Naha on China Airlines since the destination for this route is listed as "Ryūkyū" rather than "Okinawa." Perhaps it is a veiled refutation of the Meiji Government's forcible annexation of Ryukyuan Kingdom.

The Warring Period of Gusuku Aji

According to *Ryūkyū Koku Den* (流求国伝) of the *Zui Sho* (隋書) and Shoku Nihongi (続日本紀), at the beginning of the 8th century a sort of class system had formed with powerful lords unifying different regions in Ryūkyū. Leaders at the village level were given the status of "petty kings."

However, each of these small sovereignties was self-sufficient and none had large advantages over the other. The person with the highest authority acted as "petty king" who made decisions that pertained to events, marriage, and other matters connected to the status of community members based on the opinion of the people under his rule. Such petty kings expanded their territory to increase agricultural output or for other reasons. As adjacent sovereignties merged, *gusuku* (forts or castles were constructed and eventually powerful leaders emerged to control unified territories. Thus in the 11th century, we see in Okinawa the construction of *gusuku* as well as the production of pottery. In the 12th century, Goryeo tile was produced for Urashī (Urasoe) *gusuku*. Shunten became the *Aji* of Urashī Gusuku in 1180.

The Ryūkyū Kingdom period begins with Shunten's accession to the throne in 1187. The period endures 692 years until the Ryūkyū Kingdom is dismantled under the 1879 *haihan chiken* (Abolition of clans and establishment of prefectures. Starting from before Minamoto Yoritomo established Kamakura shogunate in 1192, the Ryūkyū Kingdom period stretches through Japan's Northern-Southern Dynasty, Muromachi, Azuchi Momoyama, and Edō periods and up to the 11th year of the Meiji period.

There were about 400 *gusuku* in Ryūkyū during the *aji* warring period. In 1405, King Shō Hashi defeated King Bunei. The royal line of Satto ended after only two generations (56 years). Shō Hashi installed his father Shishō as king and began working to improve the government. Shō Hashi unified the three kingdoms by defeating Hananchi, the king of Hokuzan *gusuku,* in 1416 and capturing Tarumai, the king of Nanzan in 1429. Shō Hashi had become king upon his father Shishō's death in 1421 and remained in that position until 1439 when he died at age 68.

進貢船 (Shinkōsen)

The founder of the Second Shō Dynasty, King Shō En (Kanamaru) was originally of the peasant class on the island of Iheya.

The Chinese Ming Dynasty began in 1368. In the same year, the Goryeo Kingdom on the Korean Peninsula collapsed and the Chosun Dynasty emerged to take its place. In Japan, the Muromachi Shogunate had been established in 1338 and the Northern and Southern Dynasties were unified in 1392. It was during this time of turbulent changes in East Asia that the Ming Dynasty began its Sakuhō system that established a new international order with China at the center. Under the Sakuhō system, surrounding countries acknowledged their subordination to China as vassal kingdoms. These countries also were allowed to carry out trade with China under this system.

According to the *Rekidai Hoan* (a collection of documents and drafts related to diplomatic relations during the successive generations of Ryūkyūan kings), the trade partners of Ryūkyū included Siam, Fuzhou, Canton, Annam, Ayutthaya, Pattani, Malacca, Palembang, Satsuma, Hakata, and Korea. Goods exported from Ryūkyū included Ryūkyūan sulfur, Chinese silk and porcelain, and Japanese swords and fans. From Southeast Asia, Ryūkyūan traders brought back *sappan* (for dyeing), pepper, liquor, and ivory. In the 16th century, however, Portuguese and Spanish entered Manila in 16th century and began trading with Southeast Asia and China. Wakō pirates were also making frequent raids. These factors led to the gradual decline in Ryūkyūan entrepot trade.

Ryūkyū the Country of Salute

Shō Hashi's son Shō Shin was born in 1465. He had barely reached the age of 13 when he ascended the throne. He ruled for 50 years until his death in 1526, the longest reign of any Ryukyuan king. During his reign, he increased trade missions to China from once every three years to once a year and conquered Akahachi in Yaeyama to the south. He also used the financial resources that had accumulated during his predecessor's time to back his project to gather the weapons of the *aji* in the surrounding regions and to bring them to the capital of Shuri where he could keep watch over them. By doing so, he was able to prevent any possible revolt and succeeded in bringing long-term peace. This has been the most heralded of his many achievements. The governance of Shō Shin's time is extolled in detail on the Momo Urasoe Rankan no Mei (百浦添欄干之銘: literally "One Hundred Inscriptions of the Handrail of Urasoe") inscribed on the stone monument erected in 1509 in front of the main hall at Shuri Castle.

Among other things, we must understand that the undertakings carried out under Shō Shin's rule required enormous amounts of expenditures and time. During his reign, the royal family's temple (Enkakuji) and tomb (Tamudun), Sunuhyan Utaki, Bengatake Utaki, and other structures were constructed. Enkakuji, erected in 1492, is the site of Goshōdō (which enshrines the ancestral tablets of the royal family), Hōjō Bridge, Enkan Pond, and Kyōdō Hall. Kyōdō Hall is a repository of Buddhist texts that were presented to Shō Toku by the Korean king. Tamaudun was built around 1501 and entombs the remains of kings and other members of the royal family who died after its construction.

A jeweled sword called "Chiganemaru" and *madama* (ceremonial jewel) are kept in the Kokuōkotokuhi that was built on the eastern side of the Shinkyūdō (north of the Enkakuji Soshindō). Records indicated that they were gifts from Nakasone Tuimiyā, the king of Miyako Island to Shō Shin, and signify the subordination of the Shō Shin's rule over Miyako. Nishitori, who built the stone gate of Sunuhyan Utaki located in front of the Kankai Entrance of Shuri Castle in 1524, was from Dakidun (Taketomi) in the southern islands of Yaeyama. He later returned and laid the foundation for governance over Yaeyama as he established rule as "Dakidun Shui (Shuri) Ufuyaku."

A description of Shō Shin's confiscation of weapons from the *aji* in the kingdom in 1509 is found in the Momo Urasoe Rankan no Mei. The inscription says, "Garments made of brocade, implements use gold and silver. Swords, sabers, bows, and arrows were gathered for the protection of the country. The weapons of this country are not to be used against another country." It was in this way that the peace-loving king prohibited the individual possession of swords, bows, and arrows. After making weapons national property, the king imposed central authority to encourage trade, beautify cities, and promote art. Simultaneously, however, Shō Sei also over saw the construction of Yara Zarin Gusuku to protect the kingdom from outside enemies in 1553. It is also said that he put resources into defense projects such as the 1554 erection of two cannon platforms at Naha Harbor.

The central government of the Ryūkyū Kingdom was organized under the Regent, the *Sanshikan* (Council of Three), and the Ministers of 15 administrative departments (Council of Fifteen). The regional governing structure was set up through branch offices located in each of the districts of the main island of Okinawa. The leader of a particular district was called *jitudē*. Below the *jitudē* administrative duties were divided among such officials as *banmē kata, kuraati kata, sachi aratami kata, satū ati kata, kūsaku kata,* and *yama ati kata.* All of these regional officials were under the supervision of the central government in Shuri and carried out its orders as well as the division of farmland and the protection of forests.

In Yaeyama and Miyako, branch offices of the government called *kuramutu* were set up. Officials from the central government were sent to these branch offices to oversee the governance of these regions. The head of each *kuramutu* was called *kashira* and each *majiri* (district) was assigned a *kashira*. Under the *kashira*, were *shui ufuyaku, yunchu, ufumizashi, ufuhissha, waki mizashi, mizashi, sūyukumi, waka tikugu, kūsaku hissha, subayama hissha*, and other officials. In Miyako, the *mizashi, yunchu,* and *kurahissha* elected a *kashira* from among the *shui ufuyaku*.

The central government structure started around the time that the three kingdoms were unified and was expanded during King Shō Shin's rule. It was strengthened during the era of Shō Shō Gen when government reforms were carried out. During the time of Sai On, the central governing structure took on a pyramid structure.

In 1689, the Office of Genealogies (系図座) was established and *samurē* (samurai) families living in Shuri, Naha, and Kume Village were ordered to compile genealogies that traced their blood lineage back to their founding ancestors. One copy of each genealogy was kept at the Office of Genealogies and the other copy was affixed with the Royal seal and returned to the family to which it belonged. The genealogy was the official document that proved a person's *samurē* status and anyone who had possession of one was called "*kēmuchi* (系持ち = or possessor of a genealogy)" and was accorded special privileges as a member of the ruling class. Genealogies for *samurē* in Miyako, Yaeyama, and Kume island groups were compiled later in 1729.

The king stood at the apex of the class system under the Ryukyuan Kingdom which was divided into three classes: lords (大名), warriors (士), and farmers (農民). Under the king were nine classes of *samurē*: *ū, ūji, aji, uēkata, pēchin, satunushi, chikudun, shūsē, and niyā*.

Satsuma's Ryūkyū Invasion

Satsuma and Ryūkyū shared a close, almost sibling-like, relation until 1591. The relation soured after Toyotomi Hideyoshi demanded that Ryūkyū cooperate in his mission to conquer Korea. Hideyoshi sent orders through Satsuma for Ryūkyū to supply 7,500 men and 10-months-worth of food. The dismayed Ryūkyū quickly dispatched a report to China while delaying its response to Satsuma. China did not make a response and the Ryukyuan government was placed in a difficult predicament in the face of repeated demands by Satsuma. Ryūkyū procured and sent most of what was ordered, but it did not respond to further demands. When King Shō Nei received official envoys from China in 1605, he further estranged Ryūkyū from Satsuma. Satsuma repeatedly made requests to Ryūkyū to mediate a Satsuma-China trade, but Ryūkyū made no move to respond to these requests. In 1609, Satsuma sent a force of 3,000 men armed with 700 guns on 100 warships to invade Ryūkyū. The Satsuma force quickly took over Ryūkyū and made a triumphant return with more than 100 prisoners including King Shō Nei. As a reward, the Shōgunate allowed Satsuma to rule over Ryūkyū. In 1610, King Shō Nei met face-to-face with Shōgun Tokugawa Ieyasu and presented him with tributary gifts and was allowed to return. However, Ryūkyū was now under the rule of Satsuma, which also directly controlled the Amami Oshima islands. A land assessment conducted by Satsuma determined that the total productivity of Ryūkyū was 89,000 *koku*. The 1609 Satsuma invasion of Ryūkyū is described in the *Kian Diaries*:

> The general landed from the bay and burned down the castle and Ryūfukuji Temple in Urasoe. As the enemy forces crossed Taihei Bridge (Taira Bridge), they discharged their guns in a rain-like volley as planned. Gusukuma Peechin was shot on his left abdomen and his head was taken right at that spot. Upon seeing this, every man retreated back into the castle. The enemy burned every house in the area.

The Ryūkyū Kingdom could do nothing in the face of Satsuma's overwhelming military force.

In 1631, Satsuma set up a magistrate office to oversee official relations with Ryūkyū. The magistrate, who was sent from Satsuma to Ryūkyū, served for three years and was allotted a staff of 15 to 18 and one horse. Maintaining a 100,000-*koku* territory with 18 men would seem difficult if not impossible. However, rather than ruling over Ryūkyū, it might be more accurate to say Satsuma carried out privileged diplomacy.

The Invasion of the Ryukyuan Kingdom by Japan (*Ryūkyū Shobun*)

Less than a year following the Tokugawa Shogunate's formal restoration of political authority to the Emperor, the Meiji Emperor ascended to his throne in August of 1868. The Meiji Period officially started on September 8, 1869. In 1872, an Imperial Order for the dissolution of the old feudal domains and the establishment of prefectures (*Haihan chiken* was promulgated. Subsequently, the Prefectural Government Ordinance and Secretary Bill were enacted and Ryūkyū was placed under the jurisdiction of Kagoshima Prefecture. The Ryukyuan king at the time was Shō Tai.

Ijichi Sadaka and Narahara Yukigoro were sent from Kagoshima to explain the general flow of the government since the Meiji Restoration to the Ryukyuan officials. The two men met with Regent Yonabaru *Ūji* and the Council of Three, which included Ginowan *Uēkata*, Kamekawa *Uēkata*, and Kabira *Uēkata*.

The Meiji Government's policy toward Ryūkyū was to make it a Japanese territory while severing its ties with the Ch'ing Dynasty. However, standing in the way of carrying out this policy was the almost impossible task of obtaining the consent of both China and Ryūkyū. A fortuitous turn of events for Japan that would solve its problem came in the form of the "Taiwan Incident."

In 1871, a ship returning to Miyako after bringing yearly tribute to Naha was shipwrecked on Taiwan. In a conflict with local residents, 54 of the 66 crew members were killed. Upon hearing of the incident, the Meiji

---

Government demanded compensation from the Ch'ing Government. However, the Ch'ing Government refused to take action and responded that, "Taiwan is an unsubjugated region beyond the reach of China's governance and civilization." In 1874, the Meiji Government sent a punitive expedition of 3,600 soldiers under the command of Saigo Tsugumichi to Taiwan. To counter the Ch'ing Government's protests over the expedition, the Meiji Government used the earlier Ch'ing response in subsequent negotiations. In those negotiations the Meiji Government was able to assert that, "Because Taiwan aborigines killed people belonging to the Nation of Japan, the Government of Japan recognized it as a crime and punished the culprits. This is a just action to protect its own citizens." In doing so, the Meiji Government was able to force China to agree that the people of Ryūkyū were Japanese.

In 1872, the year after the Taiwan Incident, the Meiji Government placed the Ryukyuan Kingdom within the old feudal system by converting it to Ryūkyū *han* (feudal domain) and appointed Shō Tai to the position of Ryūkyū-*han* king. By setting up Ryūkyū-*han* before the 1874 punitive expedition, the Meiji Government was able to both claim Ryūkyū as a territory of Japan and to provide the rationale for sending troops there.

In 1875, under orders from Interior Lord Okubo Toshimichi, Interior Minister Matsuda Michiyuki visited Ryūkyū where he delivered a notification to Nakijin *Ūji*, the representative of the Ryūkyū-*han* King. The notification stipulated, among other things, the prohibition of receiving investiture missions from China, the adoption "Meiji" as the era name, the implementation of Japanese criminal law, and the closing of the Ryūkyū Hall in Fuzhou, China. The Ryukyuans violently resisted the ending of relations with China. Two factions, the pro-Japan *Kaika-tō* (Enlightenment Party) and pro-China *Ganko-tō* (Stubborn Party), emerged and engaged each other in vigorous debate. In 1879, Matsuda Michiyuki again visited Ryūkyū to deliver a last notice. Because Ryūkyū did not follow the notice, the Meiji Government had Interior Lord Itō Hirobumi draft a concrete disposition plan. Matsuda was given the title of "Ryūkyū Disposition Officer" and returned to Ryūkyū for the third time.

Matsuda entered Shuri Castle with a force of 160 police and 400 infantry soldiers on March 27, 1879 and delivered to Ryūkyū-*han* king's representative, Nakijin *Ūji*, the order for the abolition of the *han* and the establishment of the prefecture. The king was ordered to vacate the castle by the 31st and stay at the residence of Shō Ten *Ūji* until he left for Tōkyō. The castle was vacated by the 31st and all official documents were sealed and sent to Tōkyō. With Shō Tai's removal to Tōkyō on May 27, the Ryūkyū Disposition was complete. Shō Tai was given the rank of a Japanese aristocrat and was made to live in Tōkyō.

The Meiji Government's abolishment of the Ryukyuan Kingdom and establishment of Okinawa Prefecture was not recognized by China. The Okinawa pro-Chinese faction also secretly sent messengers to repeatedly petition the Ch'ing Government to come to aid of Ryūkyū. In response, the Ch'ing Government asked Ulysses S. Grant, the former U.S. President who had stopped in China on a round-the-world trip, to mediate in the Ryukyuan issue. For China, which was embroiled in internal strife at the time, the Ryukyuan issue was an important diplomatic matter.

After receiving the arbitration request from the Ch'ing Government, Grant went to Japan where he met with Itō Hirobumi and others and received assurances that negotiations between China and Japan would be opened. Through Grant's mediation, negotiations over Ryūkyū began in Peking. Japan negotiated with China based on Grant's opinion that it was better to turn its attention to China's vast resources rather than stir things up over the Ryūkyū issue. The Japanese proposed the following: 1) the main island of Okinawa and islands north of it be part of Japan, 2) the Miyako and Yaeyama Islands near Chinese territory be part of China, and 3) the addition of a provision in 1871 Sino-Japanese Treaty of Amity that would allow Japan to engage in commerce in China at the same status as Western countries. The proposed treaty was called the "Island Division Treaty Draft." In response, the Chinese

22

proposed the "Three-way Division of Ryūkyū Proposal," which called for: 1) to include Amami Oshima and other islands north of it be part of Japan, 2) granting independence to the Okinawa Island group and restoring the Ryūkyū Kingdom, and 3) including the Miyako and Yaeyama Islands in China.

Because the two countries' opinions were at odds with each other from the beginning, the negotiations were deadlocked. However, the Chinese found it necessary to accept the Japanese proposal in the end. The negotiations were reestablished in October 1880 and as a result the two countries agreed that their representatives would sign a treaty the following February on Ishigaki Island under which the land and people of Miyako and Yaeyama Islands would be handed over to China. However, the Ch'ing Government hesitated signing the treaty at the last moment as confusion broke out in China's domestic markets over the fear that a Sino-Japanese friendship treaty would lead to Japan's expansion into Taiwan and Korea. In the end, the treaty was shelved and the proposal to divide Ryūkyū never materialized.

The entire period from the 1872 establishment of Ryūkyū-han to the 1880 island division issue is called the Ryukyuan Disposition (Ryūkyū Shobun).

As the international situation changed in the subsequent years, Japan advanced into Korea leading to conflict between Japan and China and finally the outbreak of the Sino-Japanese War (1894-95). Japan won the war and Taiwan become its colony resulting in the Ryūkyū issue never being resolved and Japan claiming all of Ryūkyū.

Section 2 The Era of *Tiy* (手

Early Gusuku Period (7th -12th Centuries

The history of Ryūkyū has been divided into four periods: 1) Prehistoric Period (20,000 years or more ago to the 12th century), 2) Ancient Ryūkyū Period (12th century to the Shimazu Invasion in 1609), 3) Early Modern Ryukyuan Period (1609 to Ryūkyū Shobun in 1879), and 4) Modern Okinawan Period (1879 to the Battle of Okinawa in 1945). While this is the general periodization carried out by historians, I believe that from a cultural/sport anthropological perspective, the following periodization might be appropriate: 1) Shell Mound Period (10,000+ years ago to 7th century), 2) Early Gusuku Period (7th century to 1185), 3) Late Gusuku Period (1185 to Three Kingdom Unification in 1429), 4) Ryukyuan Kingdom Period (1429 to 1879), 4) Modern Okinawan Period (1879 to 1945), and 5) Contemporary Okinawan Period (1945 to present). These periodization scheme allows for clearer observation of the different eras that are associated with the Ryukyuan Kingdom.

It is believed that humans have been living in Ryūkyū for 40,000 to 50,000 years. In the Omoro Sōshi appears the following passage: "*Chinen mori gusuku kami ori hajime no gusuku amamikiyo ga nodate hajime no gusuku* (Chinen Mori Gusuku is the first *gusuku* that the gods descended upon. It is the first *gusuku* to pray to Amamikyo)." The deity called Amamikyo came from above to create the islands and placed a man and woman to live in those islands. From this first couple were born 3 sons and 2 daughters. The first son became the first king, second son the first *aji* (lord), and third son the first peasant. The first daughter became the first *ogimi* (the priestess of the kingdom) and the second daughter became the first *noro* (regional priestess). The first king was called Tensonshi and his reign lasted 25 generations. Of particular interest is the fact the gods who created Ryūkyū first descended

---

24

upon a *gusuku*. *Gusuku* can be translated as a "castle" or "fort." The origins of the Ryukyuan Kingdom in a *gusuku* is illustrated in *Ryūkyū Koku Den*, which is part of the Chinese *Sui Sho* (隋書).

According to the *Ryūkyū Koku Den*, "The Ryūkyū Kingdom is an island kingdom. It is a five-day sea journey east of Fukien and filled with mountains and caves. The family name of the king is Kanshi. His given name is Katsurattō. His origins and the number of generations that the kingdom has been in existence are not known." The *Sui Sho* reported that the Sui Emperor ordered an expedition to subjugate Ryūkyū in 607, but it failed and was only able to bring back one prisoner. The next year in 608, another expedition was sent. However, the people there did not comply and the expedition brought back "cloth armor" as well as a few thousand men and women as captives.

The *Sui Sho* also mentions that the king of Ryūkyū was Karayō and his wife was Tabacha and that they lived in a place called *Haradandō* that was surrounded by three layers of circular moats and fences and a wall of thorn bushes. Rule of the country was carried out by 4 to 5 "governors" that were subordinate to the king. Further, there was a "petty king" in each cave and a "*chōryōsui*" in each village. People who were strong at battle were in these positions. Because swords and other armaments were few, weapons made of animal bones and horns were common.

Special attention must be paid again to the passage "Rule of the country was carried out by 4 to 5 "governors" that were subordinate to the king. Further, there was a "petty king" in each cave and a "*chōryōsui*" in each village." This passage indicates that some organizational structure was maintained in the monarchal system of the time. This is corroborated by another passage: "The *chōryōsui* made judgments regarding crimes, but appeals were brought up to the king. The king would confer with his vassals to make a decision." The *Sui Sho* also describes, "All men and women wind white ramie cords around their hair from the back of their head to their foreheads." This practice survived in the latter Ryūkyū Kingdom Period as the "*Hachimachi*" system under which a person's class ranking rank was represented by the color of his headband (*hachimachi*). Women were described as "wearing white clothes with lightly died pattern that were square in shape." Their "clothes were made of the bark of the *gajimaru* (banyan) or woven from fibers of various colors such as hemp" and the designs were "not singular." From ancient ties, Ryūkyū has had its unique Ryūkyū *tsumugi* (pongee) that is woven from *bashofu* (banana fiber), hemp, and other materials. Also, the typhoon-resistant *gajimaru* is the Okinawan prefectural tree and still grows in Ryūkyū today. It is not only strong against the wind, but it is used as the raw material for making dyes for the unique Ryukyuan textiles.

The *Sui Sho* describes Ryūkyū's has having fertile farmland that is first burned with fire put out with water. The crops that grew well were "Millet, rice, [unknown] cane, hemp, beans, *azuki*, *gozu*, black beans, and others." From this account it is clear that millet existed in Ryūkyū at the time and that the burning field technique was used for crops other than millet.

Another passage talks about a tool called a *sō* that was about 30 centimeters in length and several centimeters wide with a stone blade. "Sō" is a word that connotes poking and it is likely that the tool being described was a short stick-like tool used to stab the earth to plant seeds or harvest crops. It is imaginable that a more easily usable tool could have been invented, but this *sō* was used long after as one of the main agricultural tools.

The account ends by saying that the Ryukyuans did not comply and so the Sui soldiers swiftly defeated them and burned the royal house. The expedition ended with the taking of a few thousand men and women captives along with captured goods.

It is clear from the account that a kingdom structure had formed in Ryūkyū by the 600s. Under this structure a king was stood above 4-5 ministers who oversaw petty kings in each region. In each of these regions, leaders called *chōryōsui* administered villages. It is also evident that "powerful persons" took these positions. The term "powerful person" refers to someone who was strong in battle or, in other words, someone who was skilled in fighting arts. However, it is most likely that there was no single kingdom that unified all of Ryūkyū at the time and instead, it was divided into fiefdoms. The existence of over 400 *gusuku* sites in Ryūkyū and the historical record of three competing kingdoms in the 13th century and the unification of Ryūkyū in the 15th century support this.

Between 700 and 800 AD., warrior leaders called *aji* began to emerge. Through military means, *aji* unified the immediate territory and built *gusuku*. The *aji* strived to expand their power, maintain their wealth and authority, and protect the lives and property of the people in his *gusuku*. *Aji* fought each other in repeat vicious battles to uphold the standing of their *gusuku*. The weapons used in these battles included small swords, staffs, spears, bows, and arrows. Because iron was not produced in Ryūkyū and was difficult to get, the small swords were probably fashioned with only small amounts of iron at the edges and tip. The main weapons were bow and arrows and staffs. Staffs were especially easy to procure and those made out of the extremely hard tropical *kuruchi* (ebony) were ideal. As *gusuku* became larger, so did the scale of the battles. At the time, judging from the size of the *gusuku* finds, it is surmised that the battles involved about 100 participants. Women and children defended the *gusuku*, while young men went out to fight the opposing forces. The reasons for going to battle probably included fights over the boundaries of the gusuku, surrounding territories, mountain regions, and farmland. They were battles between the haves and have-nots. The participants in the battles were the citizens of each *gusuku* who were normally farmers and fishermen with households and were not specially trained fighters. It is believed that each *aji* was surrounded by dozens of close aides who defended him from other *aji* and also participated in administering their own *gusuku*.

Unlike Okinawa, the Japanese mainland had developed weapons from ancient times. By the 3rd century B.C., agriculture, metal implements, and Yayoi pottery had reached the Japanese mainland during the Yayoi Period. During this period, both iron and bronze implements had reached Japan at roughly the same time. While iron was used for tools used in farming and other tasks, bronze was eventually used for ritual objects and jewelry. In the later part of the Yayoi Period there were many settlements that have been described as "moat villages." Judging from the existence of such settlements, one could deduct that there was constant conflict between settlements. Further, judging from the large *kofun* tombs and large amounts of buried goods retrieved from coffins in those *kofun* tombs from the time, it is thinkable that there were differences in individual status among people from the same group of residents and that strong local leaders emerged in each region. The "Geography Section" of the *Han Shu* (The History of the Former Han) talks about Japan as divided into more than 100 countries in the 1st Century. According to the Wei Shu, there were 30 countries in Japan that China had diplomatic relations with and that in 108 A.D. Himiko of Yamatai received a gold seal (金印紫綬 *jin yin zi shou*) from the Chinese Ming Emperor. Consequently, there were over 100 small countries fighting each from the 3rd Century B.C. to the 2nd Century B.C. This number falls gradually to 30 or so countries as nation-state formation in Japan moved toward the unification.

The process in which strong leaders emerge, regional settlements unify, and "petty nations" form happens about 900 years earlier in Japan than in Okinawa. In Japan, the process begins in the 3rd Century B.C., while in Okinawa it begins from around 600 A.D. Moreover, there is a distinct difference in the weaponry used in the two places. In Japan, iron and other metals were already in use in Japan by the 3rd century B.C. The production of iron in Japan was well established and iron was used for farming tools as well as for weapons. However, iron was not produced in Okinawa and was imported from either China or Japan. Consequently, the weapons used in warfare included farm implements such as the *bo* (pole used to carry loads across one's shoulders), the *kama* (sickle for cutting grass), the *tunfā* (a wooden tool for husking soybeans and other beans or grains), and the *nunchaku* (two pieces of wood connected by rope placed in horses mouths as steering bits) or implements used in fishing such as the *ēku* (paddle that fishermen used for *sabani* boats). The only weapon-like weapons used were a few short swords. The *Sui Sho* describes how animal bones or horns were attached to staffs and sharpened to make spears.

These first weapons used in Okinawa were quite crude in their ability to kill or maim. However, such weapons were the only ones available at the time and one could say that they were merely extensions of a person's bare hands. During the fighting, one might have his or her *bo* break or *kama* or *nunchaku* yanked away by the opponent's weapon. In such a situation, he or she would have to revert to fighting with bare hands as the most primitive way of self-defense. This is the reason why *tiy* developed as a fighting art. Iron was not produced in Okinawa and was not imported in sufficient amounts until the era of Shō Hashi in the 15th Century. The availability of iron in Okinawa led to the amalgamation of the 300 or more *gusuku* that had been warring each other since the 7th century into three kingdoms and finally into the Ryūkyū Kingdom in the 15th Century. During the 800-year period prior to the influx of sufficient iron, warfare using *bo*, *sai*, *nunchaku*, and other rudimentary weapons – with bare hands as the last resort – remained relatively unchanged.

Since *tiy* was employed as a way to defend oneself in the event of losing one's weapons, it includes various barehanded techniques. The basic techniques of *tiy* include punches, kicks, and blocks and were designed to bring down an opponent with just one attack or movement. Fists, limbs, and torsos were conditioned to be as hard as rock or iron. In the event that an opponent attacked with a *bo*, it would be possible that a block with one's arm could break the *bo*. One could also break a *bo* when it was used to attack the lower body by using one's shin or thigh. This was the context for the birth and development of *tiy* over a long period of several centuries as a most practical fighting set of barehanded techniques.

Late Gusuku Period (12th to 15th Centuries)

The Late Gusuku Period began in the 12th century and extended to the 15th century and is referred to as the age of the Shunten Dynasty, King Eiso, and the Satto Dynasty. While the Early Gusuku Period was characterized by small-scale conflicts between tiny *gusuku*, the Late Gusuku Period featured large-scale wars between major *gusuku*. It was in this time period that powerful *aji* began to emerge to establish dynastic rule.

From around 1000 to 1100, the number of *gusuku* was reduced from over 400 to less than half that many as larger more advanced *gusuku* incorporated the smaller *gusuku* into their domains. In this period, *aji* arose to rule the southern, central, north-central, and north regions of Okinawa as well as the Miyako and Yaeyama island groups. One of those *aji* was Shunten. Shunten received help from the Ōzato *aji* in Shimajiri to defeat Riyū who was the most powerful leader in Ryūkyū at the time. In 1180, Shunten unified the central region of Okinawa and became the Urasoe *aji*. He became the Chuzan king. Shunten's name resounded throughout Ryūkyū and through history as the ruler of the entire central part of Okinawa. His authority even extended into Nanzan in the south and Hokuzan in the north as he was the first person in Ryūkyū to emerge as an unrivaled leader. He is said to be the founder of the Ryukyuan royal lineage and was the first to establish a dynasty of Chuzan kings that reigned for three generations over a span of 73 years.

In 1243, the sixth year of the reign of Shunbajunki, a Japanese ship headed for China from Bizen was washed ashore in Ryūkyū during a typhoon on September 17. The account of shipwrecked crew is called the *Hyōtō Ryūkyū Kokuki*. A full-size photographic copy of *Hyōtō Ryūkyū Kokuki* was published by the Imperial Household Agency in 1962. The following is an excerpt of this document.

On September 17, the crew of our ship that was shipwrecked on the southeast part of Ryūkyū debated about what country we had reached. Some argued that it was Kikai, some said it was a southern barbarian country, and some said it was Ryūkyū. In the end, we agreed that we were in Ryūkyū. Upon exploration, we found a large river from which we drank. The taste of the water was so delicious

---

30

that everyone tried to get a drink first. This greatly quenched everyone's thirst...

... On the 20th, we had a meeting and it was decided that 30 or more men would explore a different direction. When they went about 2 *ri*, they heard a dog bark in the mountains. They then saw human footprints on the mud. Right at that moment, they caught a glimpse of a person. That person had a childlike body and wore red clothes and a red cloth on the head. The person wore nothing on his feet and carried a *hoko* (spear or pike). The person climbed quickly over the rocks as if flying like a bird. At that time, everyone thought that his life would come to an end. Gathering sticks, we built a hut in which we gathered to read Buddhist sutras.

... On the 21st, when we looked out onto the ocean before dawn, we saw 2 or 3 boats. Those boats did not look like Japanese or Chinese boats. In one of the boats there was a general wearing red clothes with a red cloth wound around his head. After a while, about 10 boats sailed near. There were over 10 people riding each boat and each carried a *hoko*, shield, bow, and arrow. They shot their arrows all at once and the arrows fell like a driving rain. The arrows were very fast and travelled far and were accurate. The skill of holding the shield while floating on the water was like that of a water bird. Upon observing an arrow quickly retrieved, one could see that it had six feathers and its arrowhead was like that of the *hoko*.

On the 22nd, they loosened the strings on their bows, put down their *hoko,* and raised their hands in a gesture of peace. We Japanese put away our bows and arrows and took off our armor and helmet and did the same. As we did so, the boats came nearer. When we got a better look, their height was taller than our country's people and the color of their faces was quite dark. Their ears were long and hooked, eyes were round and black, and hair was cut to shoulder length. They wore no hoods but instead wrapped red cloths around their heads. Around their waists, they wore silver belts and on their necks they had exquisite golden jewelry. Their clothes were red or black. The language they spoke was different from Japanese or Chinese and they did not have a written language. They asked us to give us some clothes and so we gave them a single layer indigo and other items to which they all were quite pleased with. They also asked for food and drink and we gave them rice and other things to which each was happy with. From the Ryūkyū boats they brought us stewed tubers (probably taro) and *nori* (seaweed), which both tasted the same as what we have in our country. There were also women. They wore soldier's gear and carried babies. Their appearance with their hair tied up was very similar to that of women of *Tōgo* (唐五).

Since they reported that they had landed on the southeastern part of Ryūkyū, if we assume that they were on the main island of Okinawa, they would have been in the Shimajiri region. The question that is raised is where would there be a large river with good drinking water in the coastal region of Shimajiri. Further, one wonders who had the cultural and military power to have a flotilla of over 30 ships to send out to meet a Japanese ship. The answers to these questions seem to lie in the Ōzato *aji* who was the leader of the Shimajiri region at the time. The figure of the superb warrior who wore hair that hung down to his shoulders, a red headband instead of a hood, a silver belt around his waist, and beautiful jewelry around his neck had probably been in existence since the Tenson Period and at least until the time of Shunten's dynasty. This period likely continued for several hundred to a thousand years.

The *Hyōtō Ryūkyū Kokuki* was said to be written on September 28, 1244, which was seven years after Shunten had died and his successor Shumbajunki ascended the throne. Since the Ōzato *aji* had such a land and sea force as seen in the *Hyōtō Ryūkyū Kokuki* which later helped the Japanese ship, it is most likely that a similar force enabled Shunten to defeat Riyū.

The Eiso Dynasty (1228-1349) followed the Shunten Dynasty. The *Chūzan Seikan* lists the five-generation genealogy of the Eiso Dynasty: Eiso (1259-1299, Taisei (Eiso's first son: 1299-1308, Eiji (Taisei's second son: 1308-1313) Tamagusuku-*Ō* (Eiji's third son: 1313-1336) and Seii-*Ō* (Tamagusuku-*Ō's* first son: 1336-1349). According to the Omoro Sōshi, the Eiso Dynasty was centered in Urasoe and at its peak ruled over Naha, Tomari, and Shuri as well as the entire southern part of Okinawa with the exception of the Sashiki district and the Motobu Peninsula in the north.

The founder of the dynasty, Eiso, was the ruler of the Iso Gusuku in Urasoe. Eiso brought Buddhism into Ryūkyū and encouraged its propagation. It was during his reign that the original *bojutsu*, staff fighting form of *Maeda no bo* was developed. The person who devised *Maeda no bo* was the Maeda *aji* who ruled from Maeda Gusuku and was a prosperous vassal of Eiso.

The Eiso Dynasty was followed by the reign of King Satto (1321-1406), who is commonly known as the king who lived through the Three Kingdom Period. Satto was also known as Urasoe *aji*, Urasoe Shikina, and Shikina Umui. As the Chuzan King, he was the first to send a tribute ship to and begin trade with China. Buying all the iron that came on trading ships from Japan, he ordered it to be made into sickles, hoes, and other farm implements. This act made the farmers under his rule happy. The *sai*, which had been a farming tool that was also used as a weapon, was modified from its original chopstick-like form to its present form. This was probably done to improve its effectiveness in defending against other weapons.

As the Chūzan king, Satto shared power over Ryūkyū with Haniji, the Hokuzan king, and Shōsatto, the Nanzan king. Satto sent a mission to China in 1363 to begin trade relations and to send tribute to the Ming Dynasty. He also sent young men from Okinawa to study in China and invited intellectuals from China to Okinawa. While Ryūkyū had been divided into many small domains, the consolidation process and advanced to where the three kingdoms of

Hokuzan, Chūzan, and Nanzan emerged supreme. Chūzan was the most powerful of the three and was the first to be recognized as a tributary by the Ming Emperor Hong Wu. This was the first time that Ryūkyū had been externally recognized as a country. Satto was also the first actual person to be recognized in an externally written history. His rivals from Hokuzan and Nanzan followed him by sending to tribute to China. This era is referred to as the Ryūkyū Three Kingdom Period.

After Satto's death, his son Bunei (1356-1406) succeeded him as Chuzan king. Bunei sent an envoy to the Ming Court just as the Jianwen Emperor was in conflict with the Yongle Emperor. It was the Yongle Emperor that sent an envoy to Chūzan. However, soon after, he was ousted by an attack by the Sashiki *aji* named Sahachi, who later became Shō Hashi. Around that time, one of important men around Chūzan king was a man named Shirataru *Uēkata*, who devised the *bo* form that is now known as *Shirataro no kon*. Later, at the beginning of the 15th century, another man close to the Chūzan king named Ufugusuku *Uekata* (Ufugusuku Kenyu) created what is known as *Ufugusuku no kon*.

Ryūkyū Dynasty Period

The era of *tiy* did not end yet. The First Shō Dynasty began with Shō Shishō (1406-1421) and ended 63 years with Shō Toku (1441-1469). In that period, Shō Shi Shō, who had been the Sashiki *aji*, defeated Chūzan and made himself the Chūzan king. In 1416, his son Shō Hashi defeated Hokuzan and, in 1429, unified Ryūkyū by conquering Nanzan. During the reign of Shō Tai Kyū (1453-1460), Amawari, the Katsuren *aji*, vanquished his rival Gosamaru, the Nakagusuku *aji*. Fresh from his victory, Amawari proceeded to stage a revolt at Shuri Castle, but was put down by Tai Kyū's forces. Both Gosamaru and Amawari were said to be superior warriors skilled in *tiy*.

The Second Shō Dynasty began with Shō En (1469-1476) and ends with the 21st king, Shō Tai (1847-1879). The era of *tiy* extended to the reign of the 15th king, Shō Boku (1751-1794). One of Shō Boku's closest ministers, Sakugawa Kanga, traveled to China where he learned Chinese *kempō* and brought it back with him to Ryūkyū. This marked the birth of the term *tūdiy* (唐手), or "Chinese *tiy*." Up to that time *tiy* was the only word used for martial arts in Ryūkyū.

A particular battle during the Second Shō Dynasty that deserves attention is the "Oyake Akahachi Rebellion." Shō Shin (1476-1526), the third king of the Second Shō Dynasty, ordered all of the *aji* on the main island of Okinawa to move to Shuri to fortify his rule. The leaders of the Miyako and Yaeyama island groups were forced into a situation where they had to choose between capitulating to Shō Shin and becoming a part of the Ryukyuan Kingdom or fighting till the end to protect their independence. Nakasone Tuimiyā of Miyako choose the former while Oyake Akahachi chose the latter.

Nakasone Tuimiyā sent an envoy to Shō Shin to convey his wishes to become a vassal. Shō Shin ordered Nakasone Tuimiyā to contribute soldiers to an army that would be sent to conquer the recalcitrant Yaeyama.

The army that was under the command of the Ozato *aji*, left Naha and stopped at Kume Island to pick up the priestess Kimihae. After sailing to Miyako to join forces with Nakasone Tuimiyā's warriors, the army recruited *Nagata Ufunushi*, who had earlier been defeated by Oyake Akahachi, as a guide. When the army arrived at Ishigaki, Akahachi had set up his army along the coast. The combined Okinawa and Miyako army found itself bogged down in a bloody battle with Akahachi's army. The Okinawa and Miyako army waited until nightfall to split into two groups and engaged in a two-pronged squeezing attack that succeeded in defeating Akahachi's army.

The priestess Kimihae was brought on the expedition because in the religious tradition of the time, she was one of the priestesses that served the three sibling *kami* or deities of Ryūkyū. The high priestess of Shuri was the oracle of oldest sister *kami*, the high priestess of Yaeyama was the oracle of the second sister *kami*, and the Kume priestess served the third sister *kami*. The oldest sister *kami* was obviously on the side of the Shuri forces and by including Kamihae, the priestess serving the third sister *kami*, it was believed that the second sister *kami* served by the priestess of Yaeyama would be compelled to join her sibling in supporting the invading forces. After conquering Yaeyama, Shō Shin rewarded Kimihae with a jewel necklace and lands. The act of bringing of a priestess into battle is an indication of how strongly the people of Ryūkyū believed in the *noro* (priestess) religion of the time.

Nakasone Tuimiyā was rewarded the position of governor of Miyako and his wife was given the status of high priestess. Nagata Ufunushi, the man who acted as a guide for the invading force was made chief of the village of Kumi and his younger sister was elevated to the status of a high priestess in Yaeyama.

Following his defeat of Oyake Akahachi and the conquest of Yonaguni in 1522, Shō Shin solidified his rule throughout Ryūkyū by setting up administrative offices in the Miyako and Yaeyama regions called *kuramoto*. Parallel to the Gosamaru-Amawari episode, Nakasone Tuimiyā is portrayed as loyal to Shō Shin and Oyake Akahachi as powerful mutineer. However, it is important to note that both were powerful leaders in their respective regions and had needed to deal with the Shuri government to secure their authority. The *Akahashi no kon* is attributed to Oyake Akahachi who had established his rule around the beginning of the 16th century.

In Ryukyuan warfare, the weapons used were farming and fishing implements such as the *bo* (staff), *kama* (sickle), *nunchaku, tunfā,* and *ēku* (oar). When there was no weapon available, barehanded fighting or *irikumi* was used to defeat an opponent. *Irikumi* means to bring down an opponent with one's bare hands and, as such, it is *tiy* in its original form. When defending their *gusuku*, ancient warriors devised *tiy* techniques to incorporate into *irikumi*. The most outstanding characteristic of *tiy* is the use of the closed fist (*seiken*). The ancient warriors devised ways to train or condition their *seiken* that are unique to Okinawa and not found in Chinese *kempō*, Japanese judō and kendō, or other fighting arts. *Seiken* is the most important feature and lifeline of *tiy*. It is probably not an exaggeration to say that *tiy* began with *seiken*.

Bojutsu (staff techniques developed during the Gusuku Period when 300 or more *gusuku* throughout Ryūkyū were in constant warfare. This period eventually led to the formation of the three main domains of Nanzan, Chūzan, and Hokuzan, but even then there were no weapons available in mass quantities other than the *bo*. As mentioned, the *bo* was used to carry loads and the *sai* for digging up soil. The *nunchaku* was placed over a horse's nose to pull its head left or right. The *tunfā* was used to husk soy beans or other beans or grains. The *ēku* was an oar that fishermen used for paddling their *sabani* boats and the *kama* was used to cut grass.

Thus, the ancient weaponry of Ryūkyū was based on farming and fishing implements used in everyday life. During the Gusuku Period and through the era of Nanzan, Chūzan, and Hokuzan, empty-handed fighting was the last resort when such poor weapons became unusable in the heat of battle. This form of free empty-handed fighting used in combat is no doubt the origin of *tiy*. In other words, *bo* and bare-handed *irikumi* fighting developed at the same time and on the same battlefields and are thus inseparable. One can thus think of the *bo* as an extension of the human hand. The *bo tsuki* (staff thrust works on the same principle as the *seiken tsuki* (fist punch). For example, when executing the *chūdan tsuki* (mid-level punch) in *tiy*, the fist is rotated 180 degrees before it reaches its target. When performing a *bo tsuki* the *bo* is also rotated 180 degrees as it approaches the target.

琉球王朝国王の王冠 （Ryukyu Kingdom crown）

Further, *bo kata* can be performed by using ones hands instead of a *bo* and, vice-versa, *tiy kata* can be performed using a *bo*. *Bo kata* that were developed in the 13th century such as *Maeda no kon, Shirataru no kon,* and *Ufugusuku no kon* are basically the same as *Maeda no te, Shirataro no te,* and *Ufugusuku no te*. Attention must be given to the fact that "Maeda (Meeda)," "Shirataro (Shirataru)," and "Ufugusuku" are uniquely Okinawan names that are not found in China or Japan. Also, the names given to *kata* that originated in the period from the 13th to 17th century are derived from the names of military commanders. However, from the 18th century, *kata* names were derived from geographic names as in *Shui-tiy* (*Shuri-te*), *Nafa-tiy* (*Naha-te*), and *Tumai-tiy* (*Tomari-te*).

Hence, *tiy* developed as an important fighting technique until the middle of the 15th century. Around that time, political turmoil reached its peak in Ryūkyū as *aji* vied to conquer other territories while sharply watching the moves of their rivals to protect their own territory. This period was brought to an end by Shō Hashi (1372-1439) unified Nanzan, Chūzan, and Hokuzan. Hokuzan was defeated in 1416 and in 1422, Shō Hashi became the king of

Chūzan. In 1429, Shō Hashi succeeded in unifying Ryūkyū when he defeated Nanzan. However, later conflicts such as the Oyake Akahachi Disturbance in Yaeyama and the Onitora Disturbance in Yonaguni prompted Shō Shin to prevent further warfare by banning weapons.

Shō Shin put an end to armed revolts by powerful clans and consolidated his central authority by bringing all of the regional *aji* to live below Shuri Castle. In a move that is called the "first weapons ban," he gathered swords, bows, arrows, and other weapons and had them placed in storehouses. The elimination of weapons no doubt contributed to the importance of *tiy* as an empty-handed fighting technique. While the weapons ban was part of the king's attempt to bolster his central rule, the *aji* and *jitu* who ruled in the outlying regions still needed to exercise their authority. In some cases, these leaders exercised strong control in their regional localities. In such circumstances, *tiy* had an important part in the demonstration of power. As long as the weapons ban was in effect, it was inevitable that *tiy* would be refined and passed down as a clandestine tradition that was crucial in the life and death situation of battle.

Right around the time that warfare was at its peak during the Three Kingdom Period in Ryūkyū, the Onin War in 1467 brought about Japan's Warring Period. The use of the *bo* in fighting in Ryūkyū is written about in *Okinawa Issennen Shi (One Thousand Years of Okinawan History* [1924]) by Majikina Ankō. The *Shirataro no kon*, a *bo kata* that is still in existence today was created around 1314 and named after an important military commander of the time. Shirataro later married Princess Tamagusuku. It is said that, disillusioned by the fighting in Okinawa, he and his wife moved to Kudaka Island so that their descendants could live there. Throughout Ryūkyū, there are "*bo odori* (staff dances)" that have been performed at village festivals for over 400 years. Hints of the original *Shirataro no kon* can be seen in these village *bo odori*.

Okinawa Karate Shinkokai / March 1937

Further, the *Oyake Akahachi no kon* is a *bo* form that has its origins in the period around 1500 when the feudal lord of Yaeyama Oyake Akahachi rebelled against the Ryūkyū King and was later vanquished under the leadership of Nakasone Tuimiyā of Miyako.

Most of the *bo*, *sai*, and other Ryukyuan *kobujutsu kata* are believed to be derived from Shuri-te *kata*. In other words, these ancient weapons can be seen as extensions of the hand (*tiy*) in the Shuri-te style. A majority of Ryukyuan *kobujutsu kata* have the same basics as Shuri-te *kata*. That is, Shuri-te thrusts, kicks, blocks, *shiko dachi* (square stance), *zenkutsu dachi* (forward stance), *neko ashi dachi* (cat stance), and other basic elements are also found in *kobujutsu kata*. From days of old, it has been said that if one wanted to learn *kobujutsu*, it would be better to learn a Shōrin style within the Shuri-te genealogy, rather than Gojū and Uechi styles.

As mentioned repeatedly already, from the 7th to 13th century, there were over 300 *gusuku* throughout Ryūkyū on Okinawa, Kume, Miyako, Yaeyama, and other islands. Each of these 400 *gusuku* was a small kingdom in itself that was led by *aji* who engaged in constant territorial wars with neighboring *aji*. Stronger *gusuku* were able to expand by absorbing weaker *gusuku* and in the process Chūzan, Nanzan, and Hokuzan emerged in the Three Kingdoms Period. Prior to Shunten becoming king of Chūzan in 1187, there was ceaseless conflict between *gusuku* and it is conceivable that it was during long period of warfare that Ryukyuan *tiy* and *kobujutsu* developed.

Moreover, according to the Ryūkyū Kokuden (流求国伝) of the *Sui Sho* (隋書), the weapons in Ryūkyū included swords, pikes, bows, and arrows. It also reported, "That iron was scarce and that the swords were thin and small and that animal bones and horns were used in many of the swords. Armor was woven from linen or made out of bear or leopard skin." In 1477, the *Richō Jitsuroku* reported that on Yonaguni, "There are blacksmiths, but they do not make plows. Farm tools include sickles, axes, and spatulas. They have small swords, but do not have bows, arrows, and pikes. They wear small spears at all times." The same *Richō Jitsuroku* recorded observations in Naha that, "There are bows, arrows, axes, swords, and armor. Soldiers wrap their shins with iron." These accounts thus provide evidence that in the Late Gusuku Period, swords, axes, bows, arrows, and other weapons were used in battle.

尚真王（**King Shoshin**）

However, swords, axes, and other such weapons were quite costly in Ryūkyū, where iron was not produced. This is suggested by accounts of swords being thin and made with the minimum of steel. Also, we could also surmise that there were few of these costly swords in the 400 or more *gusuku*. It would follow that in the wars between *gusuku*, a few of these small, thin swords were used with farming and fishing implements – especially the *bo*, which was a everyday-use tool for both farmers and fishermen. Consequently, from the perspective of one who is trained in *kobujutsu*, the *bo* is more advantageous in actual battle than the flimsy swords of the time.

The *bo* used in Ryukyuan *kobujutsu* ranges from 6 *shaku*[1] to 9 *shaku* in length and is made of *kuruchi* (ebony) or *kashi no ki* (oak) that are difficult to cut even with a sword. *Bojutsu* incorporates a wide variety of techniques, including strikes, thrusts, penetrations, side strikes, upward strikes, and downward strikes. Further, both ends of the *bo* can be used to deliver quick and almost simultaneous blows. Also, since *bo* are made of hardwood, it can inflict bone fractures with even light blows. It is clear that a small flimsy sword would be no match against a *bo* in the hands of someone trained in *bojutsu*. This is the reason why *bojutsu* developed in Ryūkyū while sword techniques did not.

Incidentally, while we can name many famous Ryukyuan *bojutsu* and *kobujutsu* masters such as Tsuken Oyakata, Yara Pēchin, Hamahiga Pēchin, and Sakugawa Kanga, the same cannot be said for even one Ryukyuan sword master. In Ryūkyū, *kobujutsu* weapons such as the *bo*, *sai*, *nunchaku*, *tunfā*, and *ēku* are valued much more than swords, bows, and arrows. The fact that masters of *kobujutsu* weapons are exalted gives us an indication of their importance in Ryūkyū.

Let me summarize what I have covered up to now. *Tiy*, the original form of *karate* (空手), was born on the battlefields on which *gusuku* fought against each other in the Early Gusuku Period during 7th to 12th centuries. *Tiy* developed in the Late Gusuku Period during the 12th to 15th centuries as many *kobujutsu* techniques were devised and perfected as ways to deliver mortal blows. During the peaceful time of the Ryukyuan Dynasties from the 15th to 18th centuries, *tiy* and *kobujutsu kata* were formulated. Consequently, the killing techniques of *tiy* have been developing from the 7th to 18th century, or a period of over 1,000 years. Eight hundred of those years, from 600s to the 1400s, were a "world of war" period of constant warfare during which *tiy* was

---

[1] A shaku is approximately one foot.

used to kill others in battle. However, from the establishment of the Ryukyuan Kingdom with the unification of the Three Kingdoms in 1429 until the Ryūkyū Disposition in 1872, there was a 450-year "world of peace" period. The role of *tiy* was transformed during this period. As the times changed, *tiy* went from a method for killing to a method of living.

Section 3 The Era of Tūdiy (唐手)

The original form of *karate*, *tiy*, was born as a set of techniques used on Ryukyuan battlefields during the Gusuku Period that began in the 7th century. Those techniques were perfected and preserved as ways to deliver mortal blows. In the Late Gusuku Period (12th to 15th centuries), *tiy* and *kobujutsu* techniques were formalized in rudimentary *kata*. "Genuine" *kata* were developed in the period of peace after the unification of the Three Kingdoms.

While *tiy* transformed from a method of killing to a method of living during the age of peace, it also was influenced by Chinese *kempō* during a golden age of trade when Ryūkyū had had exchanges with various other countries and regions. Chinese *kempō* that entered Ryūkyū around the middle of the 18th century influenced the development of *tiy*. To differentiate between the indigenous *tiy* and Chinese *kempō*, Ryukyuan fighters called the latter *tūdiy* (唐手). In the Okinawan language, *tūdiy* means "Chinese *tiy*." Consequently, until the 18th century *tūdiy* did not exist in Okinawa. Until then, there was only *tiy*.

In describing the spread of Chinese *kempō* to Ryūkyū, *Okinawa Issennen Shi* (*The Thousand Year History of Okinawa*) writes:

> *Mēkata* (舞方) dances that are particular Okinawan martial arts performances in the country side were created by well-known martial artists in ancient times before *tūdiy* had developed, but the confirmable spread of the name *tūdiy* happened with Tūdiy Sakugawa of Akata and in more modern times. In other words, until the Age of King Shō Kō, the word *tūdiy* did not exist, as the novel set of techniques had not spread widely.

In other words, according to *Okinawa Issennen Shi*, the uniquely martial arts dances performed in the rural areas of Okinawa, or *mēkata tiy*, were created by famous martial artists before *tūdiy* became well known in the time of Sakugawa Pēchin of Akata in Shuri. In addition, until the reign of King Shō Kō (1804-1824), *tūdiy* did not exist as a word. Consequently, until the early part of the 19th century, *karate* was simply called "*tiy*." "*Tūdiy*" became used commonly in the later part of King Shō Kō's reign when Sakugawa Kanga Pēchin (1733-1815) became widely known. Tūdiy Sakugawa was born during the rule of King Shō Kei (1713-1751) and was a warrior who served as a royal personal attendant and lived through the reigns of three subsequent kings: Shō Boku (1752-1794), Shō On (1795-1802), and Shō Kō (1804-1824). It was only when Sakugawa became well known in the 18th century that *tūdiy* became part of the common vocabulary. Until then, there was only the ancient word *tiy*.

This does not mean, however, that Chinese *kempō* had not existed in Ryūkyū at all before Sakugawa Pēchin's time. There were at least three Chinese who had brought *kempō* to Ryūkyū before then.

The first time that Chinese *kempō* had been brought to Ryūkyū was in 1625 by the Ming Chinese Chen Yuan Sai (陳元賽). At the time, while *tiy* existed in all regions of Ryūkyū as secretly transmitted techniques, in places such as Shuri and Naha, uniquely regional forms of *tiy* had been developed. Consequently, the Chinese *kempō* that Chen Yuan Sai brought did not make much of an impact in Ryūkyū.

In 1682 and 1659, a Chinese official named Wan Shun (汪楫) was sent to Ryūkyū as a senior envoy. Even now, there is a *karate kata* called Wan Shun. However, the *kata* was only adopted by a segment of the Tomari-te styles and did not widely influence Ryukyuan *tiy*. Then there is the *kempō* form that was taught by a Chinese martial artist named Kūsankū around 1761. It was amended by Okinawan martial artists and later taught to Kyan Chōtoku by Yara Pēchin (1816-?), who had been born in Shuri but later moved to

Chatan. Consequently, the name of the *kata* is also known as Chatan Yara no Kūsankū. While Kūsankū was adopted by some Shuri-te styles, as will be discussed later, it was adopted only as a *kumiai jutsu no te*. In other words, it was only a part of the overall system of *tiy* as *yakusoku kumite* (prearranged sparring) or *irikumi te* (free sparring) along with *bo no te*, *sai no te*, *nunchaku no te*, and *ēku no te*. Again, Kūsankū did not have a large impact on *tiy*. The *Ōshima Hikki* (*Ōshima Notes* [1762]) gives the following account of Kūsankū:

> In a previous year, a person who did *kumiai jutsu no te* (said to be the *kempō* written about in the Bubishi) named Kūsankū (probably an honorific title rather than a proper title) came from China. He used both hands and when one hand was held near his breast, the other hand was used for techniques. He used his legs very effectively! While he looked thin and weak, when a large and powerful man grabbed him forcefully, he threw that man to the ground.

Attention should be paid to the fact that *kumiai jutsu no te* (組合術ノ手) is actually written in the above passage and not *kumiai jutsu no jōzu* (組合術ノ上手) as many translators of the passage have done up to now.[2] When doing so, the passage is mistakenly interpreted as saying that Kūsankū was a "person skilled in *kumiai jutsu* from China" even though that is not what is originally written. The fact that the actual passage talks about *kumiai jutsu no te* is an important point since it provides further evidence that *karate* at the time was referred to as *tiy*. In olden days, people used the word *tiy* to refer to a general category that included bare handed fighting techniques as well as *bo*, *sai*, *nunchaku*, *tunfā*, *ēku*, and other *kobudō* weapon techniques. A person known to be trained to fight with bare hands and/or with the *bo* or *sai* would be pointed out by others who say, "*Anuchu ya tiy chikayundo* (That person uses *tiy*)." *Tiy chikaya* or *bushigwā* (warrior) meant a person who did martial arts and a person who skilled in using the *sai* or *bo* would be referred to as *sai (nu) tiy chikiya* or *bo (nu) tiy chikiya*. That is, the *kobudō* weapon name would be the prefix to the word *tiy*.

In describing "*kumiai jutsu no te*," the *Ōshima Notes* show how Chinese *kempō* sparring was incorporated into Okinawa martial arts by adding *te* (*tiy*) as a suffix. Consequently, the notion that the original *karate* was martial arts brought to Ryūkyū from China is clearly a mistaken one.

According to the *Ōshima Notes*, a delegation of 52 Ryukyuans led by Kurayaku Shiohira Pēchin from Akata in Shuri, were on a *kaisen*[3] that was shipwrecked on Ōshima Island in Tosa during a typhoon on its way to Satsuma in 1762. The delegation stayed on Ōshima Island for over a month and was given aid by Tosa officials. During that time, a Tosa Confucian scholar named Tobe Yoshihiro interviewed Shiohira Pēchin about Ryūkyū and wrote down what he heard, including the account that, "In a previous year, a person who did *kumiai jutsu no te* named Kūsankū came from China." Interestingly, the interviewee, Shiohira Pēchin, is from Akata in Shuri, which is where Tūdiy Sakugawa was from. They were roughly the same age as well.

The Chinese *kempō* techniques brought by the three Chinese persons mentioned above did influence Okinawan martial arts, but even after their arrival, *tiy* was still the mainstream and the term *tūdiy* was not widely recognized. The people responsible for establishing *tūdiy* as part of the Okinawan vocabulary were not Chinese but Okinawan *tiy* experts or "*bushi*." First on this list of illustrious experts is Sakugawa Pēchin (Sakugawa Kanga) and he is followed by such people as Matsumura Sōkon, Itosu Ankō, Higaonna Kanryō, Miyagi Chōjun, and Uechi Kanbun. They are all referred to as *bushi*

---

[2] The character is read *te* in Japanese and *tiy* in Okinawan. Adding the character 上 to 手 creates the compound word 上手 (*jōzu*), which means skillful. Also, "*no*" (ノ or の) in Japanese is pronounced "*nu*" in Okinawan.

[3] *Kaisen* (楷船) was a ship that carried rice, sugar, and other tribute items from Ryūkyū to Satsuma.

and incorporated *kempō* from China into the original *tiy* that came to them from ancient times.

At the time, Ryūkyū had high esteem for China and children were always given both Japanese and Chinese names. The fact that most Ryukyuans had Chinese names, whether they were *bushi* or commoners, is an important key in interpreting Ryukyuan history and culture. It follows that it is premature to assume that *karate* techniques are merely Chinese imports simply because Ryukyuan martial arts masters had Chinese names. The high regard that Ryukyuans had for "things Chinese" is the reason why they called Chinese martial arts *tūdiy* to distinguish them from the indigenous *tiy*. Further, it also became necessary to distinguish the two.

What I am calling the "Era of *Tūdiy*" in the Ryūkyū begins in the middle of the 18th century when Sakugawa Kanga, an important minister to King Shō Boku, brought back Chinese *kempō* techniques from China in the 1770s. One might say that this era extends to 1922 when Funakoshi Gichin introduces both *tiy* and *tūdiy* to the Japanese mainland.

However, it is important to remember that although Chinese *kempō* was introduced to Ryūkyū in the 18th century, it was not the case in which the ancient indigenous Ryukyuan *tiy* was completely transformed by it. Rather, it was quite the opposite as Chinese *kempō* techniques have influenced only a small part of tiy. They managed to concretely influence a regional variant of tiy that was later to be known as Naha-te, but it hardly influenced Shuri-te at all. It is essential to remember that even in the "Era of *Tūdiy*," tiy was more widespread and deeply entrenched in Ryukyuan martial arts and it is more accurate to say that it was a period during which tiy and tūdiy coexisted. For lack of a better term, however, I use "Era of Tūdiy" to describe the history of tiy after the mid-18th century.

Consequently, the roots of contemporary tiy go back to the battles between gusuku from the around the 7th century onward. Tiy was well-established as a fighting art by the 10th century and by the 15th century the objective of "killing with one blow" and techniques such as striking vital points with the fist, blocking with the forearm, and kicking became its basic features. It was at that point that tiy was at a refined state that has not fundamentally changed even in the present day.

In relationship to *tiy*, *tūdiy* could be somewhat described as an offshoot in which breathing techniques and stances of *kempō*, *tai chi*, and other Chinese martial arts were incorporated to a limited extent. The mainstream of martial arts in Ryūkyū is *tiy* that has remained fundamentally unchanged even with the development of *tūdiy*.

I would like to discuss the *bushi* who taught *tūdiy*. Sakugawa Kanga (1733-1815) was, of course, a Shuri-te master. It was because of his martial arts expertise that he was one of three personal attendants to the Ryukyuan King. Sakugawa brought back a few Chinese *kempō* techniques to Ryūkyū that he learned in China and is the first Okinawan *karate* master to bring recognition to *tūdiy*. He is therefore given the name "Karate Sakugawa." Sakugawa's official title was Teruya Chikudun Pēchin Kankan and having been trained in martial arts from a young age, he was one of several *bushi* in his family.

However, although Sakugawa Kanga introduced *tūdiy* to Ryūkyū, he did not significantly change the basics of *tiy* and instead preserved it in its original form. Sakugawa's successor, Matsumura Sōkon (1809-?) also knew tūdiy techniques, but like his teacher, adhered to the traditional tiy. As a result, the traditional Ryukyuan form of tiy has been passed down intact to the present in the form of Shuri-te. If the two men had replaced tiy techniques with tūdiy techniques, the original tiy would not have survived until today. There is no doubt that Sakugawa Kanga and Matsumura Sōkon placed much importance on Ryukyuan martial arts and other traditions.

Matsumura Sōkon became a personal attendant to the Ryukyuan King before the age of 30 and it was in this capacity that he was sent to China and Satsuma. His scholarship and martial arts were at the highest levels and it is said that even in China, a mecca of martial arts itself, master warriors in Fujian knew of him. There is also a well-told episode of Matsumura's matches with a woman warrior named Ume. In their first match, he loses bitterly to Ume, but emerges victorious through superior tactics in a return match. Matsumura ends up marrying Ume and proceeds to become an important historical figure as a diligent official and martial artist. While he was a grandmaster of Shuri-te, Matsumura also had a significant knowledge of *tūdiy* as he had learned it in China as well as inherited some of its techniques from his teacher, Sakugawa.

When he was 20 years old, Matsumura passed the official Ryukyuan Kingdom test to become a *"samuree."* Because of his rare skills as a *tiy* master, his first official position in 1813 was personal attendant for Shō Kō, the 17th King of the Second Shō Dynasty. Matsumura also went on to be personal attendant for the Shō Iku, the 18th King, and for Shō Tai, whose destiny was to be the last of the Shō Kings before Japan's annexation of Ryūkyū. In his lifetime, he traveled twice each to China and Satsuma. Matsumura not only had a reputation as the personal attendant of the Ryukyuan King, but was also respected by martial artists in Fujian, China as a master of *tiy*. In Satsuma, he learned the basics of Jigen-*ryū* sword fighting techniques. However, although he is said to have received certificate in Jigen-*ryū* after training for six months, he was probably given this honor because of his status as the Ryukyuan King's personal attendant. It is unlikely that he could have received an official certificate in the style after only six months of training and to say that Matsumura was a master in Jigen-ryū does disservice to real Jigen masters. In fact, to make assumptions of other styles, whether they be other sword fighting styles or martial arts such as jūdō and tūdiy.

It follows that to the notion that Matsumura tiy was somehow connected to Jigen-ryū is absolutely false. He merely learned the basics of Jigen-ryū and was given an honorary title. Matsumura was a tiy master, but not a sword fighting master (in Jigen-ryū).

Matsumura put into practice the Seven Virtues of the Warrior: prevent violence, stop war, uphold government order, determine correct standards of achievement, work with the people in mind, keep harmony among factions, and build the wealth of society. Such was his upright standing that there was a saying that, "Before Matsumura, there was no Matsumura and after Matsumura, there has been no Matsumura." He has a very important position in the history as founder of Shuri-te, but the distinction between Shuri-te and Naha-te developed after *tiy* became associated with geographical regions as secretly practiced techniques around the 17th century. Up to that point, *tiy* was associated to individuals such as with "*Ufugusuku nu tiy*," "*Shirutaru nu tiy*," and "*Makabi nu tiy*." Consequently, both Shuri-te and Naha-te are manifestations of the same original Ryukyuan fighting techniques.

Sakugawa and Matsumura were excellent warriors in the ancient Ryukyuan *tiy* tradition to which Sakugawa introduced some Chinese *kempō* techniques and is thus called Tūdiy Sakugawa. However, the fact remains that both men were Shuri-te masters. The person who introduced fundamentally new Chinese *kempō* techniques to *tiy* was Higaonna Kanryō. It was his appearance on the scene that led to the real development of *tūdiy*.

By introducing the very novel *sanchin* from China to Okinawa, Higaonna brought about the divergence of Naha-te from the original *tiy*. Nothing like *sanchin* existed in the ancient Ryukyuan *tiy* before and its introduction led to the need to clearly distinguish between Shuri-te, which was a continuation of the original Okinawan *tiy*, and Naha-te, which evolved differently with the new arrival from China.

Because Matsumura was the leading master of Shuri-te at the time, he is seen as its founder, but it is imperative to remember that he was not its creator. The indigenous fighting techniques known as tiy were born out in the battlefields of Okinawa in the 7th to 12th centuries. In the 17th and 18th centuries, tiy became known by regional names, such as Shuri-te and Naha-te. Naha-te diverged significantly when it adopted Chinese sanchin as part of its core techniques. Meanwhile, Shuri-te was not influenced significantly by the Chinese sanchin and remained the inheritor of the original tiy techniques, which it later passed down to the Shōrin-ryū schools. Consequently, it is important to acknowledge that because Naha-te adopted Chinese *kempō* techniques, it became known as *tūdiy* and became the predecessor of the Gojū-*ryū* schools.

From the 18th century, the original ancient Ryukyuan fighting techniques (*tiy*) coexisted with the new Chinese-influenced *tūdiy*. Eventually, the more prestigious name of *tūdiy* began to be used commonly to refer to both forms of fighting. The person who introduced the Chinese *sanchin* to Naha-te and brought about the changes which led to drastic differentiation in the very concept of *tiy* was Higaonna Kanryō (1853-1914). It is no exaggeration to say that there was no one else besides him who is responsible for such a clear distinction between *tiy* and *tūdiy*. If Higaonna had not learned sanchin in China and introduced it to Okinawa, it is very likely that the ancient Okinawan fighting techniques would have still been known simply as "*tiy*" and would not have had such a convoluted genealogy.

Higaonna Kanryō was born in Nishimura, Naha as the fourth son of Higaonna Kanyō, who sold firewood that his three "*Yanbarusen*" ships brought to Naha Harbor from the northern Yanbaru region of Okinawa. Higaonna's *warabinā* (childhood name) was Mōshi and his *Tōnā* (Chinese name) was Shèn Shàn Xī. He was born in the same year that Commodore Matthew C. Perry sailed into Naha. Higaonna was small in stature and was said to have exceptionally quick reflexes. From age 17 to 22, he studied *tiy* under Arakaki Seishō *1840-1920, who was known as "Mayā Arakachi (Arakaki the cat)." Higaonna was not of the shizoku (noble) class and the details of his travel China have been the subject of different narratives. It is known that he went to China in 1876, which was a year after the Japanese government issued a prohibition on Okinawans going to China. As such, he is considered a member of the cohort of "Chinese exiles" who left Okinawa for China around the same time. Higaonna was 22 years old when he went to China with a letter of introduction from Prince Kojō. The version of the story given by Nagamine Shōshin says that he called upon Master Ryūryūkō, while another version posited by Shimabukuro Kōyū says that his teacher was Waishinzan. Further, Miyagi Chōjun says that he was taught by the plasterer

Tōryō. (Sawada Shigeru *Karate Meijin Retsuden* [*Legendary Karate Masters*]) Ryūryūkō (born 1852) had learned Luo Han Fist from his father and later White Crane Fist from the Yong Chun Family. Higaonna was 24 and Ryūryūkō was 25 when they are said to have met and former became the latter's first student. Higaonna probably returned to Okinawa in 1879. Because he was associated with the pro-China faction in Okinawa, he was not able to talk about his time in China as the shadow of Japan's anti-Chinese militarism grew increasingly oppressive. As a result, Higaonna's time in Fujian is shrouded in mystery.

A man named Kojō, who was of one of the *shizoku* families of Kume Village, was also in China learning *kempō* at the same time as Higaonna. However, the two men had different ways of teaching *sanchin*. Kojō instructed his students in the basic *sanchin* posture by telling them, "Put strength into your lower abdomen while folding it slowly as if you are folding a paper lantern." While in this posture, the feet are opened up with the toes pointed inward and the elbows are touching the sides of the body. The fists are extended outward in right angles with strong emphasis on the so-called closed fist form. It is said that a person's skill could be observable from just this posture. Higaonna's instruction greatly different from Kojō's as he told his students to "while clenching the muscles in the lumbar area as if clamping the spinal cord between the right and left sides of the pelvis, take the tension stored in the navel region and transfer it to the stomach." In other words, strength was not simply put into the region right below the navel. Instead, one first put strength in the region below the navel, then pulled it up to the region above the navel and clenched the abdomen. In doing so, the stomach and internal organs become completely separated from the outer layer of skin and are hardened. It is interesting that while both men learned at the same place in Fujian, their sanchin were very different. There are even anecdotes of "tūdiy hearing" being held to scientifically determine which sanchin was stronger. A surgeon named Okamatsu is said to have summoned both men to examine them and make a judgment.

Why is Higaonna known as the founder of Naha-te? Although he received instruction in the original Okinawan *tiy* from Arakaki Seishō, he brought back from China the very novel *sanchin* and breathing techniques and incorporated as the basics of what he taught in Naha. *Tiy* was born out of the battles between *gusuku* and passed secretly from master to student, but after the *gusuku* period ended after the 12th century and was followed by a long period of peace from around the time of the Second Shō Dynasty, *tiy* transformed into techniques for the self-defense of each *gusuku*, where they were passed down through the generations as such. Up to the 17th century, *tiy* techniques were given regional names according to where they originated from as in the case of Shuri-te and Naha-te. Around the same time that regional names were being adopted, Chinese *kempō* techniques also began entering Ryūkyū. Then in the 19th century, there was a succession of Ryukyuan *tiy* masters who trained in China and brought back *kempō* techniques. It was around this time that *tūdiy* developed as a distinct concept from *tiy* and began to be gradually recognized by the general public in Ryūkyū. Finally, the person who brought revolutionary changes to the ancient indigenous techniques of Okinawan *tiy* was none other than Higaonna Kanryō.

Kanryō Higaonna

These changes were not only through his introduction of *sanchin* movements and breathing techniques, but also through open-handed blocking and grasping techniques. Because Higaonna had brought these techniques to Okinawa from China, a distinction needed to be made between them and the indigenous *tiy* techniques. Thus, techniques that came from China, or "*tō* (唐)," were labelled as *tūdiy*.

The stance of indigenous Okinawan *tiy* was a "natural stance." The feet are at shoulder width with the front foot aimed at the opponent and the back foot pointing at a 45-degree angle from the plane of the front foot. The knees are slightly bent and the center of gravity lowered so that a kick can be made at any time with either the front of back leg. However, Higaonna introduced the *sanchin* stance that had not existed previously in Okinawa and was indeed the epitome of *tūdiy*. Of course, the horse stance (*kibadachi*) in Shuri-te's *Naihanchi kata* had the same purpose as the *sanchin* stance in that it was aimed at protecting the groin while hardening the body through the flexing of the lower limbs. However, the horse stance in *Naihanchi* is designed to move sideways and not forward as in the *sanchin*. Modifying the Naihanchi horse stance to move forward in *sanchin* was a very large innovation. It is not entirely clear whether Higaonna innovated within the tradition of *tiy* or within his knowledge of Chinese *kempō*. However, because he spent 15 years in

China and because Uechi Kanbun had also brought *sanchin* back as a core *kata* from China as well, *sanchin* is without doubt within the realm of *tūdiy*.

Breathing techniques are also fundamentally different in *tiy* and *tūdiy*. The breathing in *tiy* is again "natural." Focused power is released while exhaling and tension is released while inhaling. Emphasis is also placed on not letting the opponent read one's breathing. Saying that breathing is "natural" does not mean that one does nothing about his or her breath and it goes without saying that *tiy* required training in breath control. The complex process of breathing in while gathering power for an attack, then letting out the breath at the instant of the strike and then immediately stopping the breath to harden the abdomen is not an easily acquired skill. It is clearly evident that this "natural" breathing technique has been passed down since ancient times in Okinawa through its orthodox form through Shuri-te.

In Higaonna's *sanchin*, a full breath is inhaled through the nose and stored in the *tanden*. It is then exhaled with a "*ha*" sound from deep down in the throat. This undulating sound is overwhelming to those who hear it. This breathing technique did not exist before in Okinawan *tiy*.

It is clear that this breathing technique is an introduction from China as it exists in most Chinese *kempō* styles. It is noticeable if one observes *tai chi*. Consequently, this breathing technique is fundamental to *tūdiy* and has been passed down through Naha-te.

The heir to Higaonna's Naha-te (*tūdiy*) was Miyagi Chōjun (1888-1953). Miyagi was born in April, 1888 in Higashimachi, Naha. At the time, the Miyagi Family was well known in Naha for its wealth. Miyagi had been blessed with a strong body and was a rambunctious boy who loved sports. At age 14, he began training with Higaonna Kanryō, the unquestionably top master in Naha. From that point onward, he became part of the Naha-te (*tūdiy*) geneaology. At the time, *karate* was not well-understood even in Okinawa as it was thought to be a tool simply for fighting. The common misperception was that if one trained in *karate*, he would develop into a rough character and be marginalized by society. As a result, few people trained in *karate* and if one did train in *karate*, he or she would do it secretly as to not be seen by anyone else, including family members. Further, beginning training under a teacher required an introduction from someone of the highest reputation.

However, right around the time that Miyagi was beginning his training, large changes were happening in *karate* as it went from being shrouded in secret to being taught in public. In 1902, *karate* became a part of physical education classes at the Shuri Elementary School. From being transmitted from master to student, *karate* became to be taught in schools in groups. In April 1906, *karate* clubs were established at the Okinawan Prefectural No. 1 Middle School, the Naha Municipal Commercial School, and the Okinawan Prefectural Teachers School. Similar clubs were also established around the same time at other Okinawan Prefectural schools as it became an official part of public physical education in Okinawa.

Higaonna's training methods were extremely tough. For the first 3 to 4 years, *sanchin* was beaten into students and most left before then. Only the most patient and strong-willed students could last Higaonna's training. Miyagi was not only perseverant, but he had a strong desire to learn and often give up food and sleep to train day and night. His efforts paid off as his strength and skill surpassed everyone else's and he matured into Higaonna's favorite students with a promising future. Miyagi gained self-confidence as he became recognized for his abilities, but he always showed humility to everyone he came in contact with and became a highly respected and popular person.

In 1915, at age 27, Miyagi received permission from Higaonna to make a long-awaited trip to China with his friend Gogenki, a White Crane master originally from Fujian. However, Miyagi was forced to return a year later when Higaonna died. In the wake of his beloved teacher's death, Miyagi immersed himself even more in *karate* studies. Also, because of his character and abilities, many people sought to be his student and so in 1917 he opened up his own *dōjō*.

At that time, the Okinawan *karate* world was approaching a crucial turning point. In 1922, the Shuri-te instructor Funakoshi Gichin introduced *tūdiy* to Japan through demonstrations in Tokyo. His appearance on the stage in Japan led to a flurry of invitations for *tūdiy* instructors to teach at Japanese universities.

Karate had been included as part of the official curriculum at the Okinawa Prefectural Police Training Center and the Naha Municipal Commercial. In April of 1929, Miyagi became an instructor at both institutions, which led to many other requests to teach to workers at the court and different prefectural agencies. In mainland Japan, *karate* clubs were started at Kyoto University, Kansai University, Ritsumeikan University, and Doshisha University and Miyagi was invited annually to teach to these clubs.

In November 1930, a *karate* club was established at the Okinawa Prefectural Sports Education Association. Miyagi was recommended as club president and in that position was able to teach *karate* widely to the general public. In the same year, taking a line of Kenpō Hakku or "the eight laws of the fist," which reads "the way of inhaling and exhaling is hardness and softness (*hō wa gōjū wo donto su*)," Miyagi named the Naha-te (*tūdiy*) that he inherited from Higaonna "Gōjū-*ryū*."

Upon becoming the president of the *karate* club of the Okinawa Prefectural Sports Education Association, Miyagi also became a standing representative for the Okinawa branch of the Dai Nippon Butoku Kai (Greater Japan Martial Arts Association). In these positions, Miyagi was able to bring about leaps and bounds in the development of Naha-te and Gōjū-*ryū*. Strong connections were established between Gōjū-*ryū* and the central Japanese government through one of its wings, the Japan Sports Education Association. These linkages enabled Gōjū-*ryū* to eventually become one of the four major *karate* styles in mainland Japan. This set it apart from Shōrin-*ryū* (Shuri-te) and Uechi-*ryū* (*tūdiy*), which were not able to establish themselves as major *karate* styles in mainland Japan. It was because of Miyagi's relations to the center of Japanese power that allowed Gōjū-*ryū* to be the only one of the three main *ryū* in Okinawa to ascend to the position of one of the major karate *ryū* in mainland Japan.

In 1934, Miyagi was invited to Hawai'i to help spread *karate* there and on May 5, 1937, he did a demonstration of karate at the Butoku Sai (Martial Arts Festival) that was sponsored by the Dai Nippon Butoku Kai. In the same year, Miyagi was conferred the title of *kyōshi* (master instructor) by the Dai Nippon Butoku Kai. It was the first time in all of Japan that a karate instructor had ever given such recognition. In 1938, Miyagi was appointed to be master instructor of karate at the Okinawa Prefectural Teacher's College. Higaonna and Miyagi's *karate*, which is being passed down as Naha-te/Gōjū-*ryū*, has taken a dominant role in the Japan Karate Federation and in the decisions around designated *kata*.

After World War II ended in 1945, the newly established Okinawa Civilian Administration appointed Miyagi as an instructor at the Okinawan Police Academy. While serving in that capacity, he trained students at the dōjō at his home in Tsuboya in Naha. However, Miyagi unfortunately passed away at the age of 65 on October 8, 1953.

Miyagi wrote *Karatedō Gaisetsu* (*An Outline of the Way of Karate*), which was from a manuscript that he prepared for a lecture and demonstration entitled "About The Way of Karate (Karatedō ni Tsuite)" that he did at the Fourth Floor Lecture Hall of the Sakaisuji Meiji Store on January 28, 1931. He prepared the manuscript as the Standing Representative of the Okinawa Branch of the Dai Nippon Butoku Kai. At the time, nine years had passed since Funakoshi Gichin introduced Okinawan *tūdiy* to the Japanese mainland in 1922. In *Karatedō Gaisetsu*, Miyagi states:

What is karate? It is the practice of training of mind and cultivation of body in everyday life to protect oneself in an emergency without the use of weapons. In most cases and in principle it is the body itself that is used to defeat opponents. However, depending on the particular circumstances, weapons may also be utilized.

Miyagi also adds:

People generally mistakenly believe that the breaking of five wooden boards or several roof tiles with the bare fist are the main part of *karate*. These things are only a minor, if not trivial, part of karate training. As with other fighting arts, the ultimate way (*dō*) of *karate* is not achievable with mere teaching and words.

The mastery of karate in the realm beyond "mere teaching and words" harks back to the olden days when training was done strictly by oral transmission and nothing was written down as masters did not show or teach their *tiy* to anyone outside of their close circle and asked for their students' absolute fidelity. Of course, books, photos, videos and other materials available in the present would have constituted a violation of the spirit of *tiy* and any student found with them would be surely expelled.

Miyagi compares different theories about the origin of *karate* such as Thirty-Six Chinese Families, Ōshima Notes, and Keichō Importation theories. However, he notes that none of these theories are backed by any solid evidence and proposes that the ancient and indigenous *tiy* and the imported *kempō* merged together and underwent extraordinary historical development and that it continues to be rationally improved in the present.

Most Okinawan *karateka* support the thesis that martial techniques in the form of *tiy* existed from ancient times in Okinawa. It is no exaggeration to say that this is the mainstream opinion in Okinawa. For Miyagi, who was a successor of Naha-te (*tūdiy*), his statement that Chinese *kempō* and *tūdiy* merged with *tiy* is evidence that he also held the opinion that *karate* had indigenous roots. Further, as Miyagi was witnessing the spread of *karate* to the Japanese mainland and the development of variations of it, he mentions its "further rational improvement and development in the present." This statement was made when techniques and *kata* that had been introduced in the Japanese mainland were being modified and protective gear was being developed as karate was going toward being a competitive sport. However, the statement was made by Miyagi in his position as an officer in the Japan Sports Education Association and there is no way of knowing exactly what Miyagi felt in his heart as a *bushi* (warrior). A hundred *bushi* (or *karateka*) in Okinawa would all tell their students in their own way that "*karate kata* should not be capriciously changed." Miyagi no doubt taught the same things, but his statement reflects his need to be a supporter of what was happening in the Japanese mainland as he was entrenched in the central authority structure of Japan as the Okinawan representative to both the Japan Sports Education Association and the Dai Nippon Butoku Kai. One cannot ignore the fact that Gōjū-*ryū* was able to quickly become one of the four major karate styles in the Japanese mainland was due to both Higaonna and Miyagi having been in the important positions of Okinawan branch presidents of the Dai Nippon Butoku Kai and the Japan Sports Education Association, which were both entities related to the central Japanese government.

There was one other Okinawan *bushi*, not related to Gōjū-*ryū,* who was important in the history of *tūdiy*. Like Higanonna, he also went to Fujian to learn Southern Fist. His name was Uechi Kanbun (1877-1948), the founder of Uechi- *ryū*.

Uechi-*ryū karatedō* has the shortest history of the three main Okinawan *karate* styles. Its founder Uechi Kanbun went to Fujian, where he learned from *Zhou Zihe* (周子和). Uechi-*ryū* is based on the style that he learned in Fujian, Tiger Fist (*pangainūn kempō*). However, there exists a theory that Uechi is part of the Sai Fist (蔡家拳) lineage that goes back to Sai Chōkō (蔡肇功: 1655-1737).

We could include both Gōjū-*ryū* and Uechi-*ryū* in the same Chinese *kempō* genealogy because they both have *sanchin* as their basic *kata* and use similar breathing techniques. In *sanchin*, however, while Gōjū-*ryū* uses a clenched fist rather than the open hand, Uechi-*ryū* steadfastly uses only the open hand. It is on this point that the two styles have diverged in their own unique direction. Although *sanchin* appears to be very simple, its stances, postures, and steps contain not only the martial arts techniques that are characteristic of Uechi-*ryū*, but also the Uechi-*ryū*'s fundamental principles and essence. *Sanchin* is held with high esteem in Uechi-*ryū* as a kata of both great psychological and physical value as repetitive practice of *sanchin* results in the simultaneous development of mind, body, and technique. Further, as one progresses in *sanchin* training, he or she also develops the breathing techniques that further support mind, body, and technique. Specifically, *sanchin* training toughens the body so that it can withstand attacks and increases the practitioner's offensive and defensive speed. It also enables the practitioner to develop mental toughness, clear judgement, and good character.

One prominent feature in regular Uechi-*ryū* training is *kotekitae* or "forearm tempering," which involves two people striking each other's forearms to harden them. Such dynamic training enables one to improve his or her attacking and blocking abilities. Also, a characteristic of Uechi-*ryū* is the use of the tips of the fingers and toes for striking. In fact, strikes with the *seiken* (full fist) are extremely rare in Uechi-*ryū*, while strikes with *nukite* (spear hand), *boshiken* (thumb fist), and stiffened toes are common.

Uechi Kanbun was born as the first son of Kantoku, who was of *samurē* descent, and Tsuru in 1877 in the mountain village of Izumi on the Motubu Peninsula in northern Okinawa. It is said that Uechi Kanbun went to China to escape being drafted into the Japanese military when he was 19. He arrived in Fuzhou and stayed temporarily at the Okinawan Fellowship Hall (also known as *Ryūkyūkan* or *Jūeneki*). Uechi initially trained at the Kojō *dōjō* under another Okinawan named Makabi, but soon left there to learn from a Tiger Fist teacher named Zhou Zhi He (Shūshiwa in Japanese). For the next 10 years, Uechi trained in both *kem kempō* and Chinese medicine. In 1904, at the age of 27, he received a certificate of mastery in Tiger Fist or *pangainūn* (半硬軟) *kempō*. Three years later at the age of 30, he opened his own *dōjō* in Nansoue, a town about 400km southwest of Fuzhou. However, in the fall of 1909, a student of Uechi killed a neighbor in a dispute over water during a drought. Taking responsibility for the incident, Uechi closed his *dōjō*. In 1910, he returned to Izumi in Okinawa after having spent 13 years in China. Soon after he married a woman named Tōyama Gozei and had two sons and two daughters with her. In 1924, at the age of 47, he left his family behind to search for stable work in the industrial region of Kansai in mainland Japan. Uechi ended up working as a watchman at a textile mill run by the Hi no Maru Sangyō Company in the town of Tebira-cho in Wakayama Prefecture. A young Okinawan man named Tomoyose Ryūyū who was 24 at the time convinced Uechi to teach him *pangainūn kempō*. It was the first time that he had taught the style outside of China. A few years later, with Tomoyose's help, Uechi opened up his "*shataku* (dormitory) *dōjō*" on the compounds of the textile mill. He was 49 at the time. It is believed that Uechi only taught 3 *kata*, *kotekitae* and Chinese medicine at this dojo. In 1932, Uechi (then 52) opened up a more permanent *dōjō* in an area where many Okinawans lived. His new *dōjō* was called the Pangainūn-ryū Tōdi Kenkyūjō. The next year, "Shūbukai" was added to the name.

Uechi's son, Kanei, received his certificate in pangainūn in 1937 and began teaching in the Kansai area. Two years later, at the age of 28, Kanei married Nakahara Shige, who was from Izumi. In the fall of 1940, the students at Pangainūn-ryū Tōdi Kenkyūjō changed the name of their style to Uechi-ryū. At the same time, Kanbun (63) was given the title of Sōshihan or General Instructor and Kanei (30) was awarded 5th degree (godan) rank. In 1942, as Kanei's students were beginning to be drafted to fight in the war, he returned to Okinawa to be with his family in Nago. In Okinawa, Kanei began teaching Uechi-ryū tūdiy to his brother Kansei and other young people in his neighborhood. This was the first time that Uechi-ryū was taught in Okinawa. Uechi-ryū experienced a rare fate as it was brought from China 18 years earlier by Uechi Kanbun and was only taught in his home island after having been first taught in Japan. Eventually, however, Uechi-ryū was able to ascend to the position of Okinawa's three main *karate* styles.

The only three *kata* that Uechi Kanbun brought with him from China and incorporated into Uechi-ryū were *sanchin*, *seisan*, and *sanseirui*. Incidentally, these three kata are also found in Gōjū-ryū. Uechi Kanei subsequently added *kanshiwa*, *seirui*, and *kanchin* to the Uechi-ryū repertoire. Later, *seichin* was added by Uehara and *kanshū* by Itokazu Seiki.

While Uechi-ryū is one of the three main karate styles in Okinawa, none of its *kata* are recognized as *shitei* (designated) *kata* by the Japan Karate Federation (JKF). The *kata* that are recognized as *shitei kata* by the JKF are from broader genealogies of Shorin-ryū and Gōjū-ryū. However, while Gōjū-ryū and Uechi-ryū were two styles greatly influenced by Chinese kempō, only Gōjū-ryū *kata* became *shitei kata*. I will explain this in greater detail later.

There is one more individual who cannot be left out of this "Era of *Tūdiy*." It is the Shuri-te master Itosu Ankō, who was a student of Sakugawa and Matsumura and eventually become a senior statesman of Shuri-te as an inheritor of the ancient *tiy* its purest form. While I call it the "Era of *Tūdiy*," it is important to note that the flow of Chinese *kempō* techniques to Okinawa was not contained entirely in *tūdiy* and Naha-te. Rather, it is more fitting to think of *tiy* and Shuri-te as the mainstream in Okinawa and that the novel Chinese *kempō* only slightly influenced it. Consequently, the "Era of *Tūdiy*" was one in which both *tiy* and tūdiy came of age together. During this era of coexistence of both *tiy* and *tūdiy*, the veil of secrecy was lifted from fighting techniques in Okinawa and they entered a whole new age of being taught publically. A pioneer in opening the door to the new age was Itosu.

In April 1901, *tūdiy* made a remarkable public appearance when it was taught as part of the physical education curriculum at the Shuri Ordinary Primary School. Up to that point, *tūdiy* techniques were passed down only within closed lineages and taught one-to-one from teacher to student. Thereafter, however, an epoch-making change in the way fighting techniques in Okinawa were taught that involved modifying *kata* and teaching them in groups. It was Itosu who devised the new pedagogy. Incidentally, it was not until 1911 that *kendō* was made a required subject at middle schools in Japan.

Judō was only made so in 1931. The unique Okinawan techniques of *tiy* were already part of Okinawan school curriculum much earlier than *kendō* and judō were introduced into Japanese schools. Articles about the education superintendent of Okinawa making a report to the Japanese Ministry of Education of the results of *karate* being introduced to schools and about the Japanese Navy doing research on *tūdiy* were published in the Okinawan newspapers (such as *Ryūkyū Shimpō* on January 19, 1913).

    Tiy was completely passed on and trained in secrecy. The reason for this was because it was important in battle and to teach to to others who could use it against you would diminish its value. In order to win in battle, *tiy* was simply not taught publically.

    However, in the Era of *Tūdiy* coincided with the Ryukyuan Kingdom's period of peace. In this long absence of war, fighting techniques gradually began to emerge out of secrecy and finally, *tūdiy* was demonstrated in groups in public spaces. This was indeed a transformation for *tiy*. *Karate* originated as fighting techniques and not as exercise or sport. In its original form, breathing was completely individual. However, the impetus for it becoming a group-oriented activity was because the art of breathing, which was a crucial element of fighting, was lost. In a group, the individual needs to match his or her breath to the group, unlike in actual combat, where breathing was part of the fighting techniques. At the point when *tūdiy* began being taught in groups and in public, it began to undergo large changes as it became oriented to sports and exercise rather than combat.

    In 1904, Itosu was commissioned to be the *karate* instructor at the First Prefectural Middle School and Yabe Kentsū was commissioned to be the *karate* instructor at the Teacher's College. In the same year, war broke out between Russia and Japan and Miyagi Chōjun went to Fujian to train in *kempō*. The next year, *karate* clubs were established at the First Prefectural Middle School, Naha Commercial School, and Prefectural Teacher's College. Subsequently, *karate* clubs were established at the Prefectural Agricultural School, Prefectural Industrial School, Prefectural Fisheries School, and other schools. Around the same time, Itosu created the 2nd to 5th *heian kata* from the *pinan kata*. It is believed that the *pinan kata* was created by Itosu out of the original *chiang nan kata* since there are slight differences between the two *kata*. However, it is also believed that *pinan* was created out of the *kusanku kata*.

In 1908, Itosu, who had become the leading figure in the spread of *karate* in Okinawa, composed the *Tōde (Tūdiy) Jūkun* or "Ten Precepts of Tōde." He was 78 years old at the time. In the *Tōde Jūkun,* Itosu proposed the consistent use of only the term *tūdiy* instead of using both *tiy* and *tūdiy* interchangeably. Thereafter, the fighting techniques that had been known as *tiy* for over a millennium became to officially be called *tūdiy*. This was an important change. This important modification in terminology first occurred in schools, but among the general Okinawan population, *tiy* had much more familiarity and practitioners of Shuri-te were probably not about to quietly acquiesce to the name change. However, *tiy* gradually began to be called *tūdiy*. While it is said that there can no "what ifs" in history, if Itosu had not settled on the word *tūdiy* and used *tiy* instead, we might not have had the confusion that we experience in the present around "*karate*." What is known as *karate* today, would have been called *tiy* and spread to Japan as such. The word *tūdiy* would have gone out of usage and not givev birth to the word "*karate*." It is necessary to recognize Itosu's many accomplishments, but from a Ryukyuan historical and cultural perspective, we cannot deny that his call for the use of *tūdiy* as a term to cover both *tiy* and *tūdiy* was the root of many issues in later generations.

Section 4 The Era of Karate (空手)

1. The Spread of *Tiy*: From Ryūkyū to the Japanese Mainland

The early formation of Okinawan *tiy* took place during the 7th to 12th centuries during the *gusuku* period. Thereafter, until the 18th century, it developed as a unique collection of fighting techniques. However, in the 17th and 18th centuries, Chinese *kempō* techniques were introduced to Okinawa and were subsequently Okinawanized and called *tūdiy*. Because Chinese *kempō* techniques were amalgamated into the indigenous *tiy*, both terms – *tiy* and *tūdiy* – were used interchangeably in Okinawa. Consequently, we can say that only *tiy* existed until the 18th century, but thereafter *tiy* and *tūdiy coexisted* in Okinawa. In any case, however, it is clear that *tiy* was the main branch of this geneaology.

Tiy and *tūdiy* became "*karate*" after their introduction to the Japanese mainland. More specifically, the Era of Karate began when the *karateka* Funakoshi Gichin went to Tōkyō in 1922 at the behest of the Okinawa Prefectural School Affairs Division to introduce the secret fighting arts of *tūdiy* at the First *Kobudo Taiiku Hakurankai* (Ancient Martial Arts Physical Education Exhibition) that was organized by the Japanese Ministry of Education.

Baron Ie Chochoku, who was then a prominent member of the Okinawa Prefectural Association, had read about Funakoshi presentation in a newspaper article. He immediately invited Funakoshi and Gima Shinkin to do a special demonstration in front of military officials, government officials, and other important persons at his home. The Baron's promise to the two men to actively support their efforts to spread of Ryukyuan *tūdiy* to the mainland Japan was not only because of his important role as a representative of Okinawans in Japan, but also because he had also studied Shuri-te under Matsumura Sōkon, the same teacher as the two men.

It was not the case where *tiy* or *tūdiy* had not been spread to the Japanese mainland before Funakoshi. Gima Shinkin gives the following account:

> We cannot overlook the private *kata* training and demonstrations that were taking place at the Edō manors of various feudal *daimyo* and at town training halls from the closing years of the Tokugawa Period through the first few years of the Meiji Period. There were many *karateka* traveling between Ryūkyū and the mainland from the end of the Tokugawa Period through the first years of Meiji and some martial artists, aficionados, and such were inviting them to do demonstrations and *kata* training that they would imitate. Ryukyuans would be invited to have *bojutsu* matches at the Zōshikan and Bōnotsu Station in Kagoshima. Ryukyuan *karateka* would be invited to teach fist strikes and kicks and at the Edō manors (of the Shimazu, Hosokawa, Nabeshima, Ōmura, Kuroda, Mōri, Ichiyanagi, and Date) or at private training halls (of Yōshin-*ryū*, Tenshin Shinyō-*ryū*, and Kitō-*ryū*).

After the new Meiji Government was established, because of their suspected connection to the assassination of Assistant Military Supervisor Sera Shuzō, Ōtsuki Hiroyasu, Kodaira Genrō, and others were confined to the Date manor in Edō for two years. Ōtsuki and Kodaira's write in their journals of their observances of "unusual" Ryukyuan martial arts in the Date residence. At the Kuroda residence in the Kasumigaseki area of Edō, it is well-documented that two Ryukyuan *kempo* masters were invited to do demonstrations of *tūdiy kata*. Based on such reports, it is possible to make guesses as to the identity of the Ryukyuan martial artists who went to Japan. For example, among the members of the delegation from Okinawa that attended the coronation ceremony of the Meiji Emperor were prominent students of Matsumura Sōkon, including Prince Ie Chōchoku (Shō Ken), Council of Three Member Ginowan

Uekata Chōho (Shō Yū Kō), and Regent Kyan Pēchin Chōfu (Shō Isshin). These delegation members had learned at least two or three *kata* from Matsumura. The delegation stayed from July 1872 to February 1873 at the Ryūkyū Residence in Tokyo. To stave of the lack of exercise, the members did *tūdiy kata* practice in the courtyard. A merchant who saw the Ryukyuans practicing spread the rumor to other people in the neighborhood that, "they [the Ryukyuans] have so much free time that they are doing Ryukyuan dances every morning." Another story was gathered a few decades ago ago by Kaneko Haruji when he was writing Restoration Japan (*Isshin no Nihon*) and there might be a kernel of truth to it. In the spring of 1920, at the welcoming party for new members of the Keiō University Kendō Club, Arakaki Kōmo (新垣恒茂) performed "Kūsankū Odori," which he took the *kūsankū kata* and arranged as a dance. The captain of the club, Konishi Yasuhiro, easily saw through the dance as he commented, "You're doing a martial arts *kata*, aren't you?" In other words, the point is that students of Ryukyuan *tiy* routinely practiced kata wherever they could and whenever they had the opportunity.

Even after Prince Ie was sent back by the Meiji Government to Ryūkyū to carry out the heavy duty of dismantling Ryukyuan Kingdom, high ranking Ryukyuans went to Tokyo, including Urasoe Uekata Chōshō (Council of Three), Ōgimi Pēchin Chōkon (Regent), Yonabaru Pēchin Ryōketsu (Regent), Ikegusuku Pēchin Anki (Council of Three), Kōchi Uekata Tokukō (Finance Magistrate), Uchima Pēchin Kakun (Regent), and Oyasato Pēchin Hōgen (Regent). The men stayed in the Ryūkyū Residence in Tōkyō while working fervently to keep Ryūkyū as a territory under the rule of the Shō Dynasty as it had been for the previous centuries. Through their connections to powerful men from Satsuma who had been instrumental in establishing the Meiji Government, the Ryukyuans tried desperately to gain allies from among influential leaders from different regions in Japan who were in Tokyo.

Despite their efforts, however, in May of 1875, the new Meiji Government ordered the 19th King of the Shō Dynasty, Shō Tai, to take up residence in Tokyo. The deposed King moved into the Imperial Household

Ministry Annex in Kojimachi along with his second son Shō In and an entourage of about 100. It is highly likely that a significant number of *tūdiy* masters were in the entourage. Shō Tai ascended to the throne at the age of 6 in place of his father, Shō Iku, who died at the age of 35. Having inherited his father's weak physical and mental disposition, he began receiving *tūdiy* training at an early age from Matsumura Sōkon, his bodyguard and most respected martial artist in the Ryukyuan government. Thanks to having survived Matsumura's severe Spartan training, Shō Tai lived 24 years longer than his father.

Toyama Kyūzō, who had graduated from the Teacher's College in Okinawa, became the principal of the Tōkyō Municipal Yodobashi Primary School in May of 1895. Toyama is well known as the "Father of Hawaiian emigration" for his work to send the first group of Okinawan emigrants to Hawai'i. What is not as well-known was his mastery of *sūpārinpei*, which he introduced to different parts of Tokyo. In the half century since Prince Ie and his delegation arrived in Tōkyō in 1872 until Funakoshi arrived in the same city in 1922, there were at least several Okinawans who introduced *tūdiy* to mainland Japan. Consequently, there is the viewpoint that the spread of *tūdiy* to mainland Japan did not begin with Funakoshi and Gima's demonstration at the Kōdōkan.

Further, in 1889, *tūdiy* was brought to the Japanese mainland through the Japanese Navy. In January of that year, under the Meiji Government's revision of the military conscription system, the practice of granting draft deferments was abolished and around the same time Okinawans were allowed to volunteer to enlist in the military. In the first year that these revisions took effect, over 50 youths from Okinawa volunteered to enlist, but only three were able to pass the academic and physical examinations. The three were Yabe Guntsū (born 1868), Hanashiro Chōmo (born 1869), and Kudeken Kanyū (born 1869). All three had been students of Itosu Ankō.

With the recruitment of the three, a crucial change happened in attitude of the Japanese military toward *karate*. The officer in charge of the three Okinawan youths' physical examination had been astounded by their physiques and asked them why they were in such top condition. He found out from them that they had trained in "*tiy*." Upon further investigation, the officer was impressed by the power of *tiy*. It was only natural that he made a report as soon as he could to his superiors. As a result, Vice Admiral Yashiro Rokurō ordered his battleship to dock in Okinawa and had his crew learn *tiy*. After having been brought to Japan during the Tokugawa Period, tiy again made a return trip through the Japanese Navy.

Another individual who contributed to the development of modern *karatedō* was the Japanese naval officer of Okinawan birth, Rear Admiral Kanna Kenwa, who later went on become a member of the Lower House of the Japanese Diet. Kanna encouraged navy crewmen to train in *karatedō* and had the honor of accompanying Crown Prince Hirohito at a demonstration of *kata*. Other important individuals include Kinjō Saburō, who introduced karate to Master Kanō Jigorō, Higashionna Kanjun, who sponsored Funakoshi Gichin's lecture at the Meisei Juku Lecture Hall, Tōyama Kanken, who was the founder of the Shūdōkan Dōjō, Ōhama Shinsui, who devoted much effort to organize student *karate* clubs into coherent network, Arakaki Kōsei, who spread karate in the Nagasaki Region, Higa Kajō, who worked to spread karate in Tokyo, Gima Shinkin, who demonstrated the *naihanchi kata* at Kōdōkan, and Arakaki Kōmo, who first did the *kūsankū kata* at Keiō University. We must not forget these Okinawans who loved Okinawan culture and contributed to the development of Okinawa *karate*.

2. Okinawan karate/Tūdiy and the Japanese Navy

It is crucial to recognize one of the important factors in the introduction of Okinawan *karate* to the Japanese mainland. It was the meeting of Okinawan karate and the Japanese Navy. The debut of *karate* at the Kōdōkan, which was at the center of Japan's martial arts world, might not have been possible had the meeting not taken place. One wonders what led to the meeting between Okinawan *karate* and the Japanese Navy that went on to defeat the Russian Baltic Fleet, which was said to be the strongest in the world at the time. Why did the Japanese Navy pay special attention to Okinawan *karate*? What was the global situation in which the Japanese Navy was at the time?

In the background of the spread of Okinawan *karate* to the Japanese mainland was the advancement of Western nations into Asia and Japan's endeavor of to defend the region. In other words, in response to the colonization of China and other parts of Asia by the West, Japan embarked on a strategy of defending itself as well as China, Korea, and other countries. This strategy also involved the embarking on a policy of *fukoku kyōhei* ("rich country, strong army") and the envisioning of *daitōakyōēken* (the Greater East Asian Co-Prosperity Sphere). It was around this time that Okinawan *karate* spread to the Japanese mainland because it caught the eye of the Japanese Navy as a way to physically and mentally train military recruits.

The British East India Company had been formed in 1600 to extract large amounts of products from India. In 1840, Britain dragged China into the First Opium War. Following China's defeat in that war, it was forced to sign the unequal Treaty of Nanjing that opened up five Chinese ports to outside trade, transferred jurisdiction over Hong Kong to Britain, and made China pay a huge indemnity for the war. In actuality, the Treaty of Nanjing led to the colonization of China by Britain. In response to the actions of Western powers in Asia, Japan was deeply alarmed over the possibility of being next in line for being invaded and colonized. An opinion that grew in strength was that Japan needed to invade the rest of Asia before the Western powers left nothing behind.

In 1856, the feudal Tokugawa Government created an army called the "Bakufu Kōbusho." In 1873, the new Meiji Government instituted a universal conscription system under which all males 20 years and older were registered to be eligible for three years of military service. In 1878, the Physical Education Training Center that was under the jurisdiction of the Japanese

Ministry of Education was established. In 1893, *jūdō* became an official part of the curriculum at the Naval Academy. The Sino-Japanese War occurred soon after, from August, 1894 to March, 1895. It was the first war that Japan fought against a foreign nation in the modern era. The war was fought over the Korean Peninsula. At the time, imperialism was the word of the day as the worlds powers were embroiled in conflicts with each other and were motivated by ambitions to expand their territories. China had traditionally thought of Korea as one of its tributary nations, while Russia began setting its sights on acquiring the peninsula. For its own security, Japan was hoping remain neutral in the situation and sought a balance its influence over the Korean Peninsula with China's. However, China insisted on its sovereignty over Korea, while Russia claimed to right to be a protectorate over Korea. By then, the Russian Empire had exerted increasing influence beyond Siberia into Enkaishu (Russian Maritime Provinces) and Manchuria and was beginning to extend its reach into Korea.

Japan asserted that "Korea's autonomy should be recognized and be allowed to be a completely independent nation-state." If the Korean Peninsula fell into the hands of another powerful nation, the only thing that would stand between Japan and being absorbed by foreign imperialism would be the narrow Genkai Sea. In 1885, Japan sent Ambassador Plenipotentiary Itō Hirobumi to Tiantsin to conclude the Treaty of Tiantsin Convention. China had long fallen prey to being carved up Western nations starting with the 1842 Treaty of Nanjing with Britain following the Opium War, the 1858 Treaty of Tiantsin with the U.S., Britain, France, and Russia, the 1860 Treaty of Peking with Britain, France, and Russia.
The Treaty of Tiantsin stipulated that:

> In case [of] any disturbances of a grave nature occurring in Corea which necessitates the respective countries, or either of them, to send troops to Corea, it is hereby understood that they shall give, each to the other, previous notice in writing of their intention to do so, and

that after the matter is settled they shall withdraw their troops and not further station them there.

Under this Convention, Japan intended to uphold Korea's independence. However, the Korean Li Dynasty, which had lasted 500 years, was beset by government corruption and threatened by both Chinese and Russian force. As it was on the verge of collapse, Korea was not in the position of forging its own historical destiny.

In Korea, the Donghak (or Tonghak) Movement had already erupted and was becoming a full-fledged peasant revolt. On June 2, 1894, the Donghak Peasant Rebellion began. The Korean Government, whose troops were frequently defeated by the peasant forces, asked the Qing Chinese Government, whom it still considered its sovereign ruler, to send troops to bring the strife into order. Japan believed that it would permanently lose its right to exert influence on the Peninsula if China gained an advantageous foothold their and so it sent its own troops. In 1882, Japan and Korea had signed the Japan–Korea Treaty of 1882, which stipulated that Japan would station a small number of troops at their diplomatic legation in Korea. On June 12, 1894, the Japanese Army swiftly landed a brigade at Incheon. Using its troops as a shield, Japan tried to get the Korean Government to "to cut tributary ties to China and to expel the Chinese forces with the Japanese forces." However, because the Korean Government believed that China was a stronger country than Japan, it hesitated to acquiesce to the Japanese Government's demand. On July 25, the Korean Government eventually gave in to the Japanese demands and issued an official request for the Chinese troops to leave. On July 29, the 1st Japanese Brigade made a fierce attack on the Chinese Army at Asan and Seonghwan, forcing them to make a hasty retreat to Pyongyang. Meanwhile, on July 23, the Japanese naval fleet left Sasebo Harbor and encountered the Qing Beiyang Fleet around Pungdo. The Chinese side fired shots on the Japanese fleet and the Battle of Pungdo commenced. While in pursuit of the Chinese North Sea Fleet's Jiyuan, the Japanese Naniwa encountered the British ship Kowshing, which was carrying Chinese military personnel, and ordered it to stop. The Kowshing ignored the order and was sunk by the Naniwa. Britain was enraged by the incident, but a later judgment under international law showed that the sinking was legally justified. This string of events considered as "dependent on the Korean Government's requests," on August 1, the Japanese Government formally declared war on China.

On September 17, at the Battle of the Yalu River, Japan won a victory and established control of the Yellow Sea. Subsequently, the 2nd Division of the Japanese Army landed on Liaodong Peninsula and captured Jinzhou and Dalian and proceeded toward Lushun, which was a stronghold of the Qing Beiyang Army and Beiyang Fleet, was a large fortified area surrounded by the Jinzhoushan Battery, Mantoushan Battery, Jiguanshan, Nilongshan, Songshushan, Yizi shan. At its center was the Baiyushan Fort. Lushan was known as a port "easy to defend and difficult to attack. The Japanese attacked from both land and sea and captured the peninsula on November 21.

The Japanese forces then attacked another Beiyang Fleet stronghold at Weihaiwei. At the conclusion of the Battle of Weihaiwei, the Qing Government surrendered on February 13, 1895.

Japan had defeated the "sleeping lion." On April 17, 1895, Japan and China signed the Treaty of Shimonoseki. Under the treaty, China was forced to pay a war indemnity of 200 million Kuping taels (7.5 million kilograms of silver) and recognized Japanese protectorate control over Liaodong Peninsula, Taiwan, the Pescadores (Penghu) Islands to Japan, and Korea.

The terms of the Treaty of Shimonoseki were a source of interest to the Western powers. On one hand, it was remarkable how a small Asian country like Japan could make such demands from the great Empire of China. On the other hand, there was concern over the threat that a Japanese invasion of China would have on their profits. The country that felt the most threatened was the Russian Empire. For the Russian Empire, which had already begun constructing a railroad from the Western entry to Siberia at Chelyabinsk to its

Pacific Fleet stronghold at Vladivostok, the entry of Japan into the neighboring northeast region of China presented difficulties. It had become customary for Russia to have its main part of its Pacific Fleet dock at Nagasaki Harbor when Vladivostok was frozen over during the winters, but this became impossible following the Japanese Government prohibition on having more than two warships from any foreign country dock at one time in Japan. Not being able to dock in Nagasaki meant that Russia would have to find an alternative harbor that would be deep enough for its warships or face the prospect of not having a military presence in East Asia during the winters. The alternative harbor that Russia set its sights on was Lushun, which the Chinese had made into a fortified naval harbor. If China ceded Japan Lushan under the Treaty of Shimonoseki, the Russian Empire would suffer a marked loss of naval strength during the frozen ocean months.

Within a week after the Treaty of Shimonoseki was signed, Russia intervened by demanding that "Japan return Liaodong Peninsula to Qing China." Of course, Russia was only speaking for its own interests, but in order to justify its demands to international public opinion, she asked France and Germany to back her up. For England, who had a near monopoly of the Chinese market, and the U.S., who was shrewdly advancing her interests in the region while publically demanding a fair share with the other powers, the rise of a small and weak nation like Japan did not create much concern. For France, who was constantly being beaten out by England, and Germany, who was at the bottom of the totem pole among the Western powers, the rise of Japan was a source of unease. For Germany, having the huge Russia keep an eye on the Far East provided a sense of security. This state of affairs led to what is called the "Triple Intervention," where France, Germany, and Russia intervened over the terms of the Treaty of Shimonoseki. Japan knew that Russia would go to war if it did not comply with the "Triple Intervention." Since it was not a country that would want to take on Russia in a war, much less making enemies of Germany and France as well, Japan was forced to go along.

Japan was made to give up its claim over the Liaodong Peninsula for the ostensible reason that, "the peace of Asia would be damaged by the taking of Liaodong Peninsula." This was, of course, a thinly veiled lie because in less than two years, Russia not only sent troops to the Liaodong Peninsula and took it over, but it also occupied Manchuria under the pretext that it was leasing the territories.

Dalian after the Sino-Japanese War

Russia curried favor from Qing Chinese government by pushing Japan out of the Liaodong Peninsula and also acted as a mediator in the procurement of a huge compensation from China to Japan. In 1896, Russia obtained the rights to lay the tracks for the Chinese Eastern Railway and began construction the next year. The Chinese Eastern Railway was publicly a joint project between the Russo-Chinese Bank, which was financed by French capital, but was controlled by the Empire of Russia. In 1898, Russia obtained the rights to lease Dalian and Lushun and proceeded to make Lushun a military harbor and nearby Dalian a commercial harbor. It also stationed its army and navy and set up a military and civilian government offices in the two places. Russia purchased the Qingniwaqiao area in Dalian and built a new city which it called "Dalniy," which meant "distant" in Russian. The Siberian Railroad made a large northward turn as it followed the border between Russia and China between Chita and Vladivostok. The Chinese Eastern Railway was built as a shortcut. Also, after Russia made Lushan a military port, the Manchurian Railway was constructed between Lushan and Harbin.

The reason for this tangential discussion on war was to show the important relationships between karate and the Japanese Navy. To begin illustrating these relationships, we must talk first about Korea, which became cause of the Sino-Japanese War. The Joseon Dynasty, was established in 1392 when General Yi Seong-gye overthrew the Goryeo Dynasty. From 1392 to the Korean annexation by Japan in 1910, 27 kings ruled in the 519-year-long

Joseon Dynasty. In the 15th century, the Joeson Dynasty carried out trade with *daimyo* in Tsushima and Kyushu. After Toyotomi Hideyoshi's invasions of Korea and the later the fall of the suzerain Chinese Ming Dynasty, the Joseon Dynasty became a tributary of the Manchurian Qing Dynasty. Trade and diplomacy was resumed in the Edō Period during which 12 delegations were sent by the Joseon Dynasty to Japan. The delegations to Japan were discontinued by the beginning of the 19th century. In deference to the Qing rulers in China, the Joseon Dynasty carried out a closed-nation policy until after the Meiji Restoration.

As a result of the Sino-Japanese War, Japan's international status rose and it was able to establish a foothold for its advancement into the continent. Following the Triple Intervention after the Sino-Japanese War, the division between Japan and Russia grew worse. After the Boxer Rebellion in China in 1900, Russia refused to withdraw from Manchuria causing Japan to carry great dissatisfaction toward Russia. In anticipation of Russia's southward encroachment, Japan signed an alliance in 1902 with England, who had interests in East Asia that were complementary with those of Japan. This led to a decisive conflict between Russia and Japan.

The Russo-Japanese War began in 1904. In bitter fighting, the Japanese Army met and defeated Russian troops at Mukden (now known as Fang Yang). The Japanese Navy defeated the Russian Baltic Fleet on the Japan Sea. Japan lacked military strength and materials and the war indemnity it had received from China after the Sino-Japanese War was already depleted. However, Russia was experiencing a revolt against its ruling structure. Consequently, carrying out a drawn out war was difficult for both countries. In 1905, both countries accepted the offer by U.S. President Theodore Roosevelt to mediate a peace treaty at Portsmouth. New Hampshire. The Treaty of Portsmouth put a halt on Russia's southern advancement as Russia agreed to recognize Korea as subordinate to Japan. Russia also signed over leasehold rights over Lushun, Dalian, and other regions of southern Liaodong Peninsula and ceded ownership of a part of the Chinese Far East Railway and the southern half of Sakhalin. With the recognition of Japan's supremacy over Korea under the Treaty of Portsmouth, Japan immediately made Korea its protectorate. Itō Hirobumi was dispatched as the resident general of Korea and proceeded to bring its foreign diplomacy and military under the control of Japan. In 1907, Japan obtained administrative control of Korea. Resistance by the Korean populace against these changes grew and two years later in 1909, Itō was assassinated in Harbin, Manchuria.

In 1910, Japan used the assassination as a pretext to use the threat of military push through The Japan-Korea Annexation Treaty" and set up Governor-General Office to which an active duty Japanese general would be appointed. For 35 years after that, until the Japan's World War II defeat in 1945, Korea was completely colonized by Japan.

It goes without saying that the Korean Peninsula was placed under slave-like status under the Japanese government after 1910. As a result, until 1945, the Japanese martial arts (kendō, jujitsu, judō, etc.) dōjō that spread throughout Korea were essentially the same as those in Japan.

As the Japanese government began its full-scale invasion of the Chinese mainland in the 1930s, it also implemented a thorough assimilation program on the Korean Peninsula under a "Formation of Imperial Subjects Policy." Worship at Shintō shrines and the recital of the "Oath of Imperial Subjects (皇国臣民の誓詞)" (enacted in October, 1937) at schools became compulsory. Japanese was taught as the "mother language" while Korean was disallowed (under the 1938 Korean Education Order). In 1940, under the Sōshikaimē rule, Koreans were forced to use Japanese names. With the enforcement of the Formation of Imperial Subjects Policy, Japanese martial arts were imposed on Koreans.

In 1910, the year the Great Empire of Japan annexed Korea as it pushed forward its military preparations to prevent defeat at the hands of Western nations under the mantra of *fukoku kyōhei* or "national wealth and military strength," the Japanese Navy Training Fleet under the command of Vice Admiral Yashiro Rokurō docked at Naha Harbor. To the great pleasure of the officers and men, the Okinawan youths performed a group demonstration of *karatejutsu* to welcome them. Yashiro had been a teacher at the Japanese Naval Academy when a *judō* department was established there in 1893 and was proficient enough as a *judōka* to be an instructor in the *judō* department. It was due to his skill as a martial artist that he was able to quickly see something special in the *karatejutsu kata*. He chose from among his officers and men those who had experience doing *judō* and sent them to the Okinawan Teacher's College to learn the *naihanchi kata* in five days from Yabu Kentsū the military advisor at the school (with the title of Army Lieutenant General). The adoption of Ryukyuan *karatejutsu* as a way to train the mind and bodies of men who part of the same Japanese navy that had defeated the Russian Baltic Fleet, which was then said to be the strongest naval force in the world at the time, was an important event in the history of *karate*. This was twelve years before Funakoshi Gichin gave his first demonstration of *karatejutsu* in Tōkyō. Consequently, one can say that *karatejutsu* was already being officially spread from Ryūkyū to the Japanese mainland through the Japanese Navy from 1910. Further, Funakoshi's demonstration in Tōkyō is connected the Japanese Navy's visit to Okinawa in 1910 because Yoshiro had talked about the visit with his close friend Kanō Jigoro, who invited Funakoshi to Tōkyō in 1922.

According to Yashiro, maintaining ship crewmembers' physical fitness relying only on naval calisthenics was difficult. However, implementing *judō* training would require practice *gi* and *tatami* and, moreover, run the risk of injuries. The problem was similar for *sumō*: without sturdy *mawashi* (belts) and *dohyō* (dirt ring), participants would have to hold back from full-throtled competition. Further, *sumō* put smaller crew members at a disadvantage. Okinawan *karatejutsu* could be practiced in the uniforms that crew members normally wore and did not require any implements or equipment. It could also be done alone or by the whole crew in unison. It was for these reasons that Yashiro believed that there was no better martial art than *karatejutsu*. Eight years before Yashiro visited Okinawa, *karatejutsu* was taught in groups as an official part of the Okinawan school physical education curriculum. Okinawan prefectural authorities had already implemented an official policy to widely spread Okinawa's "ethnic sport" that had up to then been long practiced in only certain regions.

It was in this way that *karatejutsu*, Okinawa's martial art and ethnic sport, became a crucial part of the training of Japan's military force as fighting techniques and a competitive sport. Through the *judoka* Yashiro, karatejutsu transformed from being a local Okinawan martial art to being a martial art for training the military force of the Great Empire of Japan. It is generally said that *karatejutsu* was discovered by Kanō Jigoro who had witnessed Funakoshi's demonstration, but it was Yashiro who recognized its value in military training and made it part of the Japanese naval training. It is believed that Yashiro passed on information about *karatejutsu* to Kanō, who was his old friend. This is confirmed by the fact that Kanō quickly approached Funakoshi in Tōkyō and invited to teach *karatejutsu* to *judoka* at Kōdōkan. Moreover, four years after meeting Funakoshi, Kanō visited Okinawa to observe karatejutsu being practiced there with his own eyes.

Yashiro, who later went on to become an admiral in the Japanese navy, contributed to the development of *karatejutsu* in different ways through his relations to Kanō (director of Kōdōkan), Yamashita Yoshiaki (*judō* instructor at naval academy), Satō Hōken (*judō* instructor at naval academy), and Kanna Kenwa (27th naval academy class; rear admiral), and other prominent people. When Funakoshi arrived in Tokyo, Rear Admiral Kanna, who was also from Okinawa, gave him support that opened many doors for him. Kanna, who was the captain of the battleship Katori became a Japanese National Diet Member after retirement and continued to offer support to Funakoshi and to the development of *karatejutsu*.

Jiro Nangō, who was a nephew of Kanō Jigoro and had been in the same 27th graduating class of the Naval Academy with Kanna, became the second director of the Kōdōkan. Nangō was Kanna's predecessor as the captain of the Katori. Funakoshi had organized the youth group demonstration of *karate kata* in front of Shuri Castle when the Crown Prince stopped in Naha when he was on his European cruise. Also, in 1912 (the first year of the Taishō Period), the First Fleet under the command of Captain Dewa Shigehiro (出羽 重遠大将) made a stop at Nakagusuku Bay. The officers and crew of the fleet had a training camp in Okinawan *karatejutsu* at the First Prefectural Middle School. For Okinawa, such visits were big events because it was a time when Japan's fortunes as a nation were rising in the wake of the Japanese Navy's victory over the the Russian Baltic Fleet.

As seen above, the Japanese Navy and Okinawa karatejutsu have had a special affinity to each other since the period right after the Russo-Japanese War. In this period when the Japanese military advocated *fukoku kyōhei* (national wealth and military strength) and was embarking on its advancement into the continent of Asia, Okinawa karatejutsu played an important role in the education of soldiers and had thus contributed greatly to Japan's national strategy. Consequently, Funakoshi's introduction of *karatejutsu* to the Japanese mainland needs to be seen in the context of the Japanese Naval Training Fleet's having a *karatejutsu* training camp when it visited Okinawa under Yashiro's command in 1910. Okinawan *karatejutsu* already began making its way into the Japanese mainland from that point onward.

Funakoshi talked about the prospects of *karatejutsu* in the following passages:

The era when *karatedō* had to be kept in secret has come to the end; now we are in this glorious era where learning of karate is officially allowed. However, the ideal state for this art is still in the distant future. I take this opportunity to publicly propagate the truth about *karate,* which was originated and cultivated as secret martial techniques in Ryukyu, and invite criticism and further study among experts of various martial arts. Further, I express hope that protective gear for competitive matches can be standardized in the future as this issue has been for many years. In this way, *karate* will be able to integrate into the spirit of Japanese *budō*.

Funakoshi goes on to describe the spread of interest in *karatedō* throughout Japan and its colonial territories as well as to the U.S., especially in Hawai'i. He concludes this bright outlook by writing, "As shown above, *karatedō* is experiencing great success by becoming a unique Japanese *budō* and developing as a global *budō*."

The important points that Funakoshi presented were that *karate*, which was once taught in secret, should be made public and developed in the same way as other martial arts and that *karate* had spread widely not only throughout Japan, but also to the colonies that Japan acquired through war such as Taiwan, China, and Korea. This confirms the notion that *karate* did not originate from Taiwan, China, or any other foreign land. It is believed that there were about 6.6 million Japanese oversea emigrants after World War I. Of this number, 1 million were in China, 900,000 in Korea, and another 4.7 million spread out in Taiwan, the Philippines, Indonesia, Sumatra, Vietnam, India, and Australia. Japanese had been emigrating overseas since the Sino-Japanese and Russo-Japanese Wars. If Okinawan *karate* had its origins in China, Taiwan, or any other overseas region, the Japanese who had emigrated overseas would have been the first to have noticed. For example, if there had been a martial art in China that was the same as *karate*, we would have to assume that this information would have reached Japan immediately. This would be the same for Taiwan and Korea. However, in the several decades that Japanese were living in large numbers in Taiwan, China, and Korea, there were no such reports and, instead, the idea that Ryukyuan *karate* was a completely different kind of martial art than *Chuan fa*, *tai chi*, white crane fist, *kung fu*, and other Chinese martial arts developed in the same period. This attests to *karate* (*tiy*) being a unique martial art that was born in Okinawa.

Japan plunged into World War I after having emerging victorious against the great nations of China and Russia. The major nations of the world at the time, each with their own view of reality, marched toward war as they sought to expand their territories and colonies and engaged in conflicts over markets. Japan did not want to be left behind and, thus, embarked on its policy of *fukoku kyōhei*. In this era when the Empire of Japan looked to enlarge its territory by encroaching into China, Russia, Korea, Taiwan, Southeast Asia, and the South Pacific to put the ideology of the "Greater East Asia Co-Prosperity Sphere" into practice, Okinawa *karatejutsu* took on an important role as it was appropriated into the mental and physical training of Japanese imperial soldiers. In this historical context, it was inevitable that *karatejutsu* to spread beyond Okinawa to the Japanese mainland after its aforementioned discovery by the Japanese Navy.

When *karatejutsu* crossed over to the Japanese mainland, it became part of the Japan Empire's ambitions to advance overseas and to promote *fukoku kyōhei*. Further, the major individuals who worked fervently to spread *karatejutsu* to the Japanese mainland, including Kanō Jigoro, Yashiro Rokurō, Yamashita Yoshiaki, Satō Hōken, Kanna Kenwa, were *judōka*. These two factors led to subsequent far-reaching changes in Okinawan *karatejutsu*.

The Spread of *Karatejutsu* to the Japanese Mainland

The prevailing narrative of the spread of *karatejutsu* to the Japanese mainland starts with Funakoshi and Gima's demonstration of *kūshankū* and *naihanchi kata* at the Kōdōkan in 1922. The idea for this demonstration was born because Kanō, who was then the Honorary Chairman of the Japan Sports Education Association, requested Okinawan-born and Tōkyō University graduate Kinjō Saburō to provide him reference materials on *karatejutsu* for the upcoming First *Kobudō Taiiku Tenrankai* (Ancient Martial Arts Physical Education Exhibition) that was being organized by the Japanese Ministry of Education. However, it is believed that Kanō's special attention to *karatejutsu* had developed earlier because he had heard about it from Yashiro. The Okinawa Ken Karate Kenkyūkai (Okinawa Prefecture Karate Research Association) sent a request for the demonstration through the Okinawa Prefectural School Affairs Division to the Japanese Ministry of Education and Kinjō. Kinjō, who was the former principle of the Tōkyō Higher Normal School (the present Tsukuba University) then sent a request to Kanō to bring the demonstration to fruition. The moving force from the Okinawan side was Funakoshi, who was the leader of the Okinawa Ken Karate Kenkyūkai and teacher at the Okinawa Prefectural Matsuyama Girls Primary School. The site chosen for an exhibit of written materials on karate was the auditorium of the Tōkyō Women's Higher Normal School. Funakoshi was chosen to be the commentator for the event. The attendance for the event was smaller than expected and newspaper coverage was almost nonexistent. It was far from being a successful debut.

However, this was to be expected. There was a limit to how much *karate* could be explained through written materials and it was impossible to convey its true nature. Kanō knew this very well and he strongly expressed his desire to see a *karate* demonstration with his own eyes. Through Kinjō, Kanō made a fervent plea for Funakoshi to do a public demonstration of *karate* at the Kōdōkan. Since his days as a student, Kanō had trained in *judō* and had studied the history and techniques of Chinese *kempō*. Because of his broad knowledge of martial arts, he was curious about the difference between *karate* and *judō* or if there was anything in *karate* that would be useful in *judō* such as *kata* for free-style practice.

Soon after, Kanō invited Funakoshi and Gima Shinkin to the old Kōdōkan Dōjō in Shimotomisaka in Tōkyō to have an introductory demonstration on karate *kata* and *yakusoku kumite* (pre-arranged sparing). The old Kōdōkan Dōjō had been built in 1906 and was large enough for 207 *tatami* mats. On that day, the *dōjō* was filled to capacity with instructors and students. On Kanō's instructions, black belts and instructors-in-training lined up on the left side of the main entrance and high ranking black belts, invited guests, and the press sat on seats that had been prepared for them. In all, there were about 300 *budōka* in the audience. Funakoshi demonstrated the *kūshankū kata* and Gima the *naihanchi kata*. This was followed by both men doing *bunkai* (analyses and explanation of separate parts) of the *kata* and 13 *yakusoku kumite kata*.

When the demonstrations by Funakoshi and Gima ended, Kanō stood up and, together with his head instructor Nagaoka Shūichi, asked for instruction in the *kata* footwork and in the main points of the *kumite*. It was quite a sight for the 300 or more students of Kanō, the head of the prestigious Kōdōkan, to see him throw away all pretension to nonchalantly roll up the legs of his *hakama* to humbly accept lessons from the Ryukyuan *karateka*. Surely, those present knew that the moment they were witnessing was no ordinary one. The reporters in attendance were astounded and wrote about the event in great detail. As Kanō went through each movement of the *kata* and *kumite*, he avidly made comments such as, "If your stance is like this, wouldn't a punch or kick be able to come in from this angle?" "If a punch came from this angle, would it be better to deal with it this way?" "If you deal with the attack that way, wouldn't your center of balance be temporarily unstable, leading to a slow counter?" "When there is only one opponent, rather than using and elbow, wouldn't it be more advantageous to deflect the attack in this way?" Through the reports by all the major newspapers, the event soon became the topic of conversations among the people of Tokyo. The demonstration of karate, an Okinawan martial art that had hardly been seen in the Japanese mainland, had a great impact and left a deep impression on Kanō, who at the time stood at the top of the Japanese martial arts world. He immediately asked Funakoshi to teach karate to his *judō* students at the Kōdōkan.

Funakoshi was supposed to have returned to Okinawa, but many influential people including Yashiro read about the Kōdōkan demonstration in the papers. He soon received numerous invitations for demonstrations from places such as the Yagyū Aobashikan, Nikaidō Taisō Juku, and residence of the late Marquis Shō (the son of the last Ryukyuan King). Funakoshi's return to Okinawa was delayed for weeks and he was forced move from the inn he was staying at to the Meisei Juku, which was the dormitory for students from Okinawa.

Gima Shinken, who did the demonstrations with Funakoshi, was living at the Meisei Juku since he was attending a university in Tokyo. While it takes only about two hours by plane, at the time, it took over a week to travel the 1,500 kilometers between Okinawa and Tōkyō by ship. To make matters more difficult, most Okinawans spoke only the Okinawan language in their everyday life and because of the language barrier with people in Tokyo, finding places to rent for Okinawas was difficult. Further, for the impoverished Okinawan students, the rent was usually too high. As a result, the Okinawa Prefectural Educational Society used its funds to build dorms in Tōkyō and Osaka, including the Meisei Juku for students from Okinawa.

In order to teach *karate* to the *judōka* at the Kōdōkan and to the Okinawan students in Tōkyō and at the urging of Kanō to stay, Funakoshi had no other choice but to stay at the Meisei Juku, where there was a small meeting room and an apartment for a maintenance supervisor. Funakoshi received permission from the Okinawa Prefectural Educational Society to temporarily work as a maintenance supervisor and to stay in the apartment for the maintenance supervisor. He then proceeded to teach *karate* in the meeting room and in the yard of the Meisei Juku, thus establishing the first *karate dōjō* in the Japanese mainland.

Soon after Funakoshi came to the Japanese mainland and began teaching *karate*, Kanō made a visit to China. It is most likely that Kanō gathered important information on Chinese martial arts while he was there. It is also believed that he consciously made comparisons between Chinese martial arts and Ryukyuan *karate* due to the fact that the character for *tō* (唐) in *tūdiy*, which Japanese read as "*tōde*" or "*karate*," referred to Chinese Tang dynasty, but generally meant "China" in Japanese. This may have led Kanō to wonder if he would find the exact same form of Ryukyuan *karate* in China. However, what he found from his own observations was that Ryukyuan *karate* was not only very different from Chinese martial arts, but also that it was a world class martial art that was not in any way inferior to Chinese martial arts.

After returning from China, Kanō warmly encouraged Funakoshi by saying, "Okinawan karatejutsu is an impressive martial art that you should not be ashamed at all to demonstrate anywhere. If you plan to spread this martial art to the mainland, I will have no hesitation in giving you my cooperation. Please feel free to ask me for anything you need." There is no doubt that this encouragement from Kanō gave Funakoshi confidence that his *tiy*, or *karatejutsu*, comparable to any other martial art in the world.

Because of Kanō's strong urging, Funakoshi gave up on his plans to return to Okinawa and decided to stay in Tokyo. For the 54-year-old Funakoshi this was probably the largest gamble in his life. There was much uncertainty over whether he could feasibly make a living teaching *karate* in faraway Tōkyō after giving up his steady status and occupation as a school teacher. He was asked for instruction and demonstrations by numerous notable figures, and frowned upon by many others. However, there was the concern that after the temporary media fanfare, people would lose interest. He wondered if he would be able to make a living since he had no examples of anyone supporting themselves through teaching *karate*. His was the first case. There is no doubt that Funakoshi was filled with anxiety. If he had ignored Kanō's encouragement and had gone back to Okinawa, the history of *karate* would no doubt been very different. However, Funakoshi's life had largely been shaped by his position as a *bushi* (warrior). As a *bushi*, Funakoshi probably felt refusing the request of the man who occupied the pinnacle position at the top of the Japanese martial arts world would be a serious affront to martial arts. Because he was a man well-versed in both martial and literary arts, Funakoshi decided to stay in Tōkyō and follow *bushidō* (the way of the warrior) out of loyalty to Kanō.

Coming to such a decision was undoubtedly because of Kanō's extremely passionate and warm support for *karate*. The facts that Kanō had a deep curiosity in Okinawan *karate* as a martial art that was so different from *judō*, that he avidly studied *karate* techniques, and that he was an important force in the spread of *karate* to the Japanese mainland are undeniable. Why did Kanō take such an interest in *karate*? Of course, as a martial artist and *judōka*, he was naturally very interested in the "killing with one blow (一撃必殺)" aspect of *karate*. Also, he also had a practical ambition of incorporating *karate* techniques with *judō* techniques. However, we can surmise that Kanō's strongest interest in *karate* was its potential usefulness in Japan's "physical education." He had hope in cultivating *judō*, *kendō*, and *karate* for the future physical education of the Japanese people.

In October of 1926, about four years after he witnessed Funakoshi's demonstration, Kanō visited Okinawa. His main purpose was to see with his own eyes *karate* at its origins. As the honorary chairman of the Japanese Sports Education Association, he contacted the Karate Kenkyūkai, the organization of Okinawa *karateka*, to set up his observations of *karate*. He was invited by the Okinawan Association of Judō Black Belts to come to Naha City to attend a *karate* conference, where he met Mabuni Kenwa (founder of Itō-*ryū*) and Miyagi Chōjun (founder of Gojū*ryū*) who explained to him the techniques of *karate* in detail. Demonstrations were given at that time by Yabu Kentsū Hanashiro Chōmo, Kuba Kōho, Kyan Meitoku, Miyagi Chōjun, Mabuni Kenwa, and other masters. Kanō deepened his knowledge of *karate* as he learned of Naha-te, which had incorporated Chinese *kempō* techniques to evolve differently from Shuri-te, the lineage that Funakoshi was part of.

It is certain that Kanō was deeply surprised in Okinawa because he learned of many *karate* masters who were on the same level or higher than Funakoshi. He realized that if those *karate* masters went to the Japanese mainland and taught in different regions, *karate* would quickly spread throughout the country and would establish itself as a major part of Japan's physical education. As a result, Kanō began giving guidance to many *karate* masters who came to the Japanese mainland, including Mabuni and Miyagi.

One year after he visited Okinawa and five years after the demonstration at Kōdōkan, Kanō published *Seiryokuzenyō Kokumin Taiiku no Kata* (*Forms for the Good Use of Energy and National Physical Education*). In that publication, his desire to develop Japanese physical education by incorporating Okinawan *karate* is shown by his inclusion of many of its techniques such as "*ate* (strike)," "*tsuki* (punch)," "*keri* (kick)," "*uchi* (hit)," "*age* (upward thrust)," "*kake* (catch)," and "*tori* (grab)."

When he went to Okinawa, Kanō gave a lecture at the Okinawa Prefectural Lecture Hall on "Karate and Physical Education." The main organizers of the lecture were Mabuni and Miyagi. There were multiple preparation meetings leading up to the lecture and in the course of the preparations, the Prefectural Education Section Chief expressed his belief that "*karate*," written with the character for "China (唐)," was not favorable and proposed that another term that would be more suitable for a martial art from Okinawa Prefecture. In response to the proposal, the Prefectural Security Division Chief and others in attendance unanimously decided on the term "karate," written with the character for "empty (空)."

Through Kanō's mediation, Okinawan karate was recognized as a subordinate part of the Judō Division of the Dai Nippon Butoku Kai in 1933. Two years before, *karate* had been included as a part of the Judō Division of the Okinawa Prefecture Branch of the Dai Nippon Butoku Kai. Incidentally, *karate* was made an official part of Okinawa Prefecture's physical education curriculum in 1901, which was well before Japan's martial arts were made a part of Japan's public education. In 1911, *kendō* was made a required subject in Japanese middle schools and it was not until 1931 that judo followed suit.

It is necessary to talk about the Dai Nippon Butoku Kai, which placed *karate* under its Judō Division. It was a state-recognized organization that promoted and supervised *kendō, judō, kyūdō, naginata,* and other Japanese martial arts.

In 1895, in commemoration of the 1,100[th] anniversary of Emperor Kanmu's establishment of Kyoto as the capital of Japan, the Heian Shrine was built in Okazaki, Kyoto. The shrine was built as a replica of a Heian Period palace in honor of Emperor Kanmu. The Kyoto Prefectural Tax Collection Chief at the time, Torinoumi Hiroki, gathered famous martial artists from around the country to perform demonstrations to honor Emperor Kanmu's spirit. With the outbreak of the Sino-Japanese War the year before in 1894, there had been calls across Japan for a revival of martial arts. Riding on this sentiment, Torinoumi met with Kyoto Governor Watanabe Chiaki, Heian Shrine Head Priest Mibu Motoosa, and other influential men to organize the Dai Nippon Butoku Kai as a group to promote martial arts.

On April 17, 1895, the Dai Nippon Butoku Kai had its first general meeting of its founding members and key officers were selected, including Prince Komatsu Akihito as General Secretary, Watanabe as Chairman, and Mibu Motoosa as Vice Chairman. The association became the main ruling body of Japan's martial arts world as it took upon itself such tasks as propagating, promoting, and regulating martial arts; organizing conferences and tournaments; and conferring awards and titles to martial artists.

The need to support martial arts was even more heightened with the outbreak of World War II in 1941. There were many martial arts organizations that promoted and supported martial arts such as the Dai Nippon Butoku Kai, Society for the Promotion of Student Athletics, Society for the Promotion of Japanese Martial Arts, and Kōdōkan. After the outbreak of war, the Japanese government decided to consolidate these organizes into a single body under its control. The new body took the name of its largest component organization, the Dai Nippon Butoku Kai.

In 1942, the Dai Nippon Butoku Kai (also known as the Tōjō Butoku Kai) was drastically reorganized as an entity to buttress government power by giving it direct control over the martial arts world and martial arts education. This brought Kōdōkan even more into the control of the Dai Nippon Butoku Kai.

Because the up and coming *karate* was under the auspices of the Kōdōkan, it was by default placed under the control of the Dai Nippon Butoku Kai. In other words, all aspects of martial arts education in military and police training as well as in the school system were utilized in the development of people to establish the "Greater East Asian Co-Prosperity Sphere" that was being taught in the Japanese mainland and throughout its colonies. The foremost martial art at the time was *kendō*, which had been called *gekiken* (撃剣) until 1911. As gekiken, the martial art had been introduced to the Korean Peninsula in 1880. *Judō* was introduced there through the YMCA in 1909.

Due to Japan's defeat, the Dai Nippon Butoku Kai had its assets confiscated and it was dissolved in 1946. The Japanese Ministry of Education issued Directive No. 8 dated November 6, 1945 that pertained to the "Handling of Post-War Course in Physical Education." Under the order, martial arts (*kendō*, *judō*, *naginata*, and *kyūdō*) classes in physical education were terminated.

Returning to the original story, we recall that Funakoshi remained in Tōkyō at the urging of Kanō and moved into the Okinawa Prefecture student dorm Meisie Juku, where Gima Shinken had been living. There he began teaching *karate* seriously. Among his students at Meisei Juku were many people from the Kōdōkan and others such as Keiō University Professor Kasuya Masahiro, osteopath Ōtsuka Hironori (who later founded Wadō-ryū), and *kendō* instructor Konishi Yasuhiro (who later founded Shintō Shizen-ryū) An incident worth mentioning was a visit by sumo wrestlers from the Dewanoumi Stable Grand Champion including Grand Champion (*yokozuna*) Ōnishiki Uichirō and Champion (*ozeki*) Fukuyanagi Isaburō and their attendants. Even Funakoshi was flummoxed by their appearance, but he was able to give a detailed explanation of the main points of karate that satisfied his guests and barely managed to politely decline their requests to be their teacher.

After he began teaching at Meisei Juku, Funakoshi began to receive requests from various universities to teach. After teaching Tōkyō Imperial,

Keiō, Waseda, and other universities in Tokyo, *karate* spread like wildfire among university students. Funakoshi soon became extremely busy and he was not able to fulfill all the requests from universities to teach. This led to universities inviting *karateka* from Okinawa to teach and a sizeable number did come over to the Japanese mainland.

Today's karate owes much of its development to the first demonstration at the Kōdōkan. If not for the success of that demonstration, *karateka* who came later may not have achieved as much. They included: Motobu Chōki (founder of Motobu-ryū), Uechi Kanbun (founder of Uechi-ryū), Yabiku Mōden, Tōyama Kanken, Miyagi Chōjun (Gōjū- ryū founder), and Mabuni Kenwa (Shitō- ryū founder).

A person who had an adversarial relationship to Funakoshi was Motobu Chōki (1870-1946). While they were both Shuri-te masters, Motobu was a proponent of actual fighting in his *karate* training. He was invited to teach at Tōyō University, Chūo University, the Ministry of Railroads, Ministry of Communications, the Toyama Army School and other places in Tokyo. Motobu's ability to speak in Japanese was almost non-existent and he was said to have taught mostly in the Ryukyuan language. At the time, most the Tōkyō dialect of Japanese was seldom used in Okinawa.

Mabuni Kenwa (1898-1952; founder of Itō-ryū) was from a high-ranking lineage form the Ryukyuan Kingdom days and learned Shuri-te from Itosu Ankō and Naha-te from Higaonna Kanryō. He began teaching *karate* at Tōyō University where Motobu had previously taught and later moved to Osaka and taught at many different universities in the Kansai Region, including Ritsumeikan, Doshisha, Osaka, and Kansai Universities.

Taira Shinken, who was born on the island of Kume, went to Tōkyō at the age of 25 and became Funakoshi's right-hand-man instructor. He taught at the Toyama Army School and at Chūo, Waseda, Nihon Shika, Keiō, Hōsei, Tōkyō Nogyō, Kokushikan, Kokugakuin, and other universities. Taira studied Ryukyuan kobudō from Yabiku Mōden and eventually opened a *dōjō* in Ikaho Hotsprings, Gunma Prefecture. As the Pacific War became increasingly intense in 1944, upon a request by Funakoshi, he and some of his students visited Japanese army and navy facilities to give demonstrations of *karate* to cheer up the soldiers and sailors.

Yabiku Mōden (1878-1941) was born in Gibo, Shuri. After graduating from the Okinawan Prefectural Teacher's College, he became a teacher at Bitō Primary School and a *karate* and *kobudō* instructor at his *alma mater*. Upon arriving in Tokyo, Yabiku began teaching *kobudō* at Meiji University. In 1929, he established a *dōjō* for *karate*, *bojutsu*, and *sai* at the Nakano-ku Youth Hall. It was the first time in Japan that a "*Ryūkyū kobudō*" was formally taught. Yabiku continued to teach *kobudō* in mainland Japan until he passed away at the age 63 in 1941.

Miyagi Chōjun (1888-1953) added Chinese *kempō* techniques to the Okinawan *tiy* that he had learned from his teacher Higaonna Kanryō and created *sanchin* and *tenshō kata*. At the age of 16, Miyagi traveled to China alone. While receiving Spartan training from many Chinese *kempō* masters, he studied old documents on martial arts. After returning to Okinawa, he did a comparative study of Okinawan *tiy* and Chinese *kempō*. Based on his study, he incorporated scientific methods for teaching karate based on the structure of the body, such as certain breathing techniques and warming up exercises. Miyagi also continued his research and compiled the two martial art systems' strong features and his own comment in *Gōjū-ryū Karate-dō*. He was invited to teach karate at Kyoto Imperial University, Kansai University, and Ritsumeikan University in 1929.

As discussed, up to now, there were many karate instructors who went to the Japanese mainland from Okinawa. In the Kantō Region, the major figures were Funakoshi Gichin (1868-1957) and Motobu Chōki (1871-1944). In the Kansai Region, Mabuni Kenwa (1889-1952), Uechi Kanbun (1878-1946), Toyama Kanken, Yabiku Mōden, Taira Shinken, Miyagi Chōjun, Higashionna Kamesuke, and others went through many hardships to spread *karate*. There were also students of Okinawan karateka who worked to spread karate in the Japanese mainland such as Miki Nisaburo, Takada Mizuhō,

Konishi Yasuhiro, and Ōtsuka Nobuzumi. Through the work of such individuals, in 1933 karate was recognized as a Japanese martial art by the Dai Nippon Butoku Kai. It was an official acknowledgment of a fighting tradition from the small island of Okinawa as a Japanese martial art.

Another major change that took place was the replacement of karate (written as 唐手) with karate (written as 空手). A manifestation of the Japanese imperialist ideology at the time was the notion that the use of the character for Tang China or 唐 in the word *karate* was unfavorable. This led to the use of 空手 instead. Also, many *jujitsu* and *iai* techniques, such as *tsukami* (grasp), *nage* (throw), *sabaki* (whole body movement), and *kansetsu tori* (joint locks) were added to the repertoire of basic karate techniques of *tsuki* (thrust), *uchi* (hit), *keri* (kick), and *uke* (block).

The Transformation from *Tiy* and *Tūdiy* to *Karate*

I have no doubt repeated myself many times, but *tiy* was developed in the continued warfare from the 7th to 10th century during the Gusuku Period as a unique Ryukyuan fighting art with the objective of "killing with one blow." After the establishment of the Ryukyuan Kingdom in the 15th century, *tiy* was passed down and preserved in secret as self-defense techniques. From ancient times to the 18th century, *tiy* was the only term used for martial arts techniques in Ryūkyū.

In the 18th century, Chinese martial arts techniques were spread to Ryūkyū and the indigenous *tiy* and certain Chinese *kempo* techniques were merged together. To differentiate Ryukyuan *tiy* from this hybrid form of martial arts, the word *tūdiy* began being used. The period in which pure *tiy* coexisted with the hybrid *tūdiy* lasted from the 18th to 20th century. The incorporation of *tiy* into the physical education classes at the Shuri Primary School in 1901 led to its being introduced to many other schools in Okinawa. Thereafter, *tiy* went beyond just being martial techniques and there arose a need to teach it as an academic subject. Until *karate* began being taught at schools in 1901, it was referred to as "*tiy*" and "*tūdiy*." Both terms are Okinawan language words. However, if karate was to be taught in school classes, the Okinawan "dialect" could not be used to describe it. Standard Japanese words, pronounced as "*te*" and "*karate*" were used to replace "*tiy*" and "*tūdiy*." The Chinese character for Tang, which for Japanese and Okinawans also referred to China, was 唐. It was pronounced "*tō*" in Okinawan and "*kara*" in standard Japanese. Consequently, at the schools it was taught at, *tūdiy* (唐手) was Japanized in pronunciation and became "*karate*." The appearance of "karate" as a new Japanese word caused further confusion in terminology. By 1908, Itosu Ankō pointed out that there was a need for a unified word because the words "*tiy*" and "*tūdiy*" were being used interchangeably in different regions of Okinawa, but at schools the words "*te*" and "*karate*" were being used interchangeably. A word had to be decided on when Ryukyuan martial techniques were taught at schools. Because Standard Japanese was taught at schools, it seemed appropriate to use it as the language for naming those martial techniques. However, since "*te*" was the Japanese word for "hand," it was taught that it might cause confusion. Using the *kanji* 唐 (*tō* and *kara*) recognized Ryukyu's past tributary relationships with the great nation of China and so it would add dignity and academic weight if it was used in the terminology for Ryukyuan fighting techniques. Therefore, Itosu sent a proposal to the Okinawa Prefectural School Affairs Division (沖縄県学務課) that "*karate*" (as the pronunciation of 唐手) be used as the unified word. The School Affairs Division accepted his proposal and decided to adopt the word "*karate*" as the unified official Okinawan Prefectural term for Ryukyuan martial arts. The *tiy* master from Shuri, Itosu, has left a fine legacy of achievements, but his proposal may have been his one major error. The decision to use the term "*karate*" to give it some academic dignity and as a way to standardize the terminology used to refer to Ryukyuan the martial art, which had been born during the during the long Gusuku Period when there

—

was constant warfare in Ryūkyū and was known as *tiy*, would later invite misinterpretation and false historical understandings.

After 1908, the term that came into currency was *karate jutsu* (唐手術). *Karate jutsu* was first introduced for the first time in mainland Japan in 1922, when Funakoshi and Gima did their demonstration at the Ancient Martial Arts Physical Education Exhibition that was organized by the Japanese Ministry of Education. At the time, their art was described as "Ryukyuan *karate jutsu*."

Who changed 唐手 to 空手? They are pronounced the same but use different *kanji*. Various narratives exist to explain what happened, such as the Hanashiro, the Okinawa Prefectural School Affairs Division, the Keiō University, and the Dai Nippon Butoku Kai narratives. The oldest of these narratives starts with Okinawan *karateka* Hanashiro Chōmo's use of the characters 空手 when he wrote "*karate*." This is clearly documented in his book, *Karate-dō Daikan*. Hanashiro was a veteran of the Japanese military and believed that there was no problem until the turn of the 20th century that in the Okinawan language there were two terms to distinguish fighting techniques: *tiy* and *tūdiy*. However, he took great issue in how the two were lumped together as "*karate*" using the characters 唐手. His problem was with the use of the character 唐 as he felt that it was not appropriate. He believed that if the term *karate* was used with the characters 唐手, most people would mistakenly believe that Ryukyuan martial techniques were of Chinese origin. Hanashiro was afraid that this would lead to the withering away of the unique identity of *tiy* as it would be seen as something that came straight from China. Originally, before the term "*tūdiy*" came into existence, only the term *tiy* was used in Ryūkyū. Moreover, Hanashiro had honed his skills in Shuri-te, which was quite removed from Chinese *kempō* and was indeed close to the original ancient Ryukyuan *tiy*. Also, at the time, *tiy* in the form of Shuri-te was the overwhelming mainstream in Okinawa. Hanashiro no doubt speculated that unifying the terminology with *karate* written as 唐手 would cause problems in the future. It was through his writings that he took it upon himself to change the character used from 唐 to 空. Being a prominent Shuri-te master, Hanashiro was well acquainted with the structure and form of Chinese *kempō* and *tūdiy* and that was probably the very reason why he felt the danger in using 唐手 to write *karate*. *Tiy* developed together with "*kobujutsu* (ancient martial techniques)." In battle, *kobudō* weapons and *tiy* were used in unison to defeat opponents. Utilizing *kobujutsu* meant holding and using weapons in battle. These weapons included *bo, sai, nunchaku, tunfa, ēku*, and other agricultural or fishing tools and implements. However, using *tiy* meant that a person was empty handed when fighting. Consequently, *tiy* techniques were those in which a person was "empty handed" and this is probably why Hanashiro chose 空手, which used the characters for "empty hand." However, his use of 空手 did not spread widely through the Okinawan martial arts world at the time. It was mainly confined to his own individual notes. Despite this fact, 1905 was during an extremely tumultuous year. In that year, Japan emerged victorious in the Russo-Japanese War, a war which involved China. We might conjecture that for Hanashiro, who had participated in both the Sino-Japanese and Russo-Japanese Wars as a soldier, using the *kanji* 唐 to write *karate* was felt problematic because of China's contentious relationship with Japan.

Further, a few years earlier in 1901, *karate* began being practiced in public when it was introduced to the physical education curriculum of the Shuri Primary School. This was also the start of *karate* being taught to groups. In 1905, *karate* clubs were established at Shuri Middle School, Naha Middle School, and the Teacher's College. Around the same time, *karate* clubs were started at other schools throughout Okinawa. Because of its public spread to schools as an official part of the curriculum, Hanashiro most likely felt an urgent need to correct the *kanji* used for *karate*. At the time, it is probable that Hanashiro may have been in dialogue with his fellow Shuri-te master, Itosu, who was lobbying the School Affairs Division to officially adopt the term *karate* using the *kanji* 唐手, which it did in 1908. It is believed that there was vigorous debate between the two men after Hanashiro began writing *karate* as 空手 in 1905. If so, it was only natural that the former teacher Itosu's proposal would be adopted over the former military man Hanashiro's proposal by the School Affairs Division. However, at the time it was probably unimaginable that 20 years later in mainland Japan, 唐手 would be replaced by 空手.

The Okinawa Prefectural School Affairs Division narrative involves Kanō Jigoro, who came to Okinawa in 1926. The reason for his visit was to observe authentic *karate jutsu* at its source. He had realized quickly after watching Funakoshi's demonstration of *kata* and *yakusoku kumite* that *karate jutsu* was unique to Okinawa. Also, after having been to China he was beginning to be convinced that Chinese *kempō* and Okinawan *karate jutsu* were not the same and as a martial artist wanted to confirm his thoughts. After watching Mabuni Kenwa, Miyagi Chōjun, and others demonstrate styles that were different from Funakoshi's, he profoundly understood the depth and diversity of other forms of *karate jutsu*. At the Okinawa Prefectural offices, Kanō gave a lecture on "Karate (唐手) and Physical Education" that had been organized by Mabuni and Miyagi. In preparation for Kanō's visit, a committee was set up. As part of the preparations, the members of the committee held a panel discussion during which they debated over the terminology for *karate*. The School Affairs Division Chief argued that, "the term *karate* (written as 唐手) is not favorable. On this occasion, perhaps we need to think of another name that would be more fitting for martial techniques from Okinawan Prefecture." Starting with the Security Division Chief, all members present agreed with the School Affairs Division Chief. According to this theory, that is how *karate* became 空手.

While the School Affairs Division settled on *"karate"* written as 唐手 based on Itosu's recommendation 1908, 18 years later, its members it reversed that decision in response to its own internal proposal. It was a time when the whole of Japan was racing towards imperialism and militarism. Officials representing the central government were sent to all reaches of the nation to see that national policies were uniform. In those conditions, both the School Affairs Division and Security Division Chiefs were not Okinawans, but Japanese mainlanders. It was most likely that these mainland Japanese appointees believed that 唐手 was too Chinese and an affront to their pride as Japanese. They took the opportunity of Kanō's visit to propose a change in the term and swayed the preparatory committee toward their opinion. However, it is not clear what the reasoning was behind their choosing 空手, but there is speculation that they referenced Hanashiro's 1905 notes.

There is also the Keiō University narrative. Following his sudden fame after arriving in Tōkyō in 1922, Funakoshi began to teach at the Meisei Juku and *karate* clubs at several universities. The first karate club was established at Keiō University in October or 1924. Among his the Keiō University students were those that wanted to replace the character 唐 because it referred to China and objected to the notion that Japanese should learn a "Chinese martial art." As a result, it is said that an article appeared in the first newsletter of the Keiō University Karate Research Association that was published in 1930 which talked about the profound meaning of the character 空. A student took the character 空 from such Buddhist teachings on 色即是空 and 空即是色 (*shikisokuzekū kūsokuzeshiki*: The form is nonexistence, and nonexistence is the form) and proposed that it be used to replace 唐. He took his proposal to Funakoshi, who is said to have given him permission to carry it out. According to this narrative Funakoshi himself had deep ties to the Shingon Sect of Buddhism and it is in respect of its founder's teaching that he decided to adopt the *kanji* 空手. As a result, the Keiō University Karate

Research Association replaced the *kanji* 唐手 with 空手 for its name in 1929. This may have been the first time that such a change was formally made at a Japanese university. Funakoshi had previously used the 唐手 in the titles of his books in 1922 and 1925, but in 1935, he began to use 空手. Incidentally, Funakoshi is buried in the compounds of a Shingon Sect temple.

Finally, there is the Dai Nippon Butoku Kai Narrative. When the Dai Nippon Butoku Kai incorporated *karate* as part of its *judō* section in 1936, *karate* had become formally subordinated to Kōdōkan *judō*. In the spring of that year, the Shōtōkan Dōjō in Tōkyō was constructed and a ceremony to commemorate the establishment of the Japanese Students Karate-dō (空手道) Federation was held (at the Aoyama Hall). The next year in 1937, the Dai Nippon Butoku Kai officially replaced 唐手 ("*karate*") with 空手道 (*karate-dō*) and established a *karate* section within its organizational structure. Consequently, with the formal recognition of the change from 唐手 to 空手 by the Dai Nippon Butoku Kai, the latter term was publicly made official. The first public use of the term "*karate-dō*" by the organization is believed to be in the published program for the 44th Butoku Sai that was held in 1940 in Kyoto.

The Spread of *Tiy*, *Tūdiy*, and Karate in Mainland Japan

The propagation of *karate* in mainland Japan through universities began in 1922. Many excellent *karate* masters have been recognized for helping to spread *karate* in mainland Japan including those on the chronological list below.

1924 Keiō University Karate Research Association (Master Instructor Funakoshi Gichin, from Okinawa)

1926 Tōkyō University Karate Research Association (Master Instructor Funakoshi Gichin, from Okinawa)

1927 Tōyō University (Master Instructor Motobu Chōki, from Okinawa)

1929 Ritsumeikan University (Master Instructor Miyagi Chōjun, from Okinawa)

1930 Takushoku University (Master Instructor Funakoshi Gichin, from Okinawa)

1933 Waseda University (Master Instructor Funakoshi Gichin, from Okinawa)

1934 Tōkyō Agricultural University (Master Instructor Taira Shinken, from Okinawa)

1934 Hōsei University (Master Instructor Funakoshi Gichin, from Okinawa)

1936 Meiji University (Master Instructor Yabiku Mōden, from Okinawa)

1936 Rikkyō University (Master Instructor Ōtsuka Hironori, student of Funakoshi Gichin)

1937 Doshisha University (Master Instructor Miyagi Chōjun, from Okinawa)

1938 Kyōto University (Master Instructor Miyagi Chōjun, from Okinawa)

1939 Nihon University Medical School (Master Instructor Taira Shinken, from Okinawa)

1949 Kansai University (Master Instructor Mabuni Kenwa, from Okinawa)

Other schools that invited the above master instructors and established their own *karate* clubs included Tōkyō Commerce University, Shōwa Medical University, Shōwa Pharmacy University, Nihon Dental University, Akita Kousen, and Yokohama Senmon. It is through universities and other schools that karate *jutsu* spread throughout Japan. Soon after Funakoshi introduced *karate* to Keiō and Tōkyō Universities, he was inundated with requests from other universities for master instructors. It was impossible for him to accommodate all the requests alone and this led a large demand for *karate* masters in mainland Japan. Kanō's role in the exodus of *karate* masters from

Okinawa to mainland Japan is largely because he passed the word on to other universities that he had observed and met many *karate* master instructors in Okinawa who were on the same level as Funakoshi. Motobu, Taira, Yabiku, Miyagi, Mabuni, and other apt representatives of Okinawan *karate* were invited to teach at mainland universities. *Karate* could not escape becoming less authentic. Not only did its name change from 唐手 to 空手, but because *karate* was made a subordinate martial art to *judō,* it incorporated such *judō* techniques such as *tsukami, nage,* and *ashibarai.* As a result, many modifications were made to the *kata* and techniques of *karate* and this led to wide divergence between traditional Okinawan and Japanese *karate kata.* Okinawan *karate* still retains elements of its traditional indigenous roots, while Japanese *karate* is a result of changes that took place after Okinawan karate was introduced to the mainland. From the perspective of Okinawans, it is "Yamatu (Japanese) *karate*." We now often see practitioners doing acrobatic *kata* to loud American music. Few Japanese are phased when they see such performances because they are quickly becoming the accepted norm for *karate.* Similarly, after reaching the mainland, liberties were taken to change Okinawan karate kata to resemble *judō* or to take two or three traditional Okinawan *kata* and choreographing a single *kata.* Ryukyuan *karateka* are appalled when we see such things. In Ryūkyū, taking liberties to change traditional *kata* is a serious violation of tradition.

Chapter 2 Cultural Aspects of Okinawa Karate Part 2

Kata and its transformation

Section 1. Culture of *kata* (forms)

Karate, which was developed as a combat skill by the people of ancient Ryukyu during its long warring period, can be perceived as a culture, and I intend to probe deeply into its *kata* (forms) that cultivated the foundation of karate. Before discussing exclusively about the *kata* of karate, I would like to first summarize how the term *kata* is used in other traditions.

Japanese culture is often expressed as a culture of *kata*. The origin of the term *kata* is not certain, but as written in Chinese character, *kata (型)* appears to primarily mean a "mold" or a "principle." We are surrounded by many *kata* in our daily lives. *Kata* can be interpreted diversely: *kata* of martial arts such as *Kendō* or *Judō*, *kata* of flower arrangement, *kata* of serving manners, *kata* of drinking manners and etiquette for tea ceremony, *kata* of postures for traditional performing arts such as Kabuki play, and more. These types of *kata* are simple and basic; therefore, they can be defined as "*kata* in the narrow sense". In comparison, "*Jo-Ha-Kyū*" (literary: introduction, development, climax) can be defined as a *kata* that represents sequence of an entire performance of a Noh play and "*Syu-Ha-Ri*" (literally: obey, detach, leave) as a *kata* to represent the stages of mastering *kata* of tea ceremony or theater arts. This type of *kata* consists of several simple *kata*, and it can be defined as *"kata* in the broad sense".

Also, visual artists' styles, monks' religious precepts, and rules, courtesy, etiquette, manners and rites of Samurai class family and royal court can all be defined as behavioral *kata* (forms) at the social level.

Kata, as described above, can be defined diversely, and its developmental process was strongly related with person's body movements. Body movements of ancient worshiping rituals or religious rites and its incidental dances were gradually stylized, and in the process, *kata* were established. After established *kata* were popularized among people, they were eventually perceived as a form of art.

One of the characteristics of *kata* is that *kata* can be used in an amphibolous way. *Kata* can mean positively and negatively. For instance traditional artists, martial artists and religious ascetics use *kata* in a positive meaning. As such, *kata* is emphasized as an important aspect of training and religious austerity. On the other hand, *kata* can be perceived negatively as formalized or conventional words or actions and as thoughtlessness. A saying *monkirigata no kōjō* (to give a conventional address or set speech) is one example. You can see how *kata* can take both positive and negative meanings. By the way, in our human society, it's unstable how people want to keep or discontinue practicing certain *kata*. Also, various personality types of people exist; one may strive to detach from existing *kata*, one may create new *kata*, and others may try to preserve existing *kata*.

In considering how human beings relate with *kata*, traditions take an important role. Tradition consists of, more than anything else, historical senses. Nothing can be regarded as a tradition without physical presence. Traditions become diverse when it contains *kata*.

In this book, I focus on types of *kata* that are based on physical movements of body instead of those compounded and abstract *kata* of cultural or social levels.

I'd like to briefly mention how Japanese people perceive *karada* (body) and *kokoro* (heart/soul). Modern generations understand *karada* as body, but this has started only in the recent history. In pre-modern history, *karada* was defined and understood as having two different aspects; (1) mi and (2) *kara* or *karada*. In this case, mi means a body that inhabits a soul or a spirit meaning a body with life. On the other hand, *kara* has the same origin as a homonym *kara* (empty shell), and *kara* and *karada* meant a body from which its soul is completely detached. It's the mental activity that gives life and energy to a body, and ancient Japanese people called it *tamashī* (spirit) or *kororo* (heart or soul). In ancient times, the antonym of *shin* was *tama* or *tamashī*, but in the later time, it was shifted to *kokoro* (soul). Seen in historical records like *Kojiki* or *Manyosyū, kokoro* was used in many poems as a term to express a comprehensive mental activity consisting of intellect, emotion and consciousness. The term *kokoro,* equipped with intellectual functions while containing emotion as its core, continued to be used as the same meaning in the Heian period. Furthermore, the term *kokoro* had a heavier emphasis on capability for aesthetic sentiments. The relation between *shin* and *kokoro* became one of the main themes of Tanka poetry, and the connection between the two became tighter as history progressed.

Amidst the era of upheaval from the end of the Heian period to the beginning of the Kamakura period, people realized how unreliable humans were, and most of all, realized unreliableness of their own selves. People began seeking transcendence in their mental capabilities. For Kamo no Chomei and Fujiwara no Toshinari, their ways of transcendence was the construction of their aesthetic world of *yugen* (a graceful and subtle beauty). Furthermore, Fujiwara no Toshinari's son, Fujiwara no Sadaie, established a concept of *ushin*. In contrast to his father, Sadaie's teachings involved the beauty of voluptuousness and emphasized the creation of poems with *unclouded mind*, and Sadaie called such mind *ushin* in contrast to *mushin* (empty mind). By the way, a Buddhist term, *mushin*, first appeared in Japan in the Kamakura period. The first Tanka poem in Japan that focused on the theme of *mushin* was, "your mind, regard it as a foe of your mind, having a mind is to have no mind (*Kokoro wo ba, kokoro no ada to kokoroete, kokoro no naki wo kokoro wo ba to seyo*)" written by Ippen. Ippen was a Jōdo (pure land teaching) sect Buddhist. *Mushin* as a creed of Buddhism was introduced into the art world as Zeami's concept of *mushin* (written in "*Kakyo*"). Besides a Buddhist teaching about body and soul relation, the perception of *mushin* was spread among people's beliefs and daily lives through the three core elements of traditional arts and martial arts, *Shin-Gi-Tai* (literally: mind, skill, body), which emphasized *mushin* as its foundation. *Kokoro* (soul) with the core element of emotion was transformed into *kokoro* of *mushin*; Furthermore, it was the positively defined *mushin* that was redefined by Zeami and not the negatively defined *mushin* as lacking thoughtfulness or sympathy. Of course, this transformation was caused by the shift of people's aesthetic senses.

The concept of *mushin* with negative impressions was replaced by a positively valued new concept. As the influence of *zen* became stronger amongst *bushi* warriors during the Middle Ages (around the Kamakura and Muromachi periods), people's focus shifted from aesthetic contemplation to actual actions and intentions. As a result of such transition, new social class appeared which valued taking physical actions and having an unshakable and unclouded mind more than wavering, hesitating and susceptible mind. The practice of *zen* was a key for such a social class to be born. Dōgen's *zen,* which emphasized physical practice, and the life style of *bushi*, which experienced physical and mental agony through various practices in the *bushi* society, had fundamental commonality. Dōgen created *shingi*, which sets the rules for training to emerge one's body and mind into standardized forms; one of his teachings included *shikantaza* which means to single mindedly practice *zen* meditation without doing absolutely anything else. *Mushin* was a part of the ascetic practice of Buddhism which subconsciously created the principle that mind and body are together and inseparable.

Waza (a skill) can also be written in Chinese character as 業 *gyō* (a job) or 態 *tai* (a circumstance). The practice of religious ascetics was adopted by artists as an attitude towards their training. This commonality between religion and art was generally accepted in the Middle Ages. For calligraphy, training had to be based on superior examples; an example had to be copied multiple times a day and continued for several days until the disciple could write exactly as the example, and then he or she was allowed to move on to the next step. About the balance between mind and *kata* (form), it was expressed that mind should be prioritized over *kata*.

Appearance of the *waza* concept played an important role in the society of the Muromachi period. A treatise *Tsurezuregusa* ("Essays in Idleness") served a function to establish a new concept of body, mind and *waza*. Keikō Yoshida was a poet, but besides Tanka poetry, he also wrote about Japanese archery. That was the era when schools of archery such as the Ogasawara-ryū or the Hiki-ryū were founded. In the Muromachi period, Chōgen brought architectural styles of the Sung Dynasty which drastically transformed wooden building structures in Japan. Performing art made a remarkable progress as seen with *Dengaku* play flourishing in Nanbokuchō period and Noh play making a surprisingly drastic improvement in the Hokuzan period of the shogun Ashikaga Yoshimitsu, and such progress could be realized because of the improvement of *waza*. Further, *waza* of performing arts was the skills tied with aesthetic senses, and the skills were supported by sophisticated mentality of the performers.

Kata is performed by body movements which consists of body, *kokoro* (a mind) and *waza* (a skill). Japan was not the only place with the concept of *kata*. In fact, there isn't any civilization without *kata*. Religious ceremonies are a type of *kata*, and etiquette or manners are also *kata*. For poetry, beginning in the Heian period throughout the Kamakura and the Muromachi periods, it has a significant meaning that the culture was developed while treating *kokinshū* and *shin-kokinshū* as classics. *Manyoshū* didn't receive its recognition as a classic until the Meiji period, until then, *kokinshū* and *shin-kokinshū* were studied as classics and used as the standards for training in poetry. Poetry style called *honkatori* (adaptation of famous poems) was developed, and without sharing these cultural standards, *yokyoku* (Noh songs) or *haikai* (seventeen-syllable verse) couldn't be established. Also, a system to preserve secret teachings of poetry called *kokin denju* and *Iemoto* system to make schools and styles (-*ryū* or –*ha*) were also born. The second transformation of *kata* arose from the development of the court etiquette in the

Heian period. *Reihō* (etiquette) was established based on Chinese etiquettes. There are historical documents from back then such as *reihō* of Shinto shrines and Buddhist temples and accounts describing etiquettes of royal court such as *Saikyūki, Jōgangishiki,* and *Hokuzanshō.*

The third transformation was the acceptance of Buddhism. There are several *kata* for Buddhism ceremony; and because of the influence of Jianzhen's teachings, there are strict rules for initiation ceremonies in Japan. Also, *giki* (rules of rites), an esoteric Buddhism brought by Kūkai, emphasized the importance of *kata.*

I addressed the culture of *kata* in Japan, and before discussing *kata* of karate, I'd like to touch basis on *kata* of other Japanese traditions: Zeami's Noh play and swordsmanship.

Kata in Nohgaku theory

Physically performed *kata* can be described as a *kata* in the narrow sense which consists of standardized body movements, and the process of practicing and assimilating oneself into such *kata* can be seen as another form of *kata* (Kawakami Fuhaku described such *kata* with *Syu-Ha-Ri* principle). Furthermore, the process of mastering and preserving *kata* is a process of human growth, and it requires a constant endeavor to improve oneself, which also can be interpreted as a type of *kata,* a *kata* of culture. As a result of different ideals of *kata* and performance styles appearing, multiple branches of schools and *Iemoto* were born, and that can be seen as *kata* of society. Zeami recognized physical movements as *kata,* then organized it as a theory, and performed on stage according to his theorized *kata.* Of course, there were several *kata* existed before Zeami such as *kata* of *kagura* dance, *giki* (rules of rites) of esoteric Buddhism, etiquette of royal court, *dengaku* dance, *zazen* performed by monks from the Kamakura period on, etc. Most of those *kata* weren't documented, and even if it were documented, it never probe into the relation between performer's mind and body. Some of them were taught only orally because documenting the subtleties of teachings were believed impossible.

Zeami's treatise about *Nohgaku* wasn't completely open to everyone. It was taught only to those who were approved by him; in fact, there is a section called *Besshikuden* (secret teachings to be given separately). In there, he elaborates on concepts of *kata* and thoroughly describes the principle *Shin-Gi-Tai* (literally: mind, skill, body).

Underwent during the civil war era up to the beginning of the 17th century during, the transformation from mere skills of sword fighting into *kendō* (swordsmanship) with sophisticated mentality was greatly affected by *Nohgaku*. Zeami's *Nohgaku* theories are often referred to for its aesthetic concepts such as *hana* (a flower) and *yugen* (a graceful and subtle beauty); however, it's also interesting to view it differently from the standpoint of *kata*. *Kata* in the narrow sense can be witnessed as *jittai* (various types of role-playing) in his treatise *Fūshikaden,* and *nikyoku santai* (Noh songs and three role-playing subjects), *goi* (five styles of role-playing) and *kui* (nine styles of role-playing) in his treatises *Shikadō* and *Nikyokusantai Ningyōzu.* The term *katagi,* which is often used by Zeami, is basically a synonym of *kata,* which is a sequence of individual techniques. *Te*, the term used in his treatises, can be assumed as each individual technique that make up *kata*.

His concept of "*Jo-Ha-Kyū*" (literary: introduction, development, climax) can be seen as *kata* to construct an overall Noh play, in other words, *kata* in the broad sense. Also, his idea of placing *waza* (skills) at the core of the relation between body and mind can be conceived as a type of *kata* in the broad sense, and *kendō* shares the same principle. Therefore, in that sense, Zeami is the pioneer of *kata* of culture.

Monomane (role-playing or mimicry) was the most basic training for *Yamato Sarugaku* since Kan'ami, father of Zeami, was the head of the theater. Inuōami from *Ōmi Sarugaku*, who was the elder disciple of Zeami, was the one who strived to perfect the beauty of a graceful and subtle beauty. Though, his lineage was extinct along the way. Zeami placed role-playing as the foundation and further absorbed the idea of a graceful and subtle beauty. Role-playing was originally the core philosophy of Kan'ami and Zeami's performance theory. On top of the foundation, essence of *Ōmi Sarugaku* was incorporated, and as a result, the treatise *Kakyo* was developed. Since *Kakyo*, concept of *nikyoku santai* was established which served as a system for teaching disciples. Now, the question is, what is role-playing? The original meaning of role-playing was to imitate a subject exactly the same and is based on realism performance theory; however, Zeami further added a philosophy "to know appropriate levels of intensity depending on the subjects." Zeami's performance theories after *Kakyo* became further pragmatic and systematic. Also, he mentions that a graceful and subtle beauty can be achieved when appearances of aged body, woman's body and soldier's body can be performed beautifully, meaning that appearance has to be beautiful as a well-integrated role-playing parts. His consideration for appearance touches on the physical appearance and the internal relation of performer's mind and body. For example, woman's egoism or self-will is said to be the most important and difficult role-playing subject. Zeami describes that woman's true fate and egoism can be depicted only when the performer has reached true *ushufu* (a performance of which *kata* is truly mastered by the performer).

In *nikyoku santai*, *nikyoku* refers to Noh songs and *santai* refers to role-playing of three appearances: elderly, woman and soldier. *Nikyoku santai* is the fundamental concept of Zeami's teaching. He asserted that until this basic *nikyoku santai* is adequately learned, training should not include any other performances or skills. This explains how he was well aware that the process of mastering *kata* involved the process of overcoming internal conflicts and assimilating one's mind into *kata* besides merely learning physical movements. Also, how did he perceive the relation between performer and *kata*? That can be described with his concept of *katagi*. *Katagi* otherwise means a patterned stamp for dying cloth or a woodcut for printing, but in this case, *katagi* refers to a standard form to be modeled in training, in other words, a *katagi* meant a *kata*. Furthermore, there were general *katagi* and specific *katagi*, and Zeami described, "a Noh play learned with general *katagi* must also learn specific *katagi*, and a Noh play grew from specific *katagi* must learn general *katagi* to avoid unbalanced weight on both."

Performers' attitude towards physical practice and training was one of the characteristics in the Middle Age. The essence of that was to train and discipline mind and body to reach the mastery of *dō* principle. *Fūshikaden* is a treatise elaborating on how to conceive practice. In the treatise, Zeami repeats to "practice rigidly and have no arrogance and stubbornness." He asserts to strive in practice thoroughly but eliminate arrogance and have modesty and flexibility. Also, *te* (hand), a term used in the treatise, means *kata* of individual techniques that are the constituents of a sequence of dance, and it's interesting to notice that "*te*" referred to karate in Okinawa. He mentions that practice isn't to be purported to improve one's performance skills, but practice itself should be the purpose. Dōgen's teachings of *zen* from his treatise *Shūshōfuji* has the same principle; *zazen* meditation shouldn't be treated as a way of reaching the enlightenment but meditation itself should be the purpose. Also, Zeami describes seven levels of practice phases according to physical and mental growth of a person. In *Fūshikaden*, his philosophy on practice according to physical and mental growth is elaborated; however, in *Kakyo*, he describes that practice should be based on performer's skill level. Young performers sometimes change their performance styles or skip some learnings, and he calls it *tendoku* (originally means a way of shortening sutra chanting by skipping some lines); he asserts that this is because they merely imitate and doesn't truly learn. Also, he elaborated on the concept of *mushufū* and *ushufū*. *Mushufū* is a performance of a mere imitation without truly assimilating the performance skills into the body, and in contrast, *ushufū* is a performance of which *kata* is truly mastered by the performer.

There is an inverse relation between body and mind in the process of learning a basic *kata*; it has forces working in opposite directions that keeps a dynamic equilibrium. Then, body and mind become closer and eventually inseparable in the process of mastering a *waza* (skill). The fact that Zeami uses the term "*tai*", which means a physical movement or condition, to refer to a *waza* explains how he aimed to achieve integration of body and mind in mastering a *waza*. The term *waza* used for traditional performance art fundamentally means a skill, and mental aspect takes an important role in it. Even though Nohgaku stories are fictitious, a well-trained performance is capable of making audiences forget that it is a fiction.

Kata in Sword Fighting Theories

In this section, I will focus on *kendō* (swordsmanship) as a representative of Japanese martial arts and intend elaborate on issues related to *kata*. There are many martial arts including *kendō, kyūdō* (Japanese art of archery), *jūdō, yari* (spear), *bajutsu* (horsemanship), *bōjutsu* (staff fighting technique), karate, *iaijutsu* (sword drawing technique), etc., and of course, various *kata* are taught at different schools. Development of old martial arts culminating in the era of Tokugawa shogunate (the Edo period), *kendō* produced more principles than any other martial arts. Until the early modern history of Japan, *jūdō* was treated as *jūjutsu* (self-defense technique) and along with *iai-jutsu*, they were part of *kenpō* (sword fighting skill). Furthermore, the social status of *jūjutsu-ka* (*jūjutsu* practitioner) was comparatively lower than of *kendō-ka* (*kendō* practitioner). *Kyūdō* was established before *kendō*. Archery had been adopted in Japan as a recreational sport at royal court since the ancient times for having influences from China where archery was one of *rikugei* (six kinds of basic culture). Also, bow and arrow had been one of the main weapons on battlefields, and in the Muromachi period, proprieties of archery were established by *Ogasawara-ryū*. However, as a result of change in war strategies in the 16th century, bow and arrow lost its practicality and was replaced by swords and rifles. In the 16th century, sword became the main weapon on battlefields. The sword fighting skill was an old martial art which was based on the *shinpō* principle (a sophisticated mentality aimed to refine one's mind) besides merely improving physical skills required on battlefields. Teachings of *shinpō* questions the current state of mind and probe for an ideal state of mind, and asks for disciplines, actions and training to achieve such ideal state. Issues of *kata* should be examined by carefully looking into the 300 years of history with treatises on sword fighting skills from the Edo period to the beginning of the Meiji period.

Before discussing about *kata*, I'll first look into the historical overview of sword fighting philosophies. A treatise *Kenpō Sekiun Sensei Sōden* describes that "seeing the truth behind the teachings of various schools, those who can defeat opponents can do so not because of what they studied but because of their luck and determination." I presume that was the true beliefs during the warring period. A legendary swordsman Miyamoto Musashi mentions in his treatise *Gorin no sho* that "when I looked back at my past at the age of 30, I noticed I didn't win battles because I perfected my philosophy on combat tactics; it may have been because my opponents' skills were insufficient. I realized at the age of 50 that without any particular philosophy, if you train day and night, you will naturally be following a principle of a warrior." Miyamoto Musashi was at the age of 29 when he had a duel against Sasaki Kojirō, and he never fought a duel again. Miyamoto didn't win his battles based on his combat theory. Rather, his philosophy was built up as an accumulation of desperate battles using his innate talent as a warrior. The history of treatises on sword fighting philosophy before establishment of the modern *kendō* principles in the Meiji period can be generally divided into the following three categories. The first period starts at the end of the warring period until the establishment of *Kenpō Sekiun Sensei Sōden* in the 17th century. The second period is from the establishment of *Kenpō Sekiun Sensei Sōden* to the beginning of the Tenpō era which is the last period of the Tokugawa Shogunate. The third period is from the Tenpō era to the Meiji 27 at the year of death of *Jikishinkage-ryu*'s Sakakibara Kenkichi.

In the first period, in transition from the warring era to the peaceful era, Takuan Sōhō elaborated on *shinpō* (way of mind) in his treatise *Fudō*

Chishin Myōroku ("The Unfettered Mind"). Also, a swordsman Yagyū Munenori left a treatise of sword fighting philosophy titled *Heihō Kadensho* ("a hereditary book on the art of war") which comprehensively covers subjects from mental aspects of training based on *zen* practices to political governance theories along with technical aspects of sword fighting. The account describes that *waza* (skills) and *shinpō* are the two inevitable and inseparable concepts. The characteristics of the second period was its focus on competition matches and development of protector equipment such as *men* (a face mask), *kote* (gauntlet gloves), *shinai* (a bamboo sword), etc. to ensure safety of competitors. This equipment was developed by Naganuma Shirozaemon Kunisato of *Jikishinkage-ryū* in the Kyōhō period. Before such protections were available, wooden swords were mainly used for training for the safety reasons. However, learning without actual duels became a mere imitation of *kata* and lost interests of disciples after all. When the protector equipment were developed and competition matches were encouraged, *kendō* became popular again. During the same era, a school *Shingyōtō-ryū* was established, and that was the beginning of the movement to standardize the relation between mind and *kata*. The second period can be divided into the first half that valued forms and the second half that valued both mind and forms.

The situation was completely different in the third period. The Shogunate ruling system was faced with a danger of crisis, and the pressure from foreign countries was becoming an actual threat. The number of *kendō* disciples increased drastically in this period. At the time, there were more than 500 schools of *kendō*. Including Kondō Isami, majority members of *Shinsengumi* (shogunate police dedicated to suppressing anti-shogunate activities) came from farm families in Mitama area. Three major schools in this period were *Jikishinkage-ryū* of Otani Nobutomo, *Hokushin Ittō-ryū* of Chiba Shusaku, and *Shintō Munen-ryū* of Momonoi Shunzō. However, when the new period Meiji started, the long history of class system was abolished with the edict *Hanseki Hōkan* (returning property of land and people from the feudal lords to the Emperor) and *Haihan Chiken* (abolition of *Han* system and establishment of prefectures), and with the establishment of *Haitōrei* (an edict for abolishing the wearing of swords) in the Meiji 9 (1876), the people who lost samurai class privilege also lost their symbol to represent their identity.

Kendō's *kata* in the narrow sense was initially established during the 16th century through the beginning of the 17th century. Many of treatises written in the period contained collections of experiences of duels or legendary stories of masters. One example of such a treatise is *Shinkage-ryū Heihō Mokuroku no koto*, which was given by Yagiyū Sekishūsai Munetoshi to Konbaru Hachijō in the Keichō 6 (1601). In the account, there is a section titled, *kyūko*, which describes nine ways to use swords: *hissyō, gyakufū, jūtachi, waboku, ōzume, kozume, yaegaki, jōkei*, and *murasame.* Yagiyū writes that it is an assortment of core teachings from various schools. However, Yagiyū Jūbei, in his treatise *Tsuki no Sho*, structures various ways to use a sword based on the principle *Jo-Ha-Kyū* and presents how to train based on it; it is evident that a well-established *kata* for training was present around this period.

A principle *Jo-Ha-Ri*, originally Noh's *kata* in the broad sense, can be found as sword fighting theory of Yagiyū Shinkage-ryū. In his treatises *Shinkage-ryū Heihō Mokuroku, Heihō Kuden-sho*, and *Tsuki no Sho*, the concept of *Jo-Ha-Kyū* is further subdivided into *Jo (jōdan 3, chūdan 3, gedan 4)*, *Ha (sekkō 2, tōboku 3, uchiai 3)* and *Kyū (jōdan 3, chūdan 3, gedan 3)*.

Further, Chiba Shūsaku describes his theory based on *sadō*'s *Shu-Ha-Ri* (principle for tea ceremony). "There is a principle called *Shu-Ha-Ri*. *Shu* means to preserve the tradition, for instance, a disciple must not alter the standard posture of his school in striking an opponent such as *gedan-seigan* for Itto-ryū and *hira-seigan* for Munen-ryū. *Ha* means to train in order to breakthrough his standards to step up to the next level, and finally, *Ri* means to leap towards a superior level by leaving the *Shu* and *Ha* concepts by keeping his mind free from any distractions. It's important to contemplate on the concept *Shu-Ha-Ri* in training."

Influenced by Takuan's teachings, Yagiyū-ryū's sword fighting style evolved from *ushin* that prioritized keeping alerted and attentive at all time to the superior mentality *mushin*. Sword fighting theories developed after the treatise *Heihō Kadensho* were based on the concept *Shin-Gi-Tai*. Describing the relation between body and mind in a duel, Miyamoto Musashi asserted "to keep your mind reactive (state of *tai*) and keep your body anticipated in making an attack against an opponent (state of *ken*). The reason is that if your mind anticipates in making the first move, you stumble as your mind jumps ahead of your body; therefore, maintain your mind reserved and have your body ready to attack, and defeat the opponent by letting him make the first move. If your mind hurries to attack, you will be defeated in trying to make your move." *Ken* means to strike single-mindedly with all force as soon as facing an opponent. That is to say mind and body has an inverse relationship; when body is ready to attack, the mind is reserved, and if mind is to make an attack then body is kept reactive. This inverse correspondence between mind and body is surprisingly similar to the basic style of aforementioned Nohgaku theory of Zeami.

Elaborating on the term *waza*, there are visible *waza* and invisible *waza*. Visible *waza* would be sword skills, and each school of *kendō* have their own skills. Sword skills are mainly taught by masters to their disciples through visible and verbal means. For *Hokushin Ittō-ryū*, there were three levels of teaching: first level, intermediate level, and mastery level. Invisible *waza* is more important than those that are visible, and it's not an exaggeration to say that exchanges of invisible *waza* decides the winner of a duel. Invisible *waza* consists of observant eye, timing, distance, etc., and they are especially important for martial arts.

The uniqueness of Japanese performance arts and martial arts came from its emphasis on *shinpō* (way of mind) in pursuit of *waza* instead of simply learning physical skills. *Shinpō* originally was based on the philosophy of *zen* practice and Confucianism later became an additional influence. Also, while some schools of *kendō* prioritized *kokoro* (heart/mind) in their teachings, the mainstream was the schools of *kendō* that prioritized learning *kata*. At the same time, concept of *ki* (*chi*) was becoming a significant element. Then, near the end of the Edo period, there was a social phenomenon that children in rural areas started learning *kendō*. Also, swordsmen like Katsu Kaishu who learned *kendō* while learning European teachings started to appear.

If *shinpō* philosophy is overly prioritized in *kendō* training, a false concept can appear; practicing *zen* as a *shinpō* training can leads to achieving mastery of *kendō*. Kubota Sugane of *Tamiya-ryū* asserted that *kendō* can't be taught with such a false concept and training of *kendō* must begin with learning correct *kata*.

Further, Okada Takehiko describes about *waza* and *chi*. "*Waza* is an outbreak of force; therefore, the origin of force is also the origin of *waza*. Then what is the origin of force and *waza*? The answer is *chi*." Also, *Ittōsai Sensei Kenpōsho* writes "a body is moved by *chi* and *chi* obeys *kokoro*'s direction; therefore, *chi* changes when *kokoro* changes and body changes when *chi* changes." This is important as to show the relation between body, *chi* and *kokoro*.

Sword fighting philosophy from the middle of the Edo period was influenced by the social system and was further developed based on the treatises of the past masters. In the era where contest match was majorly prioritized, Muneari Nakanishi of *Ittō-ryu* asserted that his *shinpō* principle as to resist the trend of prioritizing ostensive *kata* and training. Nakanishi achieved the mental state of *ken zen ichinyo* (sword and *zen* are one) after studying sword fighting treatises of Sekiun, Ichiun, and other masters. It's important to note that Nakanishi developed a breathing technique to cultivate *chi* based on Hakuin's introspective meditation called *rentan*. You can now see how *kendō* evolved from a killing skill into an act with sophisticated mentality.

Section 2. *Kata* of Karate （型）

    Kata is essential for karate because it is the foundation of it. Now what is *kata*? *Kata* are compilations of basic combat skills such as thrusts, kicks and blocks that were developed in actual battles to achieve the purpose of defeating an opponent with a single strike, and were organized into established sequences so that such combat skills can be learned effectively and efficiently.

    In the olden days of Ryukyu, *aji* developed *tiy* to defeat opponents with bare hands. Such techniques were developed to take opponents' lives with single strikes with bare hands or legs.

    Those *bushi* (warriors), who used *tiy* back then, trained and hardened their fists as rock so those could be used as weapons of lethal attacks. That is to say that the fundamental of karate is to use *seiken* (clenched fist). Using well-trained fists, it isn't a difficult task to crush roof bricks or break a cinder block into halves. A strike with such a fist to the face can even kill a person. Combat skills with bare legs were also developed. By strengthening one's soles, toes, insteps and shins, a single strike can end an opponent's life. Legs that are trained to such a state can be strong enough to kill a person with a strike to the head. The same can be said about strikes to the stomach or torso. Such strikes can easily disable opponents by fracturing bones. Well-trained legs can be lethal weapons that can even fracture a bundle of two baseball bats. Needless to say that achieving such level of strength requires a considerable amount of time and training. It's the ultimate *waza* (skills) that only those who rigorously trained for 10, 20, or 30 years can achieve.

    Some people, who are unfamiliar with karate, say that karate isn't difficult to learn and even women can learn it. I agree that may be true to some extent. Karate may be easy enough for anyone to learn. However, if you made such a comment in front of a person who has spent a substantial amount of time in training for karate, you must realize your life may be at stake. Karate is a dreadful killing technique. A blow of a well-trained karate master must be considered as a strike of an untrained person with a baseball bat or a brick. Conversely speaking, without training and hardening fists and legs, it can't be called karate in its original sense, which is to train one's body as a weapon to achieve the fundamental of *tiy* as a killing technique.

The point I'm stressing here is that karate training begins with hardening one's fists and legs. The next step is to challenge one's trained body to actually defeat opponents. In that phase, *kakidamishi* (real fight) becomes important. Karate-*ka* (karate practitioner) in the past often measured their actual strength by *kakidamishi*. In today's society, however, *kakidamishi* can turn into a crime so it is not advisable. Therefore, one's strength has to be measured in sparring at a dōjō. Furthermore, sparring has to be done without the non-contact rule. Strikes have to have actual contact to challenge the outcome of training and to measure real strength.

Let us return to the subject. *Kata* includes elements of thrusts, kicks and blocks so that each technique can be effectively learned in sequence. Reaching an ideal form is difficult to achieve, for instance, practicing *seiken zuki* (thrust of clenched fist), a fundamental technique of *tiy*, 300 times a day isn't quite enough. The same can be said for upper thrust, lower thrust, upper block, lower block, etc. Normally, each technique has to be repeated for 300 to 500 times a day to make an effective training. However, it would take hours to cover all techniques. The benefit of *kata* is that it allows one to practice several techniques efficiently at once, and also practicing techniques in a flow of body movements gives another merit. Thus, by practicing *kata*, which cover several techniques, one can train for all skills of *tiy* until all techniques are adequately mastered.

Training for karate includes; strengthening fists and legs, challenging those fists and legs against live opponents, and practicing repeatedly and consistently to master *kata* which were developed and passed down from past masters. It can be considered as real karate training only when all three conditions are satisfied. With any of the three missing, it can't be a true training of karate.

Origin of *Kata* of Karate

When, where and how did *kata* of karate get developed? Originally, karate was born as a combat skill on battlefields during the early *gusuku* period in Ryukyu, and it was originally called *tiy*. During the warring period that lasted about 800 years from the 7th century until the unification of *sanzan* (three kingdoms) in the 15th century, *aji* from more than 400 *gusuku* fought against each other to protect and to expand their territories. In Ryukyu, where weapons were not available, a bare handed combat technique called *tiy* was developed, and consequently, karate was born. Combat technique developed primary to kill opponents can only be born in actual battlefields. *Tiy* was created and developed to defeat opponents with a single strike. If one couldn't defeat his opponent with a single strike, he then faced a risk of getting killed by the same opponent. Such technique could only be born in where one's life was at stake. Ryukyu was a perfect place for such technique to be cultivated. Firstly, there weren't real weapons in Ryukyu. *Bō* (staff), *sai* (traditional Okinawan weapon originally a hair ornament with a forked stick), *nunchaku* (two linked sticks)*,* and *ēku* (oar) were some of the tools used as weapons (currently used in Ryukyu *kobujutsu*.) There were short swords, but it was difficult to be procured in Ryukyu, where iron wasn't produced, so it was rather a luxurious item. Secondly, during the warring period that lasted for about 800 years with more than 400 established *gusuku*, lack of weapons made bare hand combat skills or *kobujutsu* developed, and such skills were passed down for many generations. In such an environment, it was natural that *tiy* and *kobujutsu* were born. Because the combat skill was born in actual battlefields and was cultivated and passed down for many generations, karate rooted in Ryukyu as a culture. There is a theory that combat skills were imported from

China to Ryukyu as a foreign culture after the unification of *sanzan*, but such a foreign culture would have been absolutely useless during the peaceful period. I don't believe a mere art form of combat skills could be rooted so firmly in Ryukyu society. Combat skills so unique to Ryukyu, *tiy*, was born on battlefields between *aji* of several *gusuku* 1000 years before Chinese *kempō* was introduced to Ryukyu, so it's absolutely untrue that karate was imported from China.

It is presumed that *tiy* was born during the warring period in the 7th century, eventually *kata* was developed to standardize the skills by the 12th century, and then those *kata* were passed down generations after generations. Considering the fact that *shirataru no kata* or *ōshiro no kata* are still present today as *kata* of *bōjutsu* and techniques were treated as part of *tiy*, it can be presumed that by the 13th century some *kata* of *tiy* were already prevailed among commoners. From this, it is considerable that, during the 11th and 12th centuries, *aji* were developing their original *kata*, practiced them secretly, and inherited them only to their descendants. Generally, *kata* were shown and taught only to their own descendants. Those *kata* were developed and constantly improved over a long period of time to satisfy a single purpose that is to know how to defend oneself and defeat opponents, and that's what were taught by *aji* to their descendants. Those *kata* gradually became open to some commoners and certain *kata* were popularized. Those popularized *kata* includes *shirataru no kon* and *ōshiro no kon* which later became *shirataru no te* and *ōshiro no te* and were practiced among commoners and are preserved until today.

Tiy was born on battlefields, preserved by formulating it as *kata*, and utilized in actual battles. When Ryukyu Dynasty was born as a result of the unification of *sanzan*, peace prevailed in the 15th century, and by then, *tiy* was taught more openly which was originally kept as secret skills within family members. *Tiy* was then called *shuri-te* as it was being popularized in various communities. In the process of *tiy* being popularized and diversified, names of *tiy* techniques gradually shifted from individual masters' names to names of areas such as *shuri-te*, *naha-te* and *tomari-te*. Also, names of each *kata*, originally named after individual masters such as *naihanchi*, *pinan*, or *bassai*, were gradually changed to names that meant characteristics of each *kata*.

While *shuri-te* preserved the way of Okinawa's traditional *tiy*, some Chinese *kempō* techniques began to be incorporated into *tiy* during the 17th and 18th centuries. It was the beginning of *tudity*.

After Shōshin king established the centralized governing system in 1526 and placed a ban on possessing any weapons and collected all swords, bows, arrows, etc. at the government warehouse, peace prevailed in Ryukyu and there was no war for 500 years. This exceptional fact can't be emphasized enough. *Aji* and farmers who previously fought aggressively against each other followed Shōshin king's ban on weapons and kept peace in Okinawa. In such peaceful society, there wasn't any actual battles to make a use of *tiy*. Those trained *bushi* (warriors) and farmers lost opportunities to use *tiy* on battlefields, and then *tiy* gradually became a privilege of *bushi* who were the protectors of *gusuku*. However, besides *bushi*, some commoners and farmers felt necessity to continue practicing and preserving *tiy* to prepare for any upheaval break out. This is evident by the fact that, in the mid-18th century, in a continued peaceful society, Arakaki Seishō and a few others performed *kata*, *bō jyutsu* and *kumite* of karate at a welcome ceremony for an official convoy from China. Ancient Ryukyu's combat skills originally developed in actual battles between *gusuku* were integrated and organized for various situations and were preserved in the form of *kata*. And those have been handed down ceaselessly until today from generation to generation as *kata of shuri-te*, *naha-te* or *tomari-te*. Today, those *kata* are truly important tradition and culture of Okinawa.

Two different *kata*: *kata* (型) and *KATA*(形)

The term *kata* is used in a broad range of fields and in various aspects, but creation of any *kata* is unexceptionally related with person's physical movements. It can be presumed that body movements and incidental dances of religious rites or worshiping rituals in ancient times were gradually stylized in time, and each of such body movements became recognized as standardized skills, then those skills were integrated and organized; it was the first form of *kata*. Those *kata* were eventually popularized, and it gradually evolved into performance art.

In Japan, people began recognizing the concept of *kata* in the Middle Age to modern history. From the point of view of audience, an overall performance carried out by a performer's body movements is a *kata* (型) that consists of multiple *KATA* (形) or skills. *(In this section, the homonyms are differentiated as kata and KATA, written in Chinese character as* 型 *and* 形 *respectively. Definitions of each words are explained below.)* Thus, without presence of *KATA*, *kata* can't exist. However, *kata* and *KATA* are not the same. *Kata* is created by carefully choosing multiple *KATA*, which are person's conscious or unconscious body movements, and is mastered by repeatedly practicing in order to acquire the ability to consistently perform such *kata*. *Kata* is a sequence of *KATA* (skills). The point is that *kata* is a compilation of *KATA*. Such type of *kata* holds functionality, rationality and stability and presents certain sense of aesthetic. When a sequence of *KATA* is improved in a thorough trial and error to shave off everything but its essence, it can be called a *kata*. Establishing a *kata* requires presence of audience that are severe critiques. Also, another type of critique is necessary, which is the objective eyes of the performer self.

Once a *kata* is established, the *kata* leaves the performer and acquire an independent identity. This kind of *kata* is called anonym *kata*. Anonym *kata* holds canonicity and ideal form and has power to enforce its performers to perform it correctly. In other words, those *kata* become the model which performers shouldn't be derailed from.

There are different opinions whether it should be referred as *kata* or *KATA*, and each school, association or organization has different policies on how to call it. Japan Karatedo Federation uses *KATA*. In Okinawa, some *dōjō* use *kata* and others use *KATA*. There was a major debate in the karate society of Okinawa over this *kata* and *KATA* issue. It was a truly interesting debate. Kinjo Hiroshi wrote about *kata* in a newsletter of Japan Karatedo Kenshukai that "I recently saw some people revising the term *kata*, which was used by master Itosu, to *KATA* at their discretion. The reason for such revision seems to be because *kata* in Chinese character can be associated with inflexibility and stereotyping while karate-*dō* values flexibility and ability to cope with various situations. I shall leave it to the scholars to debate whether *kata* represents inflexibility and *KATA* represents flexibility, but according to my memory, *kata* refers to mental activities to model something, and *KATA* is used to express *katachi (形)*, literally meaning mere objects. *KATA* represents objects without a soul such as *keigai (形骸)* which means a skeleton or *ningyō (人形)* which means a doll. As master Itosu was a secretary to the Ryukyu dynasty, it's natural to presume that he was well acquainted with his language. Also, for *sumō* wrestling, *kata* is used."

A counterargument was made by Nagamine Shōshin, a founder of Okinawa Shōrin-ryū. He writes that "I don't know where such interpretation can be found in the *10 rules of* karate by master Itosu written in October of Meiji 41 (1908). Furthermore, the definitions of *KATA* and *kata* according to *Kōjirin* (a Japanese language dictionary) edited by Kanazawa Shōjirō are; "*KATA*" is (1) a shape, (2) to trace, (3) a mortgage (e.g. mortgage for debt), (4) an object fabricated to imitate something (e.g. a doll), (5) a custom, a convention (e.g. conventional way), (6) to mimic, a model, and (7) a movement or conventional way that is standard for traditional or martial arts; comparatively, "*kata*" is (1) a mold or a frame to be filled with soil or metal to form a certain shape, (2) a mold to press patterns on cloth, (3) a standardized size or dimension, (4) a pattern paper or a pattern, (5) a figure with which its characteristics clearly evident, (6) a typical type, and (7) a type. As indicated in *Kōjirin*, the category (7) of *KATA*, 'a movement or a convention that is standard for traditional or martial arts' would be an appropriately fit for karate.

Therefore, without any further contemplation, use of *kata* is incorrect and *KATA* should be used.

Also, cultural assets in Japan are defined according to Chapter two of the Cultural Asset Protection Act as; "(1) building, painting, sculpture, craftwork, book, historical written document and other tangible cultural products that are highly valuable historically and artistically and other historical documents (hereinafter referred to as 'Tangible Cultural Asset'); and (2) theatre art, music, craft skill and other intangible cultural products that are highly valuable historically or artistically in Japan (hereinafter referred to as 'Intangible Cultural Asset'). In the account, cultural assets are categorized into *yūkei (*有形*)* translated as tangible and *mukei (*無形*)*translated as intangible using the Chinese character of *KATA (*形*)* . Furthermore, *7 ōtachi* and *3 kotachi* are referred to as *kendō*'s *KATA,* and old style *jūdō* also uses *KATA,* not *kata*. Also, on September of the Minkoku 58 (1969), I received a book about Chinese *kempō, Keiiken,* from its author. This account proves that the term *KATA* is used in the country where Chinese character was originated. With above evidences, I confirm *KATA* is the proper way for karate."

The argument evolved into a major debate involving some eminent masters of Okinawan karate society. Both arguments have valid points and are both convincing, but I personally believe *kata* is the correct term. To give an example, *kata* of *1 st naihanchi* has 25 actions, and each action includes one karate technique. One action consisting of one technique can be conceived as one *KATA*, and 25 of *KATA* are integrated to form one *kata*. The aggregate of such 25 *KATA* make up the *1 st naihanchi*. If it is short or over with 24 or 26 *KATA*, it can't be acknowledged as the *1 st naihanchi*. Further, if the 5 th action becomes upper thrust while it should be a *KATA* of upper block, it is not a correct *1 st naihanchi*. Thus, it is conceivable that each *KATA* must always be the same action, and *kata* is an integration of *KATA* in the right number and order as if they fit into a frame. Therefore, it can be said that the overall *1 st naihanchi* is a *kata*, and each body movement or action is *KATA*.

The first step to learning *kata* is to mimic. Zeami called it role-playing which means to mimic, and he called the object to be modeled a *katagi* (形木). In trying to learn a *kata*, often times the learning doesn't pass beyond mere imitation of *KATA*. However, *kata* can't be truly learned without considering the issue of *kokoro* (mind/heart). A learning process of *kata* is advanced through repeatedly going back and forth between working on *KATA* and *kokoro*. According to Minamoto Ryōen, there are two types of people who learn *kata*; those who prioritize *KATA* first and those who prioritize *kokoro* first. Former is *kata* supremacist such as Yamaga Sokō, Ogyū Sorai and Dazai Shundai. Latter is *kokoro* supremacist such as Nakae Tōju and Kumazawa Banzan.

Tiy, which was originally developed as skills to kill opponents and protect oneself on battlefields, became a self-defense technique and a status for *bushi* who resided in *gusuku* castles after peace prevailed. Consequently, how to live as a martial artist became an important aspect of learning karate besides simply learning *tiy* skills, and *tiy* was conceived as humane combat skills for protecting *gusuku aji* and community, one's family and most of all, upholding justice. How could *tiy*, which was standardized in a peaceful society, be preserved for many generations? Answering to the question, *kata* worked as the medium to make it possible. Impressive fact is that more than 50 kinds of Okinawa born *kata* are still preserved and taught at local karate *dōjō* in Okinawa. For those local *dōjō*, there aren't any opportunities like the Olympic, the National Athletic Meet, or the inter high school athletic competition. There isn't any tournament to aim for in Okinawa, Japan, or the world. A karate practitioners keep facing their straw boards in training, carefully listen to what it tells them, and thrust with their fists into it to respond. They repeat such a routine task for years, even decades. After decades of training, their straw board wouldn't approve of their mastery. There is no answer to when they can finally hear that they've trained enough, but they must keep facing the straw board until they hear it. However, there is a tacit understanding that they will continue the work for their life time.

What's the best way to learn *kata*? We are in the age of information. Traditional Okinawa karate can be instantly viewed on screen in Brazil that is on the opposite side of the earth from Okinawa. We are flooded with all kinds of information through TV, radio, newspaper, magazine, book, video, etc., and the same is true for karate. There is an oversupply of books and videos about *kata* of karate; *kata* can be learned easily through them, and Okinawa's traditional karate is not an exception. However, can those books and videos truly teach karate? In the olden times, *tiy* was a combat skill that were secretly preserved within each family; but today, karate is not a secret. Of course, there may be secret teachings which can only be taught to masters of each school, but in general sense, there isn't any secrecy in karate. This fact can lead me to a conclusion that "karate can be learned through books and videos." That, however, is limited to learning generally and shallowly.

Objections can arise against learning karate by such means. Since the olden times, it has been said that exquisite beauty of martial arts can't be taught by words or letters. That is to say the core understanding of martial arts can only be taught and learned through desperate and curious training and by heart to heart communication between a master and a disciple; it can never be taught through verbal explanations. Karate could survive till today because it was inducted as a result of true communications between masters and disciples. I'm doubtful that authentic *kata* can survive in the modern society where people forgot the importance of *kokoro* (mind/heart) of martial arts and fell into opportunism of the materialistic world.

When a *kata* is established, another concern arises; that is the concept of *dō* (a road). *Dō* is the term to identify the ideal characteristics of *kata*. If learning stays at mere mimicking of a *KATA* without considering effects of *kokoro*, true understanding of *kata* can't be achieved; it requires a self-control discipline and undying ambition to improve oneself every single day.

Seeking ways to preserve *kata*, sect, schools and *Iemoto* systems (Iemoto is the head of a school) were developed. Also, it became common to involve *kokoro* in preserving *kata;* however, there were both positive and negative aspects to it. The positive side of it was that cultures could be successfully passed down and old traditions could survive drastic changes of a society. The negative side was that intellectual curiosity weakened because creativity and originality wasn't valued so much anymore. Needless to say that unrestricted originality and creativity could potentially harm the foundation (or tradition) of *kata*. It was fragile as to keep or to change was up to the persons who inherited the traditions.

Tradition becomes the key when contemplating how people are related to *kata*. The most significant aspect of tradition is its history. Without physical presence which survived for a long period of time, it can't be called a tradition. It usually contains the original forms of *kata* and so is diverse.

Mentioned earlier in this chapter but one of the characteristics of Japanese art is that pursuit of skills doesn't stop at merely learning skills but goes beyond; work of *kokoro* becomes a significant aspect, especially for martial arts. Furthermore, Confucianism became part of the fundamental philosophy of work of *kokoro* in addition to the conventional *zen* theory. Bushidō philosophy prevailed among the *bushi* class in the Kamakura period and was developed in the Edo period as corroborated by Confucianism especially neo-Confucianism and was promoted as the national ethic in the Meiji period.

Investigating the western fencing and sword techniques in China or in Korea, I haven't seen anything that stressed so much about mental aspect. Even in Japan, sword techniques were teachings without so much focus on mentality at first. However, work of *kokoro* was placed as the core philosophy of sword techniques in the treatise *Shinkageryū heihō kokoroe* in 1626 and *Heihō Kadensho* in 1632 written by Yagyū Tajimanokami Munenori.

These two accounts were influenced by *Fudōchi Shinmyōroku* ("The Unfettered Mind") written by Takuan Sōhō. It writes, "in performing a skill, when his mind becomes conscious of his action, his hands becomes heavy" and "use the sword but without mind, strike in absence of his mind to strike, slash the opponent but without placing his mind on the opponent, know the opponent is air, you are air, hands and swords are air; his mind can't stay in air." *Fudōchi* means one's mind is immovable, that his mind is bound or obsessed by nothing. This is the fundamental teaching of Takuan; and, as he placed mentality as the core aspect of sword technique. It can be said that he created a *kata* of sword technique.

Let me introduce a story about training of *kata*. Jyūyonse Kita Roppeita, a master who revived Kita-ryū (a school of Noh), performed the program, *Dōseiji,* in Meiji 25 (1892) for the first time. 40 years later, he performed the same program for the last time on stage. Later he said, "since this was going to be the last time to perform this program, I was going to perform it in a completely new style, but then I rethought that such a performance may harm this school's *kata*. And it would be an immense problem. I decided to perform it strictly according to the *kata* especially because of this occasion for this school and the disciples." Underlying veneration for *kata* is uniformly held in all disciples of art, and their goal is to assimilate themselves with *kata* by performing them; commonly they are aware of such a goal can be achieved only by continuous practice. As mentioned above, creativity could invade the boundary of tradition, thus training is based on the philosophy "to begin with *kata* and never to leave *kata*."

Gotō Tokuzō, a disciple of Kita Roppeita, left an impressive comment about the importance of observing and studying that is the core element of mimicking. He was an attendant of his master for 50 years. He said "it was the best experience I could ever have. Audiences watch the performer from the front, but you can actually better recognize the emotions of the performer from the behind. Chorus members of the play have to concentrate on singing so they can't watch the performer carefully; but an attendant can observe attentively even to hear the performer's breath."

I went over the issues of mentality that serves an important role in forming *kata* from multiple angles. But, mentality only functions together with skills, which can only be actualized with a body that is trained and conditioned. A disciple who prioritizes mentality has to eventually come to probe oneself for actual physical movements in performing *KATA*. The relation between mentality and *KATA* must be studied within oneself continuously, and in the process, the understanding of it deepens. And the process never halts. A disciple who proceed with such process is called an ascetic. This endless journey of training, however, has a satisfying moment; that is when one feels no boundary between mind and *KATA* as mind completely assimilated into *KATA* and *KATA* into mind. That's the moment performance ripen. Same can be said for performance arts or martial arts.

Cultural Trait of *Kata*

How can *kata* be conceived as a culture? Answering to this specifically and definitely is not easy. Different approaches can be assumed depending on how the term *culture* is defined. Although there may not be anyone objecting that Okinawan traditional karate is not a culture, I still believe it's important to demonstrate that it is.

Master Takamiyagi Shigeru, a successor of a Uechi-ryū school, addressed his theory of martial arts that is an art. He treated Okinawan karate as a martial art; and from the perspective of its skills and *kokoro* (mind/heart), he recognized three values in it that are mental, dynamic and aesthetic values.

Takamiyagi Shigeru elaborates on the topic of his theory of martial arts that is art in his treatise *Overview of Okinawan Karate-dō ~various aspects of karate as a martial art~* that "there are three necessary elements in order for karate to hold the characteristics as an art, which are the mental, the dynamic, and the aesthetic values. Karate can take a form of art when those three elements are held within it," and he described those three elements in detail as follows.

131

First, considering the mental element, *kata* of karate has a function to unexceptionally lead a performer to reach the level of unclouded mind once certain amount of time is spent for training. In other words, in the process of learning *kata,* performer naturally cultivates purified and sophisticated mentality and spirituality.

For the dynamic value, when a performer's combat skills reach a level of mastery, his/her *kata* performance also becomes practical in serving its purpose of defeating his/her opponent with a single strike; and at such a level, his/her *kata* hold the dynamic value. Repetitious engagement in the action that focuses on lethal attacks would eventually develop a healthy body subsuming the mentality of selfless spirituality.

Lastly, as for the aesthetic value, *kata* moves the emotion of its audience and cause sympathy, and the halts and flows of physical movements have beautifully controlled rhythm. The beauty of each intangible *KATA* has its own flow according to a certain dynamic principle, and as an aggregate, a *kata* performance flows with a consistent rhythm.

When all three elements are expressed within a *kata*, it can be conceived as an art. Such *kata* can silence an audience. Karate is a combat skill and at the same time it is a form of art. This art is a culture thus I conclude karate is a culture that is an art.

Takamiyagi Shigeru also writes in the section titled *the important points of Okinawan Karate-dō (3)* in his abovementioned treatise that "training of martial arts has two purposes. One is to perfect self-defense techniques and another is to develop one's morality." He further mentioned that if one trains long enough under appropriate conditions, the process of training for skills would merge into the realm of development of morality, in other words, training of technicality would eventually move the learner into training of morality."

As a process of sublimation from mastering skills into cultivating morality, development of mentality can be seen through disciplined behavioral patterns and intellectual understanding of technicality of skills, and at such a level, combat skills assume the characteristics as a culture and the qualities as a form of art. He is calling a skill, which is present in the process of creating cultural value, an art. That can be called a martial art and also a performance art. Combat skills that only purported to defeat opponents on battlefields in the past was sublimated during the peaceful era into a martial art that focused on refining mentality by training for skills, and such skills were further evolved to hold values as an art.

According to a treatise "Study of Art" by Watabe Mamoru, "art isn't cultivated during the time that skills to kill people with weapons are used to satisfy its primary purpose; however, when weapons are used but not meant to kill his/her opponent in the 'competition matches', the concept of 'martial arts' becomes significant." I have an objection in his writing for using the term "competition match," but this isn't a serious objection if it can be translated as "training."

Written by Takamiyagi Shigeru, "art as is defined here is a function that creates cultural values by performing a certain *kata* which consists of movements of entire or a part of body. This function is a process of creation or reproduction of artistic actions, and such actions are neither objectified nor materialized. They are intangible culture and are intangible cultural assets." He recognized that it is a historical fact that martial arts cultivated artistic characteristics, and he asserts that, as mentioned earlier in this chapter, karate-dō is a typical form of performance art.

Furthermore, he mentions about Funakoshi Gichin, who was a master and a historical figure that opened the door for Okinawan karate to the mainland Japan and to spread it to the world. "Funakoshi emphasized the concept of 'martial art that is art' in his teaching at universities or *dōjō* and probed symbolism, logicality, principle, artistry, etc. of karate-dō as a sinologist and a Japanese classical scholar. He devoted his life seeking and clarifying the characteristics of modern karate as a martial art and making a road for it to be further cultivated."

More than 50 *kata* of Okinawan traditional karate were originally created by selecting, integrating and practicing essential combat skills from many that were developed amid the warring *gusuku* period. People have been and will continue observing and inheriting those physical expressions of *kata* of karate. Those skills that are performed by a master hold characteristics of performance art, and it has energy to touch emotions of audience with its destructive force as a lethal combat skills and beauty of efficient and effective body movements.

Section 3. *Kata* of Okinawan Traditional Karate

In the beginning, there weren't any schools for Ryukyuan *tiy*, which was developed as lethal combat skills on battlefields in the early *gusuku* period, but there were styles such as *oshiro no te, shirataru no te* and *oyakeakahachi no te* that were named after *bushi* (warrior) who developed the style. Until 17th century, *kata* of Ryukyuan *tiy* had names of *bushi* who created them, and beginning in 18th century, when Chinese *kempō* techniques were brought to Ryukyu, those styles were differentiated by regions or areas such as *tiy* (traditional Okinawan style), *tudity* (*tiy* that incorporated Chinese *kempō*), *shuri-te* and *naha-te*. The traditional *tiy* style was mainly inherited by *shuri-te*, and *tudity* was inherited by *naha-te*. Furthermore, uechi-ryū that was greatly influenced by *tudity* became one of the three major schools of Okinawan karate. Today's three major schools of Okinawan traditional karate are shōrin-ryū, which mainly inherited Ryukyuan traditional *tiy,* and gōjū-ryū and uechi-ryū that were influenced by Chinese *kempō*. In this section, I'll describe these three schools more in detail.

Okinawan traditional karate are *shuri-te* (*shōrin-ryū* and its branches), *naha-te* (*gōjū-ryū* and its branches) and *uechi-ryū* (*uechi-ryū* and its branches). There is also *tomari-te,* but it is conceived as a mix between *shuri-te* and *naha-te. Shōrin-ryū* has a direct connection with the traditional Ryukyuan *tiy* which was first developed around 7th or 8th century and stylized in forms of *KATA* or *kata* around 10th century and has been passed down through family lineages. Thus, shōrin-ryū, which has the direct roots in *tiy*, is truly the pristine karate with a history of a millennium. *Gōjū-ryū* was developed by Higaonna Kanryō, who was a disciple for the traditional Ryukyuan *tiy*, as he visited China and tempered *tiy* with techniques of Chinese *kempō*. *Sanchin* technique had never been seen in Ryukyuan *tiy* techniques until Higaonna. *Gōjū-ryū* was started in 19th century when he returned from China and taught his techniques in Okinawa. It has about 150 years of history. And, *uechi-ryū* was developed in a very similar fashion as *gōjū-ryū*; it was developed by Uechi Kanbun who studied in China and made *sanchin* technique as his base form. *Uechi-ryū* has its history of about 110 years.

Currently, over 50 schools and branches exist, but the above three schools are traditionally the main stream of Okinawan traditional karate. *Shōrin-ryū* is also known as *shuri-te* and has the longest history with its direct roots in Ryukyuan ancient combat skills *tiy*. Despite the influences from Chinese *kempō* since 17th century, the schools preserved mostly original forms of Ryukyuan *tiy*. On the other hand, *gōjū-ryū* was significantly influenced by Chinese *kempō* as it was developed by Higaonna Kanryō, also known to be the founder of *gōjū-ryū*, who was inducted by Ryū Ryū Kō, a master of Chinese *kempō*. *Uechi-ryu* also was influenced by Chinese *kempō* as Uechi Kanbun, the founder of *uechi-ryū*, was taught by Shu Shiwa (Zhou Zihe) a master of Chinese *kempō*.

In the society of Okinawan karate, Karate *Kenkyū-kai* (literally a society for studying karate) was inaugurated in 1918 with main members of Funakoshi Gichin, Oshiro Chodo, Chibana Chōshin, and so on. On the other hand, *Okinawa karate kenkyujo* (literally Okinawan karate institute) with main members of Kyan Chōtoku, Miyagi Chōjun, Motobu Chōki, Shiroma Koki, and so on. They all used *shurit-te* except for Miyagi Chōjun, who used *naha-te*.

Funakoshi Gichin is describing important points in learning *kata* in his *Karate-dō kyōhan* ("teachings of karate-do"), "in the past, learning one *kata* took as long as 2 to 3 years, so it was common for even a master to know only 3 to 5 *kata* at most. It is better to know less *kata* profoundly than many shallowly. It took me 10 years to learn three levels of *kata* of *kibadachi*. However, it is equally important to learn different *kata* broadly as each *kata* contains important techniques, so being obsessed with only few *kata* can't be encouraged either. People in the past learned narrowly and deeply and people today tend to learn broadly and shallowly. I personally don't advise neither; there should be a balance between both poles. To explain how I learn and practice *kata,* I first decide a breakpoint, for instance, if I decide to learn up to *heian godan* (5th level) or *kiba sandan* (3rd level), I continue moving onto new *kata* once I generally learn the important points of each *kata*, and when I reach the breakpoint, I go back and practice those *kata* repetitiously. Mere knowledge of *kata* isn't useful, so *kata* need to be persistently practiced to the point where it can be performed right when it's needed." It's said that master Motobu Chōki only knew 3 or 4 *kata*. I often meet people in the U.S. who are proud of themselves for knowing 40 to 50 *kata*. Masters in Okinawa don't trust such people. Number of *kata* is not the point.

(1) *Kata* of *Shurite* · *Shōrin-ryū* and its branches of *Shuri-te*

Shuri-te is the mainstream of and in direct descent from *tiy*, which originated as a killing skill on battlefields during the warring period from the 7th or 8th century to the early *gusuku* period and was later developed by warrior class families who resided near the Shuri castle. Today, *shuri-te* is being taught as *shōrin-ryū* and its branches. Among the three major schools of Okinawan karate, *gōjū-ryū* and *uechi-ryū* incorporated techniques of Chinese *kempō* such as *sanchin* into *tiy,* but *shōrin-ryū* (*shuri-te*) is truly the traditional Okinawan karate that is preserving the original form of Ryukyuan *tiy*.

Chūzan king had his *gusuku* in Urasoe area before he moved his base to Shuri area in the middle of the 14th century. In 1180, Shunten *aji*, who was an outstanding martial artist, became the king of the Urasoe castle (Urasoe-jō). He successfully accumulated wealth by conducting imports and exports with China and South East Asian countries, and eventually became the most powerful *aji* in Ryukyu history. During this period, *tiy* skills of Urasoe were taught in the style of *gusukuma-no-te (tiy)*, and eventually it was inherited by *shuri-te*. The original style of *urasoe-no-te (tiy* of Urasoe) influenced *shirataru-no-te* (*kon*) in the 14th century, *ufugusku-no-te* (*kon*) in the 15th century, and *oyakeakahachi-no-te* (*kon*) in the 16th century. The main characteristic of *shuri-te* is the fast thrust or kick that is initiated in a relaxed position. The essence of *shuri-te* is its offensive style. *Tiy* that originated in Ryukyu was practiced by *bushi* (warriors) and referred to as *urasoe-no-te* when the center of Ryukyu was in Urasoe area and later as *shuri-te* when it moved to Shuri area.

As time went by, the three major schools of Okinawan traditional karate grew to hold about 100 schools, organizations and branches with about 360 *dōjōs* in total, and *shōrin-ryū* (*shuri-te)* and its branches has the majority of 56% with about 200 *dōjōs* in Okinawa. Of course, it excludes those *dōjōs* that are not considered as traditional karate such as *dōjōs* of Union of Students, All High School Athletic Federation, Nippon Junior High School Physical Culture Association or other Japanese karate, *dōjōs* that only teach combative sports, and *dōjōs* of newly established schools of karate. Just as a piece of information, *gōjū-ryū* has 91 *dōjōs* that makes 25.6% of total, and *uechi-ryū* makes up about 18.5% with 66 *dōjōs*.

The main characteristic of *shuri-te* is its speed with the main focus on its offense and to teach breathing naturally.

While breathing in one is relaxed and strong just before breathing out completely. Breathing and power releasing is correlated; a strike should be at the strong point in breathing to focus on releasing power outward from the body, internal organs are under minimal pressure. Also, breathing is trained to be under control with minimal disturbance that keeps muscles from wearing out unnecessarily, allows easily focusing on power release, achieves quicker motion, and consequently allows strikes to be actualized fully and effectively. Furthermore, it emphasizes the integration of strikes and blocks. It teaches to practice *kata* and train with straw board with a focus on making its defense to be powerful and destructive. The defense shouldn't be merely blocking opponent's attacks but to break it instead, which leads to the principle of integrated strikes and blocks. And, it teaches to be more destructive by striking the space beyond the object.

Prominent masters in the past probed in two or three *kata* deeply instead of learning many and strived to master their original styles which couldn't be imitated easily by others. And those masters didn't teach their *kata* to others unless they were entirely satisfied with it. *Naihanchi* is the most basic *kata* for *shuri-te*. It's said that first *kata* to be learned is *naihanchi* and the last should be the same, and also for daily training; a training is opened with *naihanchi* and closed with the same. *Naihanchi* is the most important *kata* for *shuri-te/shōrin-ryū*. It's even said that there is no need for learning other *kata* if you practice *naihanchi* every day.

Today, there are three level of *naihanchi* as master Itosu invented *naihanchi* second and third based on the old traditional *naihanchi*. *Naihanchi* consists of advanced techniques such as knifehand strike, middle *seiken* (clenched fist) thrust, middle block, backfist blow to face, *sokutō* (edge of the foot) kick, etc. Besides *naihanchi*, there are *pinan* up to level five, *passai-shō* (small), *passai-dai* (large), *kūshankū-shō* (small), *kūshankū-dai* (large), *chintō*, *gojū-shō* (small) and so on.

(1) *Naihanchi Shodan*: This *kata* has been taught around the Shuri area since the olden time. *Naihanchi*, along with *pinan*, is the most basic *kata* to be practiced by beginners. This *kata* was developed by a master in the past but his

138

name is unknown. This *kata* focuses on lower body to develop necessary muscles for a stable stance instead of learning practical combat skills.

(2) *Naihanchi Nidan*:   a *kata* invented by Itosu Ankō.

(3) *Naihanchi Sandan*:   a *kata* invented by Itosu Ankō.

(4) *Pinan Shodan*:   a *kata* existed from the olden time.

(5) *Pinan Nidan*:   a *kata* invented by Itosu Ankō.

(6) *Pinan Sandan*   a *kata* invented by Itosu Ankō.

(7) *PinanYondan*:   a *kata* invented by Itosu Ankō.

(8) *PinanGodan*   a *kata* invented by Itosu Ankō.

(9) *Passai shō (small):*   Also referred to as "*passai* of Itosu" or "*passai* of Matsumura". This *kata* consists of most basic techniques of *shōrin-ryū* with variety of striking and defensive moves. It includes many techniques that focus on reversing an unfavorable situation by making a counterattack after a blocking move. *Passai* of Matsumura is especially said to be one of the best *kata* of *shōrin-ryū*.

(10) *Passai dai (large):*   This *kata* has different styles depending on whom it was taught by. Today, there are *passai* of Hanashiro, Matsumura, Oyadomari, Tawata, Ishimine, Chibana, Matsumora, Kyan and Motobu. It can be conceived that this *kata*, originally a same *kata*, became so diverse because it was arranged by the past masters who had a profound understanding of *karate*; also, their physique and personality might have affected their arrangements. Hanashiro Chōmo, who taught "*passai* of Hanashiro," used side to

side movements and the waist rotations for *soto-uke* (outside-to-inside block) and *uchi-uke* (inside-to-outside block) in the first half of his *passai*. "*Passai* of Matsumura" has been performed by the circle of master Matsumura; it was taught by master Tawata to Chibana Chōshin. *Passai* of Matsumura was favored by many. "*Passai* of Oyadomari" was taught in Tomari area, and it was studied by Oyadomari Koukan.

(11) *Kushanku shō (small)*: It is said that master Itosu invented this *kata* based on a *kata* "*kūshankū*." It includes dynamic moves like two-step kick, picking up a staff (or a stick), and an attack with a time lag (make a feint, dodge and observe the opponent's move).

(12) *Kushanku dai (large)*: According to an account *Ōshima hiki,* this *kata* was brought over by Kōshōkun, a military officer of Qing dynasty. Just like *passai,* there many styles of this *kata* such as *Kōshōkun* of Itosu, Chatanraya, Kuniyoshi, etc.

(13) *Chintō*: This *kata* was practiced in Shuri area and is said to be one of the best *kata.* The movements are made on a straight line and has many moves with integrated block-and-attack moves. It includes many vibrant motions and one of the main characteristics of this *kata* is to have vertical weight shift and one-legged stance (anticipating unfavorable situation) as purported to train lower body strength. It is taught by the name of "*chintei*" in Shuri area. This *kata* was called "*Chinsū*" when it was taught by Itosu Ankō to Mabuni Kenwa, but it's no longer taught because it wasn't inducted completely.

(14) *Gojūshiho:*   This is an old *kata* that has been taught in Shuri area and is the *kata* that represents the school of master Itosu of *shuri-te*. Along with a *kata, sōchin, gojūshiho* was one of Mabuni Kenwa's favorite *kata* to perform. Also, Tōyama Kanken often chose to perform the "old-style *gojūshiho.*" The characteristic of this *kata* is its unique tempo and varying speed, the basic moves are from and to front, back, right and left, but there are also some diagonal moves. Unlike other *kata* of *shōrin-ryū,* it only has few clenched fist thrusts and front kicks and has many spear hand strikes and knifehand guards, and it also includes techniques like clawhand, cat stance, pulling down.

(15) *Anankū:*   *Kata* performed in Tomari area.

(16) *Wanshū:*   It's said that Itosu Ankō created this *kata* by arranging main techniques of Matsumora school's *kata.*

(17) *Wandau:*   This *kata* is no longer taught. *Kata* performed in Arakaki school.

(18) *Nīsēshī:*   *Kata* performed by Arakaki school.

(19) *Jion:*   *Kata* performed in Tomari area.

(20) *Jiin:*   *Kata* performed in Tomari area.

(21) *Jitte:*   *Kata* performed in Tomari area.

The main characteristic of *kata* of *shōrin-ryū* (*shuri-te*) is to have clenched fist thrusts and front kicks as its basic strikes with a focus on defeating opponents with single strikes; therefore, there is only few grabbing and throwing techniques. If grabbing is anticipated, then guarding techniques to the same have to be considered. Jūdō would be much better fit for such techniques as it specialized in it. Therefore, grabbing techniques weren't used in old Ryukyuan *tiy. Shuri-te* adopted some grabbing techniques after Sakugawa Kanga incorporated Chinese *kempō* techniques. Until then, *shuri-*

te's only focus was the single and deadly strikes without grabbing techniques. In that sense, *shuri-te* has completely different techniques from *gōjū-ryū* and *uechi-ryū* that are later explained. Another unique characteristic of *shōrin-ryū* (*shuri-te*) is its focus on natural breathing. It's completely opposite from *gōjū-ryū* and *uechi-ryū,* which has a controlled breathing that is seen in their basic *kata "sanchin."*

"Kata" of *Gōjū-ryū*/*Naha-te*

Higaonna Kanryō (1853~1915) is said to be the central figure for revitalizing *naha-te*, and also was the one who transformed *naha-te* from the traditional *tiy* to *tudity*.

The essence of *naha-te* is said to be the breathing technique that is used for its fundamental *kata*, *sanchin*.

Practitioners aim to master the breathing technique so that, in contesting an opponent, breathing can be under control even when his/her body is moved vigorously in order to effectively shift his/her body weight, to step forward or back, to attain concentration, quickness, explosiveness and endurance, etc. Also, the training includes developing the reproducibility of fighting skills by repetitiously practicing *kata* and to cultivate physical strength equipped with strong skeletal muscles. Furthermore, the basic fighting style is to stay reserved, and it's strong in infighting; flexible legs and abundant hand skills are emphasized, and strikes are made by leaping in the range of an opponent and quickly bounce back to defend. One of the main characteristics of *naha-te* is that it teaches to train his/her mind and physique by strengthening entire body utilizing traditional supplementary training equipment such as *makiwara* (straw wrapped punching board), *chīshī* (a stick with weight on one end), *sāshī* (stone padlocks), *akuryoku-kame* (grip training urn), etc. and supplementary trainings without any device.

Kanryō was a disciple of a famous master Ryū Ryū Kō and some other masters of Chinese *kempō* in Fujian province, China, and after 10 years of training, he was certified of full mastery and approved to return to Okinawa. After moving back, he was running a business for a while, but many people saw his exquisite *tudity* skills and earnest personality and asked him to teach karate. In the mid-Meiji period, at the age over 50 years old, Kanryō started teaching karate at police stations and middle schools; over time, he had many disciples and taught *tudity* skills and how to train for strong physique and mind.

In the Meiji period, the society of karate wasn't yet well organized; for *naha-te* and *shuri-te,* there wasn't any established structure or method for teaching *kata.* Karate was originally secretive skills that was taught only within family members, but Kanryō, in responding to the demand of people, started teaching martial arts as part of physical education at schools. In Meiji 38 (1905), karate was adopted as a regular subject at the Prefectural Normal School and Prefectural First Middle School. His effort and accomplishment contributed to the development of karate and cultivated many masters of *naha-te* including Miyagi Chōjun (1888~1953), Kyoda Jūhatsu (1887~1968), and Higa Seikou (1903~1973). Later, Mabuni Kenwa moved to Kansai region, and Kyoda Jūhatsu moved to Kyusyu region to distribute their teachings. One of the elder disciples of them was Iranami Chōkō.

The contribution of Miyagi Chōjun, the founder of *gōjū-ryū* school, can't go unmentioned. Miyagi became a disciple of Higaonna at the age of 14 and endured rigorous training and became one of the best among other disciples for his strength and techniques. Even at a young age, he was expected a lot for the future for his calm and modest personality and academic brilliance, and he certainly did contribute to spreading Okinawan karate to the world. In 1915, as Miyagi received a permission from his master, he moved to Fujian province in China and studied about famous martial artists while living in the cities of Fuzhou and Shanghai for about one year. After moving back to Okinawa, he reviewed *tudity* skills and principles that were taught by his master and organized them in a logical and scientific way while incorporating his ideas of effective teaching method both as physical education and martial art; he developed a modern karate-do principle. Consequently, many great teachers of *gōjū-ryū* (*naha*-te) were cultivated by following Miyagi's teaching method.

Chōjun Miyagi

Some names of Miyagi Chōjun's disciples are: Shinjō Jin'nan (1901~1945); Yogi Jitsuei (1912~); Yamoto Meitoku (1910~2003), the chair of Federation of All Okinawa Karate; and Miyazato Eiichi (1912~1999), the chair of Okinawa Goju-ryu Karatedo Kyokai. After Higaonna Kanryō passed away, Higa Seikou (1898~1966), a member of Federation of Goju-ryu International Karate Kobujutsu, learned from Miyagi, his senior disciple, strived to preserve *tiy* in its original style. There were also Fukuchi Seikou (1919~1950), a disciple of Higa, and Toguchi Seikichi (1915~1998), the chair of Okinawa Karatedo Goju-ryu Shoreikan, who was taught by both Miyagi and Higa.

Gōjū-ryū (naha-te), founded by Miyagi Chōjun, adopted teachings of Southern Chinese Shaolin Kung Fu in Fujian province in 1828, and after studying and developing his own style, it was established as *gōjū-ryū, a tudity* style karate. The three main techniques used in *gōjū-ryū* are the basic *kata* (*sanchin*), open-handed *kata,* and closed-fist *kata. Gōjū-ryū* has twelve *kata* in total including *kata* that were taught by Arakaki Seishō and Higaonna Kanryō, which are the old style *sanchin, saifā, seiyunchin, shisōchin, sanseiryū, sēpai, kururunfā, seisan,* and *pecchūrin* (or *sūpā-rinpei*), and *kata* that were developed by Miyagi Chōjun, which are *gekisai first, gekisai second*, open-handed *kata* and *tenshō*. Achieving mastery of the core value of *naha-te* requires mastering of *sanchin* with unique hand technique, basic techniques and its reverse training of *tenshō*, which were invented by Miyagi Chōjun.

For open-handed *kata, pecchūrin* (or *sūpā-rinpei*) has the most tempo variance with powerful techniques and is the representative *kata* of *gōjū-ryū*. There is a record that, in 1867, Aayakaki Seishō, a *bushi* resided in Naha area, performed *pecchurin* at the *Ochaya Goten* (the tea ceremony palace) in Sakiyama in Shuri area for the celebration for completion of the Chinese official envoys for Shō Tai king.

Naha-te/gōjū-ryū and its branches currently have about 28 schools and has about 91 *dōjō. Kata* of *gōjū-ryū* are as follows:

(1) *Gekisai dai ichi*

(2) *Gekisai dai ni*

This is the first *kata* to be taught at many *dōjō* of *gōjū-ryū*. It was invented by Miyagi Chōjun in 1935 as a part of physical education curriculum for Okinawa Prefecture. Basic moves such as punching, guarding, dodging, standing, etc. are adopted abundantly in a ceaseless flow, and it's appropriate to cultivate basic stamina for karate.

By the way, *gekisai dai ichi* uses clenched fists, but the *gekisai dai ni* uses open hands, and its movements are a bit more advanced.

(3) *Sanchin*

This *kata* is seen as the backbone of *gōjū-ryū*. "Sanchin" doesn't only teach its striking techniques but also cultivate body endurance from attacks by stably locking his/her joints by simultaneously controlling flexed and relaxed muscles.

(4) *Tenshō*

This is a unique *kata*, which mostly consists of blocking, while *sanchin* mostly made up of thrusts. Even though *sanchin* and *tenshō* are *kata* of simple moves, these have the basic elements of *gōjū-ryū,* and even those who have higher level *dan* come back to practice these *kata*.

(5) *Saifa*

Relatively short *kata* that often uses elbow strikes.

(6) *Sanseirū*

Kyoda Jūhatsu, a fellow disciple of Miyagi Chōjun, often performed his own *kata*, which was created based on *sanseiū;* a video of an 8 mm film camera of Kyoda performing his *kata* has been preserved.

(7) *Seiyunchin*

This *kata* was used to be written in Chinese character as 制引戦 (combat of suppressing and pulling), but it was changed to more militaristic name as 征遠鎮 (suppressing on expedition) because of the influence of the WWII. As indicated by the old name, this *kata* has many techniques to grab opponent's collar or wrist and pull in closer. It has a strong *jū* element (of *jujutsu* or *jūdō*) and is unique that it doesn't include any kicking technique.

(8) *Shisōchin*

Similar to above *seiyunchin,* the name was originally written as 四向戦 (four directional combat) but was changed to be written as 士壮鎮 (combat of a great warrior). This *kata* includes dynamic blocking moves and it can be conceived that it anticipates weapons with a long handle.

(9) *Seipai*

This *kata* has the strongest *jū* element (soft techniques of *jujutsu* or *jūdō*) of all *kata* of karate schools, and there is a theory that this *kata* originated in the Northern or Eastern dessert area instead of the Hwang Ho (Yellow River) area in the Southern China. Normally, martial arts techniques get modified and improved to fit the climate and culture when it is taught in different places, but for *seipai,* it is said that its original style has been unchanged since it was brought over from the inland of China.

(10) *Seisan*

If *seipai* has the strongest *jū* element, *seisan* is the *kata* with the strongest *gō* element (hard techniques with blows). The moves are very dynamic, and it is often performed by people who prefers attacks like punches and kicks.

*Kururun*fā (written as 久留頓破 and 来留破)

sūpā-rinpei or *pecchūrin*, (written as 壱百零八手 and 百歩連)

That's all the *kata* of *gōjū-ryū*, there are: *gekisai first* and *gekisai second* designated as *fūkyū-gata* (promotional *kata*); *sanchin* as fundamental *kata; saipua, seienchin, sanseirū, seipai, shisōchin, seisan, kururunfā, pecchūrin* (or *sūpā-rinpei*) as open-handed *kata*, and *tenshō* as closed-fist *kata*.

"Kata" of Uechi-ryū (上地流)

Uechi-ryū was founded by Uechi Kanbun (1877 ~ 1948) and is the youngest of three major Okinawan karate schools. Teachings of *uechi-ryū* is based on Chinese kung fu *pangainūn* of which Uechi Kanbun learned under Shu Shiwa (Zhou Zihe) in Fujian province, China. Following are the *uechi-ryū* schools' eight standard *kata*.

(1) *Sanchin*

A *kata* initiated directly from *pangainūn-ryū,* a school of Southern Chinese Shaolin Kung Fu. This *kata* is to develop the basic stance, keen eyesight, and endurance for opponent's attacks and to cultivate mental strength to emerge oneself into an unclouded and pure state of mind. It's not allowed to perform any other *kata* before *sanchin*. Every *kata* of *uechi-ryū* is based on the principle of *sanchin*. This is the most basic and obligatory *kata* for the school.

(2) *Kanshiwa*

This *kata* was created by Uechi Kanei in 1954. This was named after two masters, Zhou Zihe and Uechi Kanbun. It was originally called *Kan sha bu,* but when *Shu Shabu* was changed to be referred to as *Shu Shiwa* in the beginning of 1970s', the name of this *kata* was respectively changed to *Kan Shiwa*. Originally, this *kata* used *shōken* (one-knuckle punch) but the first three punches were later modified to *Seiken-zuki* (closed fist punch). This is the only *kata* that has *Seiken-zuki*, and this is practiced by beginners.

(3) *Kanshū (Seisan second)*

This *kata* was invented by Itokazu Seiki and was named after two masters, Kanbun and Shu Shiwa, just like *Kanshiwa*. It was originally referred to as *"seisan second"* but was changed *kanshū* in 1970. As it includes several movements of *seisan*, this *kata* was purported to prepare learners before starting *seisan*. This *kata* is for beginners, but it includes many advanced techniques such as *hirate mawashi-uke* (open hand roundhouse block), *furi-hiji* (angled elbow strike) at lowered body position, *boshi-ken* (thumb fist) strike, etc.

(4) *Seichin*

A *kata* invented by Uehara Saburo in 1963.

This is seen as the most difficult *kata* at *kyū* level. This *kata* adopts many moves from Okinawan *tiy* and *pangainūn*.

(5) *Seisan*

This *kata*, along with *sanchin* and *sanseiryū*, originated in China and it is still practiced in China today. In China, they are referred to as *ryūsō-ken* (dragon style), *kosō*-ken (tiger style) and *kakusō-ken* (crane style) and are called *ryūkokaku* altogether.

Seisan was created based the *tsuru-ken* (crane style), and this *kata* is for training practical combat skills to be used in actual battles. It mostly uses open-handed techniques, and it's unique that it includes toe-tip kick and crane style one legged stance. This *kata* requires speed and quickness of the performer.

(6) *Seirui*

This *kata* was invented by Uechi Kanei.

This is unique how it includes cat stance. Also, it has many techniques with open-hand such as *hirate mawashi-uke* (open hands roundhouse block) and *boshi-ken* (thumb fist), etc., and it requires perseverance in the lower body.

(7) *Kanchin*

This *kata* was invented by Uechi Kanei.

It has similar moves as *sanseiryū*. It is the seventh *kata* of *uechi-ryū* and is unique in including many techniques that are initiated from a lowered body position and make a sharp step towards an opponent followed by a body twist for *hiji-zuki* (elbow strike), *kobushi sukui-uke* (scooping block with fists), or *gedan harai-uke* (lower-level sweeping block).

This requires a whip-like flexibility and strength to make a sharp body twist, and its speed and dynamic moves are the uniqueness of this *kata*.

(8) *Sanseiryū*

This *kata* was brought over from China and is the last of eight *kata* of *uechi ryū karatedo*.

It assumes opponents in all directions, and it has flexibility in the moves initiated from the "natural stance," "forward stance" and "lowered stance." Its controlled tempo and speed hold a characteristic as an art that integrates beauty, strength and speed in a perfect balance.

(9) *Ryūko*

In 1949, Uechi Kanei started the "Uechi-ryū Karate-jutsu Kenkyūjo" in Ginowan city in Okinawa after the World War II to teach karate again, and in 1957, the name was changed to "Uechi-ryū Karate Dōjō. This was the beginning of *uechi-ryū* to be spread to the world. Today, *uechi-ryū* and its circles have 19 schools and branches with 66 *dōjōs*.

Section 4. Kata of karate in mainland Japan

Japanese karate (karate in the mainland Japan is referred to as "Japanese karate" in contrast to "Okinawan traditional karate") has four major schools: Shōtōkan-ryū, Shitō-ryū, Wadō-ryū and Gōjū-ryū. All of these schools of Japanese karate were brought to the mainland from Okinawa after 1916. In that year, Funakoshi Gichin showed karate performance at Kyoto Butokuden, and in 1922, Funakoshi attended, performed and made commentaries of karate at Kobudō Exhibition hosted by the Ministry of Education. This was the first time Okinawan karate was introduced in the mainland Japan.

Later, Funakoshi Gichin opened a karate *dōjō* named Meisei-juku in Tokyo and visited universities mainly in Kanto region to teach karate, and in 1934, he founded Shōtōkan.

Shitō-ryū was founded by Mabuni Kenwa from Okinawa who taught karate mainly in Kansai region, and the name Shitō was named after the first letters of Mabuni's teachers' names: Itosu Ankō of *shuri-te* and Higaonna Kanryō of *naha-te*. Gōjū-ryū was started by Miyagi Chōjun of *naha-te*, who was a police officer at the Okinawa Police Department. Miyagi taught karate at Ritsumeikan University and other places mainly in Kansai region and named his school Gōjū-ryū in 1930. Wadō-ryū was founded by Ōtsuka Hironori who was a student of Funakoshi Gichin. Ōtsuka integrated *jū-jutsu* and Okinawan karate and created Gōjū-ryū. As seen above, the origins of all Japanese karate are Okinawan karate.

Karate that was brought over from Okinawa quickly became popular and prevailed all over Japan. In such a phenomenon, it was discussed to promote and further popularize karate as a sport. Consequently, Japan Karatedo Federation was established, and *shitei-kata* (designated *kata*) was created. There are 8 *shitei-kata*: *seipai, saifa, aki, kankū dai, seienchin, bassai dai, seishan* and *chintō*. These are based *kata* of *naha-te* and *shuri-te* and are modified in various ways. Therefore, it is obvious that they are far different from the original *kata* of *naha-te* and *shuri-te*.

Kata was completely modified when it was introduced to the mainland Japan. The traditional style *kata* was transformed in time in the land with different culture from Okinawa. The tradition of Okinawa was changed so easily. Also, the names were changed; *naihanchi* was changed to *tekki*, *pinan* to *heian*, *chintō* to *gankaku,* and *kūshankū* to *kankū*. They were originally written in Katakana characters but were corrected to Japanese with Kanji characters.

Furthermore, various parts of *kata* were changed; an upper block was changed to a middle block, a turn to the left was changed to a 180 degree turn, a knifehand strike was to a slapping, and so on.

All the dangerous strikes and moves were modified so that they are safe to perform and looks beautiful. The traditional karate emphasized its lethal strikes and strong defense, but those were changed completely. Change in traditional *kata* means to destroy the tradition of Okinawa.

The same can be seen in the karate competition match with no-contact rule. This rule is far from the original concept of karate that valued actual duel of *kakidamishi* (challenge match on street) in olden times. Low kick is prohibited, and speed is the only focus of all strikes in those competitions. And fierce strikes that follow the concept of *niku wo kirashite hone wo kiru* (take a flesh wound from your opponent before cutting him/her to the bone) are not valued highly, and sometimes it's seen as a violation of the rule. For competition karate, it's unnecessary to follow the traditional training method that is to use a straw board to harden his fists so that he can defeat opponents with a single strike. Without ever training his/her fists with straw board, he/she can win the National Athletic Meets by training his/her lower body with long standing jumps and alike training every day for quickness to jump close to the opponent to make strikes and back off quickly. I wonder if this can be called karate. This is another transformation with having competition matches.

In the essay Hōjōki, here is a line, "the flow of the river is ceaseless and its water is never the same. While along the still pools foam floats, now vanishing, now forming, never staying long."

Is there anything unchangeable in this world? Society adjusts itself to changes within it, and as society transforms, each era forms its own culture. It's same for martial arts; karate has been transforming in time. Culture of arts and crafts is always present within people's daily lives and is subject to change according to transformation of people's way of living and thinking. The difficulty of preserving the culture of *kata* in its original form can be witnessed through the popularity of the competition based karate.

Chapter 3 The Martial Arts Characteristics of Okinawa *Karatedo*

The Transformation of Martial Arts Techniques

Section 1: Warfare

Before talking about martial arts, it is necessary to talk about the martial techniques that gave birth to martial arts. However, we must also look at the warfare that brought about martial techniques. This is because martial techniques can only be born on the battlefield.

It is surmised that warfare was common from around the late Jomon Period in Japan based on the frequent observations of bones with weapon-induced damage excavated from that period. However, large numbers of human remains that show intentionally caused deaths by weapons in large scale battles show up from fortified ring moat settlements from the later Yayoi Period. It is generally believed that full-scale warfare began with the spread of agriculture and subsequent pressures to gain territories through invasion. The accepted theory is that warfare was widespread in Yayoi agricultural society in an area that stretched from northern Kyushu to the Chuugoku, Shikoku, Kinki, and Tokai regions from the fifth century B.C. to the third century A.D. The material used for weapons rapidly evolved from stone to bronze and iron. The remains of war dead with signs of wounds by weapons made of various materials have been discovered in large numbers.

Paddy rice farming, iron and written language were the factors that spurred the development of Yayoi culture in Japan. Paddy rice farming became the main agricultural method, and with that, people's mode of life was transformed to living in settlements. The formation of settlements gave birth to the concept of territory. In Ryukyu, several *gusuku* were formed to establish and protect territories, then the era of territorial disputes amongst *gusuku* lords, *aji* (or *anji*), began. Similarly, in the mainland Japan, introduction of rice farming was a significant factor in establishment of small nations. Settlement formation was progressed as a consequence of the introduction of rice farming in 300 B.C., and around 100 B.C. small nations formed. In 57 A.D. and 107 A.D. the King of Wado in Japan sent envoys to the Latter Han Dynasty in China. In 239 A.D., Queen Himiko of Yamatai sent an envoy to the Wei Dynasty in China. Based on these records, it is probable that many small nations had formed in Japan in a much earlier period. These nations engaged in warfare with each other and there was a process in which the smaller nations were unified into a larger entity. Yamatai is thought to have emerged supreme around 300 A.D.

From where and how was rice farming introduced to Japan? Two theories place the origin of upland slash-and-burn rice cultivation in China. One theory place the beginning of such cultivation in the present Yunnan Province 4,400 years ago while the other asserts that it began in present Hunan Province 12,000 years ago. Paddy rice farming is believed to have originated 7,000 years ago in the region around the lower Chang Jiang River in present-day Zhejiang Province. Rice farming methods are thought to have been brought to Japan from China through three routes: the Korean route (from Liaodong peninsula to northern Kyushu via the Korean peninsula), the Tsushima Warm Current route (from the Yangtze River region directly to Northern Kyushu), and the Kuroshio route (from the Jiang Nan region through the Ryukyuan Archipelago to southern Kyushu). It has been generally speculated that rice farming reached Japan around 300 B.C., but recent research points to the possibility that this happened as early as the 9th century B.C. Further, as the tropical Japonica variety of rice is believed to have entered Japan during the Jomon period, it can be surmised that rice farming was introduced to Okinawa at a very early period. While the conventional theory holds that agriculture was established in Okinawa only after rice farming was introduced around 12th century, it cannot explain the much earlier emergence of *gusuku* and *aji* (*anji*). Recent research may reverse the conventional historical theory by showing that rice farming was introduced much earlier during the Jomon period, thus enabling a more logical explanation of the Gusuku period of Ryukyu.

In Ryukyu, the nascent political entities of *gusuku* engaged a long process of incalculable battles with each other, resulting in their eventual unification. In the mainland Japan, after Yamato Dynasty unified the country in 300 A.D., the subsequent Kofun Period was when the Monobe and Soga Clans fought each other. The Heian Period that followed was marked by the Ezo Rebellion. Record of foreign affair of Japan can be found in the Chinese historical account "Sōsho" (or "Book of Song") written in 478 A.D. under the section *Ibanden Wakokujō* that, during the Northern and Southern Dynasties period in China, Waōbu (emperor of Yamato) presented a memorial to the emperor of the Song Dynasty. It says, "our nation in a far land that is bestowed peerage by China is the protector of your imperial majesty against Yezo (non-Yamato people from the Northern land). We wear armor and patrol mountains and rivers and have been fighting seamlessly since generations ago." Waōbu (the Emperor Yūryaku) also known as Wakatakeru Ōkimi, in the memorial he sent to China, placed his country periphery of the Song Dynasty and indicated that Yamato fights against *Yezo* or *Yenishi* from Eastern and Northern land as a protection for the Chinese empire.

The Yamato Court was controlling a part of the present Tohoku Region by the 7th century. In the Nihon Shoki we can find references to "Michi no Oku," "Mutsu," and "Mutsu no Kuni." Later, during the reign of the Emperor Kammu (781~806), Sakanoue no Tamuramaro was appointed to subjugate Yezo people. Consequently, in 802 A.D., Isawa castle was constructed and Morioka city became under the rule of the Court. Large scale rebellions and battles followed in the period such as the rebellion of Gangyō (878 A.D.), the Early Nine-Year War (1056~64 A.D.) and the Later Three-Year War (1083~87 A.D.). Also, when Fujiwara clan in the Ōshū province, who had authority in the Hiraizumi and the surrounding area, was overthrown by the shogunate, the northern end of the Honshu (main island of Japan) became under rule of the Court.

In the process towards a unified nation, strong nations and settlements take over weaker entities with aim to conquer the entire land. And the process naturally entails fierce battles. The condition was the same in Ryukyu. The Gusuku period was the era of over 400 *aji* fiercely fighting against each other to expand their *gusuku* territories. It was the age of wars.

Several significant ancient battles in Ryukyu are worth mentioning. From 607 to 609 A.D., Emperor Yang of the Chinese Sui Dynasty attacked Ryūkyū. However, Ryukyuan resistance repelled these attacks. In the 8th century, warfare between *gusuku* began. In 1180, Shunten became the *aji* of Urasoe. In the "Riyu Conflict," Shunten brought down the Tenson Dynasty. In 1260, Eiso became the king of Chūzan. In 1322, Haniji emerged as the king of Hokuzan. Thereafter, for about a century the "Three Kingdoms," Chūzan, Nanzan, and Hokuzan, existed side by side in Ryūkyū. The Three Kingdoms Period, differed greatly from the previous age in that instead of having a plethora of petty *aji*, it was characterized by the emergence of a few powerful *yu nu nushi*. Hokuzan was at the north end, Chūzan in the central part, and Nanzan on the southern end of Okinawa. Chūzan was the strongest of the Three Kingdoms. Each kingdom had a *gusuku* that served as its stronghold. Hokuzan's *gusuku* was in Nakijin, Chūzan's was in Urasoe, and Nanzan's was in Ozato in Shimajiri. In 1393, Shō Hashi became the *aji* of Sashiki (in Nanzan). In 1406, Shō Hashi defeated Bunei, the king of Chūzan. Bunei had taken over Chūzan after the death of Satto, but because of his unpopularity, the Sashiki aji Sho Hashi took power from Bunei ten years after Satto's death. Shō Hashi installed his father Shi Sho as the first king in the First Shō Dynasty. Shishō established a tributary relationship with the Chinese Ming Dynasty and Chūzan prospered.

Katsuren Castle

In 1416, Shō Hashi attacked Nakijin Gusuku and defeated Hokuzan. Earlier, Shishō ordered Shō Hashi to attack Hokuzan upon hearing that its king, Hananchi, was preparing to attack Chūzan. Shō Hashi assembled a force of 3,000 to attack Nakijin Gusuku (population of the main island of Okinawa at the time is estimated to have been about 80,000). However, because Nakijin Gusuku was built upon terrain that provided natural protection against invaders and because Hananchi had put much effort into reinforcing his military, the Chūzan army made little headway even after three days and nights of fighting. Consequently, Shō Hashi sent his own spy to convince Hananchi's trusted vassal Mutubu Teibara to switch sides. The next day Mutubu Teibara convinced Hananchi to go out of Nakijin Gusuku as a way to show his vassals his bravery as a warrior. In the ensuing battle with the Chūzan forces, the Hokuzan forces were defeated. While Hananchi was being pursued by the Chūzan forces, Mutubu Teibara set fire to Nakijin Gusuku. Having nowhere to flee, Hanachi cursed the gods and cut the stone figure that represented his own protective deity in half before killing himself. Following the battle, Shō Hashi declared that, "not only are the Hokuzan territories far from Chūzan and the population difficult to educate, but both the character of the people and the geography is wild making it difficult to prevent a

157

rebellion." Consequently, he decided that he needed "to place an overseer there to keep watch" and thus sent his brother to oversee the former Hokuzan territories or what became known as Kunjan (Kunigami).

In 1429, Shō Hashi defeated Nanzan to finally unify Ryūkyū. Earlier in 1421, Shishō died and Shō Hashi was made king of Chūzan. The king of Nanzan had been the materialistic Tarumi. Shō Hashi offered his own gold leaf screen in exchange for the abundantly flowing Kadeshigaa River that flowed through Nanzan. Tarumi readily agreed to the proposition, but this raised the ire of the farmers who not only depended on the river but also saw it as sacred. The loss of support from his subjects contributed to Nanzan's defeat by Chūzan.

Section 2: Martial Techniques

Life or death survival skills that were born and cultivated on battlefields are called *bujutsu*, or the martial techniques. Such techniques were developed as result of desperate search for the ways to kill opponents in order to survive. It is evident from the history that people have been killing each other on battlefields ceaselessly since the before century periods. Depending on nations and times, military strategies and martial techniques were different. Further, in the times before weapons were created, as evidently shown by the Olympic of the ancient Greek, people fought with bare fists.

The ancient Olympic game was first held in 776 B.C. It was a religious event for Greece and the surrounding Hellenic cultural region and was a festival to celebrate human history of battles. The first established event was the race. It was for deciding who could run fastest, in other words, how fast can one run to catch and kill a running away enemy. Next event was the wrestling. It was first an event included in the pentathlon, but from the 23rd

Olympic game in 668 B.C., wrestling was treated as an independent event. The competition was to grab and throw an opponent from a standing position (it was allowed one knee to touch the ground in order to throw the opponent), and without a time restriction, it was a harsh competition that could take a long time before the winner was decided. On the same year, boxing was included as an event. Similar to wrestling, there was neither time restriction nor intervals, and even if one was beaten to the ground the match didn't end unless he admitted the defeat; in other words, they fought to death. Further, there wasn't any weight classes, and competitors' fists were wrapped with leather strap to increase damage (later, metal rivets were embedded in the strap to make it even further destructive).

From the 25th Olympic game, chariot racing was started to compete in 48 stadium distance with four-in-hand chariot. Also, from the 33rd Olympic game, a combat competition called Pankration was added as an event. In Greek language, *pan* meant as *"of all"*, and *kration* meant as *"powerful"*. The only rule was that any attacks were allowed as long as bare hands were used; so joint-locking techniques or choking were allowed, and similar to boxing, a match didn't end until a competitor accepted defeat. As symbolized by the ancient Olympic games, combat techniques have existed all over the world.

Long warring periods took place in both the Japanese mainland and in Ryūkyū. It is in such times of war that martial techniques to kill are born. In Japan, the martial techniques that developed included archery and fighting on horseback. In the war between the Minamoto and Taira, the *naginata* (halberd) was used extensively. In the Kamakura Period, the *katana* (sword) became the main weapon. In the Muromachi Period, the weapons of most importance on the battlefield were in order the *yari* (spear), *tachi* (long sword), *kodachi* (short sword), and bare hands. In the guns appeared for the first time at the Battle of Nagashino in 1575.

In the 16th century Tokugawa Bakufu, a long lasting peace was achieved. However, with the ending of war, martial techniques were not discarded.

Martial techniques that lost their practicality didn't become mere hobby of *bushi*. Certificates of martial techniques affected their retainer's stipend. Furthermore, without receiving appropriate certificate or number of enumerations for each clan or family status, there were occasions that their hereditary stipend was lowered. Namely, it was an obligation for *bushi* to endeavor in martial techniques. For instance, Asahi Monzaemon of Owari-han became a disciple of several schools for mastering various martial techniques. In 1692, he became a disciple for spear fighting technique; archery technique in three months; *suemono-giri* (fixed object cutting) and jujutsu in 1693; military science and *iai-jutsu* (sword drawing technique) in 1695; firearms technique in 1696; and sword fighting technique in 1697. Of all martial techniques, he learned the widest and deepest was of course the sword fighting technique. The sword was a symbol of the soul of the samurai. In the opening of the edict *Buke-shohatto,* it writes "one should work hard to study and to improve martial techniques." *Bushi* couldn't neglect sword training because of the above. Just like Tokugawa shogunate made Yagyūshinkage-ryū and Onoha Itto-ryū their designated schools, each *Han* had teachers for sword fighting from specific schools. Towards the end of the Edo period, most of the *han-kō* (school for children from samurai class families) annexed a training room or a dōjō for martial technique courses, and masters for each martial technique were employed. Teaching of sword fighting techniques was considered as a family business, and the occupation was normally succeeded from father to son. By the end of Shogunate period, schools for sword fighting could be counted up to 700 and more.

Meanwhile, martial techniques developed differently in Ryūkyū. The weapons used in Ryukyuan warfare included the *bo* (staff), *sai, tunfā, kama* (sickle), *nunchaku, ekū* (oar) and other farming and fishing implements. In the absence of iron and steel production, *katana* were not made in Ryūkyū. Consequently, *kenjutsu* (sword fighting) was virtually non-existent in Ryūkyū. However, *tiy* was developed as bare handed techniques to defeat opponents. Evidence of this can be taken from the *Omoro Sōshi.*

The *Omoro Sōshi* is a collection of songs that were passed down orally in Okinawa from ancient times. It is the oldest collection of Okinawan songs and has been compared to Japan's *Kojiki* and *Mayōshū*. Upon orders from the Ryukyuan government, *omoro* (songs of the gods) that were sung in Okinawa and Amami were written down over a period from 1531 to 1623. Twenty volumes of the *Omoro Sōshi* were collected, including 1,553 songs of varying lengths. The first volume was compiled in 1531 during the reign of Shō Sei. The second volume was compiled in 1613 during the reign of Shō Nei. The third through twenty-first volumes were compiled in 1623 during the reign Shō Hō. The twenty-second volume was a compilation of songs taken from each of the previous volumes and later used in official ceremonies. Many of the *Omoro Sōshi* songs were sung by women priestesses in their capacity as oracles for the gods. The *Omoro Sōshi* also included songs used in ceremonies, songs composed by poets, work songs, and song sung by commoners in groups. However, a majority of the songs are religious and magical in nature that pre-exist the development of music as entertainment in Ryūkyū. Until recently, linguistic theory explained Ryūkyūan dialect was branched off from Japanese language before the Nara period, however, the grammar used in the *Omoro Sōshi*, although it got corrupted into Ryūkyūan local dialect, is correctly following the grammar of Japanese language during the Muromachi period when trade between Ryūkyū and Japan flourished. The original copy of the *Omoro Sōshi* was destroyed in the fire of the Shuri Castle in 1709. In the following year, copies from Gushikawa aji family and Adaniya family, who was the successor of songs of the gods, were transcribed to make one copy to be kept at the Shuri castle of which exists today.

The *Omoro Sōshi* is a legacy of a period that stretches from the Early Gusuku Period (5th to 12th century), the Late Gusuku Period (12th to 15th century), and the Early Ryukyuan Dynasty Period (15th to 17th century). As time passed, the subject and contents of the songs became richer and the songs themselves give us an idea of how people lived in the past. In the early Gusuku Period, the gods were the main topic of the songs, which were mainly for religious ceremonies. In the late Gusuku Period, songs about castle construction, shipbuilding, tribute collecting, trade, and the virtues of particular *aji* became more common. These songs, known as *wesa omoro*, were used for dances done in groups. In the Ryukyuan Dynasty Period, songs extolling the king and about temple building, tree planting, tribute collection, shipbuilding, ocean voyages, conquering other islands and other songs that were not related to agricultural village life became more prevalent. In the same period, a form of work song called *weto omoro* came into being.

In later volumes of the *Omoro Sōshi,* tension in ideas and song become visible as the epic-type *omoro* start to transition toward the lyrical 30-syllable *Ryūka* form of songs. The formation of a class of society that was free from the constraints of village communal life and could engage in the cultivation of individualistic self-reflection can be seen in this transition. Further, geographical names began to appear in the songs, including Okinawa, Amami, Miyako, and Yaeyama and more faraway places such as Kamakura and Kyoto in Japan, China (Ming and Qing), Vietnam, and Thailand. Many of the songs praised the Ryukyuan king and government.

An official history, the Chūzan Seikan, was compiled after the unification of the Three Kingdoms in the 15th century, but the *Omoro Sōshi* has been valued as the only window to the more distant. There are 41 songs in the first volume of the *Omoro Sōshi* and, remarkably, 13 of those songs are about war. This is an indication of how much war was a part of the Gusuku Period. Below is one of the Omoro songs that is about war.

> The supreme shamaness
> famous woman filled with power
> let the lord among lords rule the realm
> choosing a good day for going out to attack
> choosing a good day for controlling the realm
> bringing down invisible power for the troops
> bringing down power to keep them alive

the men splendid and standing tall
the men so lovely you want to stroke them
let the lord among lords
their hearts truly filled strength
their livers truly filled with power
protected by the shamanesses
protected by the lordly women
against the soldiers sent from Yamato,
monk-like men with half their heads shaved
the shamans send fear into their hearts
the shamans send doubt into their livers
with both hands they throw them down
with their legs they knock them down
chopping them up like deep-sea fish
eating them up like shallow-water fish
all the way to the Yamato islands
all the way up to their capital
extending the borders of the king's power
spreading the strong rope of his rule
until they send riches to Shuri castle
until they pay taxes to the sacred shrine
now his soldiers receive prayers of thinks
now they receive the shamans' blessings
let the supreme shamaness
inform the spirit of the sun[4]

Of special interest are the lines, "with both hands (*kumute*) they throw them down" and "with their legs (*atasu*) they knock them down". The lines suggest that in those times of bare handed fighting, there was an expression "*kumute*," or what is now called *kumite* was used. This *omoro* song provides evidence that hands and feet were used by Ryukyuans from ancient times in battle to engage in *kumite*. This particular song is valuable in showing that *tiy* was used as a weapon of war in Ryūkyū and that its use was recognized widely enough to be sung about.

There are those who posit that Ryukyuan karate came from China based on the the *Bubishi* text, but this text had not been compiled by 茅元儀 until 1621. The *omoro* song above depicts the impending Satsuma invasion of Ryūkyū strongly suggesting that it was being sung before that invasion happened in 1609. Consequently, it is doubtful that *tiy* has its origins in the *Bubishi*.

Incidentally, there are two types of martial techniques. *Dai no heihō* ("large martial strategy") refers to the techniques honed to prepare a soldier for an attack that would come unexpectedly in terms of place, time, and type. It also refers to battles involving large numbers of soldiers. Contrastingly, *Sho no heihō* ("small martial strategy") refers to the refinement of individual soldier's skills in such things as archery, horseback riding, and the use of swords, naginata, firearms, and other weapons. Man-to-man fighting is also part of *sho no heihō*.

Miyamoto Musashi personally presented Hosokawa Tadatoshi with the Thirty-five Articles of Martial Strategy (兵法三十六箇条) in 1641. Two years later in 1643, he wrote the *Book of Five Rings* that was largely based on the Thirty-five Articles of Military Strategy. I would like to discuss *Dai no heihō* as it appears in the *Book of Five Rings*.

The *Book of Five Rings* is divided into chapters on Earth, Water, Fire, Wind, and Sky. The chapter on Fire is mainly devoted to *Dai no heihō*.

In a section entitled "Concerning Place," Musashi writes about the importance of assessing the immediate conditions. For example, he writes that

---

[4] Masachie Nakahodo, Minoru Higa, Chris Drake. Omoro: Ancient Ryukyu Rhymes (中本正智・比嘉実・クリス・ドレイク「おもろ鑑賞ー琉球古謡の世界」) 連載５４

as a principle, you should have the sun at your back. Even indoors, you should have the light or to the right of you. He also prescribes choosing a position that looks down on your opponent. Further, when chasing an opponent, you should drive him towards your left.

In "Taking the Three Initiatives," Musashi that there are only three initiatives in beginning any confrontation. The first initiative is the "Initiative of Attack" in which you initiate the attack on your opponent. The second is the "Initiative of Waiting," when your opponent attacks. The third is the "Body-Body Initiative," when you attack and your opponent makes a counterattack.

"Pressing Down on the Pillow" refers to "not letting your opponent bring his head up." He writes that in martial arts, you should check your opponent's strikes, suppress his stabs, and escape his grappling.

In "Traversing," Musashi writes about getting through the particular situation. In order to traverse, you must assess the situation, know your own strengths and abilities, and act accordingly. In other words, like a ship sometimes sailing with a tail wind and sometimes using its oars against the wind to make it to a harbor, you must adjust to the conditions of the moment.

In "Knowing the Conditions," Musashi talks about how in battle you must know whether your opponent is strong or weak. In accordance to that assessment, you adjusts the strategy toward one that would ensure victory.

"Stepping on the Sword" talks about not using the same strategy as your opponent. That is, if you merely seek to strike back with your long sword after your opponent attacks with his long sword, the battle will keep continuing strike for strike. However, the idea is to "step" on your opponent's sword in the instant that he strikes to prevent him from attacking a second time.

"Knowing Collapse" is to know the collapse in all things. The collapsing of a house, a body, and an opponent all involve a discordance of rhythm at particular moment. In a large battle, it is important to detect your opponent's break in rhythm and to take advantage of it by pursuing them with no hesitation. If you miss that opportunity, your opponent will have a chance to mount a vigorous counter attack.

"Becoming the Opponent" happens when puts yourself in the place of your opponent by thinking from his perspective. Even in a large battle, if you lead yourself to belief that the enemy forces are strong, you tend to become overly cautious. However, there should be nothing to worry about if you have a good number of troops, understands the principles of martial strategy, and knows the right points to attack your opponent.

In "Letting Go of Four Hands," Musashi writes that when the mind of your opponent and the mind of yourself become the same, the fight feels like it is not going anywhere. You should know that when that happens, it is best to discard your present tactics and find another way to win.

"Moving the Shadow" means that, even in battles involving many people, when it is impossible to judge your opponent's situation, you should act as if they are mounting a strong attack to see what their intentions are by their reaction.

Going through the major points of Musashi's *Dai no heihō*, we can see that his techniques are not limited just to swordfighting, but also include battlefield strategy. This attests to his exceptional talent and abilities.

Next, I would like to discuss *Sho no heihō*. *Sho no heihō* techniques depend on the particular weapon being used and it should be noted that the *Book of Five Rings* is focused solely on *kenjutsu*. Musashi gives a detailed discussion on the use of sword techniques in his chapter on Water.

In "Frame of Mind For Martial Strategy," Musashi advises that in the way of martial strategy, even in battle, your frame of mind should not change from your normal everyday frame of mind. In normal times and in battle, your mind should be broad and straight. It should not be too tight, nor too slack. It should be centered and not allowed to be distracted. Your mind should sway peacefully, with the swaying never stopping for even a moment as it should always be aware of your surroundings.

"Appearance in Martial Strategy" refers to your posture in which your face is not turned down, up, or sideways. Your eyes should not looking this way and that and your brow not knitted. The space between your eyebrows should be narrowed. While not moving your eyes, slightly narrow them without blinking. Keep a calm face with the line of your nose straight and your chin slightly jutted out. Keep the line of your neck straight up and put strength in the nape of your neck. Also put strength from your knees to your toes and open up your stomach area so that your hips are not bent.

"Using the Eyes in Martial Strategy" pertains to keeping your purview broad during battle. The first priority is to look deep into the essence of things, while the second priority is to look at the surface level where movements occur.

In "Holding the Sword," Musashi instructs us to let your thumb and index fingers have a sensation as if they are floating. The middle fingers should be neither too tight nor too loose. The ring and little fingers should be tightened. There should not be any looseness in your grip. When holding a sword, you should always have in mind the idea that you will cut down your opponent. In all movements of the sword, you should not let your hands become immobile. Immobility is death and mobility is living. You should understand this well.

For "Using the Feet," Musashi advocates having your toenails float slightly and your heel planted firmly on the ground. When moving the feet, there are cases when you have to take large, small, slow and fast strides, but in each case you should walk as naturally as you do usually. Feet that seem to fly, float or be immobile are all not desirable.

The "Five Stances" are Upper, Middle, Lower, Right-Side, and Left-Side. There are no other stances than these five, but you should not think of the stance itself, but about how you will cut down your opponent. In the way of martial arts, the essence of the stance is the Middle. The Middle is the core of all stances.

Musashi writes that if you know the "Way of the Sword," even if you handle the sword with only two fingers, you will be able to use it freely. When you handle the sword, it is necessary to handle it as calmly as you can. You will deviate from the Way of the Sword if you try to handle the sword quickly as you would a fan or dagger. Handling a sword becomes difficult in such a case. Cutting down a person with what is called a "knife cut" with a sword is impossible.

In "The First of the Five Fronts," you take the first Middle stance with the tip of his sword aimed at your opponent's face. When your opponent attacks, you deflect his sword to your right. When he attacks again, use your sword so that the tip of his sword goes back up. Keeping your sword in that position, which is in a downward position, strike your opponent's hand from below when he strikes again.

In "The Second of the Five Fronts," one takes the Upper stance and strikes exactly the same time as when your opponent makes his strike. If you have missed your opponent, leave your sword as it is. When your opponent strikes again, strike at him again by bringing your sword back up. When he strikes again, do the same.

"The Third of the Five Fronts," involves taking the Lower stance and lowering your sword. When your opponent attacks, strike at his hand from below. Your opponent will counter with another strike. When he tries to knock down your sword, strike at your opponent with an upward strike with the intent to cut his upper arm laterally.

In "The Fourth of the Five Fronts," you take the Left-Side stance with the sword held laterally to the left. When your opponent strikes, strike at his hand from below. When your opponent moves to strike down your sword, while keeping your aim to strike his hand, in the same breath, parry the path of his sword and strike diagonally upward toward a point above your shoulder.

"The Fifth of the Five Fronts" is when you take the Right-side stance with your sword held laterally to your right. In response to your opponent attacking, swing your sword diagonally upward and take the Upper stance and strike downward in a straight line. If you learn to use your sword with this method, you will be able to freely swing even a heavy sword.

As shown above, Musashi was giving concrete lessons on *kenjutsu* in the *Book of Five Rings*. In his 62 years, Musashi is said to have won 60 duels, but those duels happened in his 20s. He did not fight past the age of 30. His famed duel with Sasaki Kojiro on Ganryu Island happened when he was 29 years old.

Musashi called his sword fighting style *niten ichiryū* (literally, two heavens as one). It was *bushi*'s duty, for both commanders and common soldiers, to wear two swords at his side. In the olden times, it was called *tachi* (a long sword) and *katana* (a short sword), and later it was called *katana* (long sword) and *wakisashi* (short sword). Unlike other weapons like spear or *naginata* (partisan pole sword), those two swords were worn at all time. The true Way of this *niten ichiryū* was achieved by always wearing two swords since the time of being a novice. One shouldn't feel burdened to hold a sword with one hand. Long sword should be used in an open area, and short sword should be used in a confined area. Holding two swords at the same time has its merit especially when fighting against a large number of opponents or to hold down an opponent. Further, anecdotes say that Musashi always fought in battles with wooden swords. The fact that he fought with wooden swords against iron swords can be the proof for that Ryukyuan's stick fighting technique was superior in battles against soldiers with iron swords.

I would like to now talk about *tiy*, which developed in Ryūkyū, and ancient martial techniques in general. The roots of modern karate are in *tiy*, which were techniques for combat. I am repeating myself, but martial techniques were born on battlefields where people were forced to kill or be killed. Consequently, martial techniques cannot be born in places where there are no battlefields. In Ryūkyū, a long 800-year period of continued warfare between aji happened from the 7th to 15th century. I have already mentioned that *tiy* is the "ancient martial techniques" that developed on the battlefields.

Tiy and *kobudo* techniques were refined to an extremely highly level on the battlefields. These techniques were practiced day and night by people so that their bodies would remember them. As individual techniques were practiced repeatedly, they began to be combined with other techniques in series. *Kata* were born when a series of techniques were put together in a narrative. The *kata* were refined as they were practiced repeatedly and unnecessary motions were eliminated. These *kata* were then practiced day and night. This is the process in which *tiy* and *kobudo kata* were developed from actual fighting.

The techniques of *tiy* begin with the fist. That is, forming a proper fist for killing with one blow lies at the heart of *tiy*. The fist is formed by bending the first and second joints in the fingers in order and clenching the fist tightly so that that there is no open space inside of it. The fist is completely formed when thumb is bent at the first joint and clamped down firmly. When this fist used to punch the opponent from the front, it is called *seiken*. *Seiken* is the basic *tiy* fist. *Seiken* practice using a *makiwara* is done to strengthen the fists. Through decades of practice, one will be able to break concrete tile with one punch.

Development of feet and legs for kicking is next in importance. The instep, sole, *sobagatana* (outer edge of the foot), heel and shin are trained so that one can bring down an opponent with only one kick. The different types of kicks include *maegeri* (front kick), *ushirogeri* (back kick), *yokogeri* (side kick), *gedan mawashigeri* (lower level roundhouse kick), *chūdan mawashigeri* (middle level roundhouse kick), *jōdan mawashigeri* (upper level roundhouse kick), *ushiro mawashigeri* (spinning hook kick), *dō mawashigeri* (wheel kick), and others. With decades of training, one can break a baseball bat with a kick.

Next comes building up the blocking forearms. Punches and kicks from an opponent must be blocked by one's forearms. Pairs of people hit each other's forearms with their own to train them. One could also use a makiwara to hit your forearms against it. Using *gaisokutō* (outer forearm), *naisokutō* (inner forearm), *empi* (elbow), etc., opponent's' thrusts are blocked, and simultaneously, the thrusting arm is crushed by *uchi-uke* (inside-to-outside block), *soto-uke* (outside-to-inside block), *age-uke* (rising block), etc. The blockings are at the same time attacks.

Creating "iron torso and legs" is also crucial. An opponent's punches can strike your solar plexus or other part of your torso. His or her middle front kick can also reach the same region. A lower roundhouse kick from an opponent will also reach your thighs and shin. To prepare for such attacks, you can build up your torso and legs by having them be kicked on a daily basis. It is possible through decades of training to be able to withstand powerful punches and kicks to these areas without even a flinch.

Last, but not least is the development of fēsa (speed) in punches, kicks and blocks. *Tiy* cannot do without speed and power. With speed in punches, kicks, and blocks, one can take the initiative in the fight with an increased variation in the types of attacks possible. Slow punches and kicks are easy to block and punches and kicks that are too quick for your blocks will cause great damage. Also, since the equation for power is speed x weight, increasing your speed will also increase your power. However, increasing speed is easier said than done. It can only be done through training, which also involves strengthening the spine, arm muscles, abdomen, and other parts of the body.

The weapons used in battle during the 7th to 15th century Gusuku Period were the *bo, sai, nunchaku, tunfā, ēku,* and other farm and fishing tools and implements.

Bo techniques are the basics of Ryukyuan *kobudō* and the *rokushakubo* (six-foot staff) is the standard *bo*. The bo is held with both hands, one third of the way from each end. Using the *bo*, you can instantly go from an attack to the front to an attack to the rear. It can be handled with dazzling speed and offers so many variations. Its attacks and defenses mirror *tiy* techniques. This can be seen in upper, middle, and lower level strikes; upper, middle, and lower level thrusts; upper, middle, and lower level blocks; and upper and lower level parries.

Sai may have originally been a tool for softening the earth for farming. For striking techniques, there are *honte-zuki* (forward hand thrust), *sakate-zuki* (reverse hand thrust), *uchi* (strike), *kaeshi-uchi* (cross strike), etc., and for blocking techniques, there are *hiraki-uke* (open block), *jōdan-uke* (upper-level block), *chūdan-uchiuke* (middle-level inner block), *soto-uke* (outer block), *gedan-uke* (lower-level block), *jōdan-kōsauke* (upper-level cross block), *gedan-haraiuke* (lower-level rowing block), and so on. They are basically the same as attacks and blocks of *tiy* techniques.

For *nunchaku* techniques, there are stances such as *chūdan-hon-gamae* (middle-level regular stance), *jōdan-honteuchi-gamae* (upper-level regular-hand strike stance), *sakate-uchi-gamae* (reverse-hand strike stance), *ushiro-gamae* (rear stance), *koshi-game* (shoulder stance), etc., and striking techniques such as *junte-ayaburi* (regular-hand swing), *sakate-ayaburi* (reverse-hand swing), *uchi-katawa-buri* (inner half-circle swing), *soto-katawa-buri* (outer half-circle swing), and so on. For grabing the moving nunchaku, there are *junte-dori* (regular-hand grab), *sakate-dori* (reverse-hand grab), *koshi-dori* (waist grab), *waki-dori* (under-the-arm grab), *sakate-uchi-dori* (inner reverse-hand grab), *haigo-dori* (rear grab), etc.

Tunfā is an agricultural tool that was originally meant for threshing grains such as soybeans or rice by hammering on them. It's a wooden club with a handgrip and is a fist-length longer beyond one's elbow. A *tunfā* is held in both hands, and its techniques consists of thrusts, blocks and swing-strikes that are almost identical to *tiy* techniques. For blocking techniques, there are *jōdan-uke* (upper-level block), *chūdan uchi-uke* (middle-level inner block), *soto-uke* (outer block), *gedan-harai-uke* (lower-level swing block), *gyaku gedan harai-uke* (reverse lower-level swing block), and so forth. For attacking techniques, there are *jōdan-uchi* (upper-level strike), *migi yoko-uchi* (right side strike), *hidari yoko-uchi* (left side strike), *naname jōdan-uchi* (diagonal upper-level strike), *honte-zuki* (regular-hand thrust), *sakate-zuki* (reverse-hand thrust), and so on. And for grabbing techniques, there are *katsugi-hikitori* (shoulder grab) and *koshi-hikitori* (waist grab).

Section 3: Budo

The Birth of Budo

Battles emerged out of the need to protect tribal territory or interests. Superior methods for fighting are discovered on the battlefield during life and death battles. These methods are then polished to become martial techniques. The more martial techniques were refined to a higher level, the more the important aspects of the mind and spirit become. In Japan, budo (martial art) was born when ritual and spirituality were added to martial techniques. The term budo has been used in many different ways, but it can be said to be include norms and moral precepts related to how a person who engages in battle should live and die.

Samurai warriors in olden times would purify themselves before heading to battle in ceremonial tearooms. The entrance of the tearoom was a "*nijiriguchi*," a small passageway of about 69 cm high and 66 cm wide. Only one samurai at a time could enter the tearoom while stooping low. Moreover, each person had to leave behind anything in his possession that would get stuck in the nijiriguchi. This meant that the samurai would have to leave his swords outside the tearoom. Since the tearoom was a space to purify oneself, anything impure was strictly prohibited from entering. After entering the tea room, which was only the size of two tatami mats, the samurai came forward a few short steps to area in front of the hearth and slowly lowered himself into the *seiza* sitting position. He would then begin to meditate over his life and the possibility of not returning home at the end of the battle. While quietly listening to his own heartbeat, the samurai would take an observer's perspective on his life up to that point.

After the samurai achieved a sense of well-being of heart and felt purified in body, a woman of samurai class was summoned to bring the tea. The tea was poured in a bowl for the samurai to drink slowly. As a sign of awareness that the tea might be the last thing he would put in his mouth, the samurai drank the tea to the last drop before graciously returning the bowl to the woman samurai. Before leaving the tearoom, he said, "that was a splendid tea." The woman samurai would say in prayer, "May you return alive" as she watched him leave the tearoom. The samurai would then retrieve his swords and tuck them in his belt as he headed to battle.

Ritual is important in the world of martial arts and played a crucial role in the development of mind training for samurai. Samurai confronted the possibility of their death not only before a battle but in their everyday life. In doing so, they studied the path of living.

The fundamental principles of budo come from Shinto, Buddhism, and Confucianism. Further, etiquette and mind practice were indispensable in the formation of budo as a philosophical path.

Present day budo etiquette comes from samurai etiquette. Samurai etiquette is believed to have its origins in Zen Buddhism as it was taught by Ogawawara Sadamune (1291-1350) who was a student of Chinese Zen Master Seisetsu Shouchou (1274-1339) who arrived in Japan in the Kamakura Period. Ogasawara, who Emperor Go-Daigo (1288-1339) in martial techniques, was put in charge of setting the standards of samurai etiquette. This leads to the question of what were the previous norms for samurai etiquette. Takeda Nagakiyo, the governor of Shinano, took on the Ogasawara name (1162-1242). Nagakiyo and his father Tohmitsu, a master of horseback archery, were retainers of Minamoto Yoritomo (1147-1199). It was in this capacity that they began developing samurai etiquette standards. Because Tohmitsu was highly trusted as a martial techniques instructor by the Emperor Go-Shiragawa (1127-1192), he was a regular participant in imperial court rituals. Speaking of court rituals, from even before the time of Prince Shoutoku (547-622), some form of ancient religious ceremonial etiquette had already been in existence. The legacy of such etiquette remains relatively unchanged even today in the ritualistic forms of bowing, sitting, walking, *gassho* (holding hands in together), and clapping.

Prince Shoutoku created the "17 Article Constitution" in 604 and because there was an article that called for the "reformation of court rituals," we can surmise that ancient rituals had already been in existence at the time. Rituals could be seen as originating in the practices and forms through which people communicated with deities. After the arrival of Buddhism to Japan, ceremonies and prayers were conducted with much frequency and there also emerge a hierarchy among priests. Further, the Confucian ideals of justice and righteousness as found in the I Ching became taken seriously. The concept of *kei* (敬 = respect) was taken as the fundamental principle of Confucian rites. Japanese Confucianism was influenced most profoundly by Zhu Xi (1130-1200), who had advocated *kei* as the basic spirit of rituals. Japanese further developed the concept of *kei* and eventually replaced it with *makoto* (誠 = sincerity; honesty). This concept of *makoto*, which came to become the spiritual formation Japanese ritual, was from Shinto. It also became the backbone of the spirit of bushidō. Consequently, Japanese budo is strongly intertwined with Shintoism, Buddhism, and Confucianism.

However, for the samurai who had to face life and death situations, his own strength and abilities were the only things that he could depend on. From a realistic and rational perspective, it was his own skill that would save him in battle, not the gods and Buddha. This can be seen in Miyamoto Musashi's words, "I revere the gods and Buddha, but I do not depend on them." They seem to advocate non-dependency on higher powers. However, there was an intimate relationship between the spirit of bushidō and the religions of Shintoism, Buddhism, and Confucianism. This especially true for Zen Buddhism: the relationship between *ken* (the sword) and Zen is profound. In the Muromachi Period, Zen priests became important as political and academic advisors to *daimyoh* (feudal lords) and were active in such important tasks as drafting documents, educating heirs, and diplomacy. Kaisen Jōki of Erinji Temple was a Zen priest who was renowned for being martyred by fire for his support of the Takeda Family and for his last words: "My name is Joki

Kaisen, to the focused mind, the flames are but a cool breeze." Other notable Zen priests were Daigen Sohfu, who served as military advisor to Imagawa Yoshimoto, and Ankokuji Ekei, the highly trusted diplomat of the powerful Mohri clan, who commanded four regiments in the Battle of Sekigahara and was later executed by Tokugawa Ieyasu.

Thus, since the days of old, *ken* and Zen have been thought of as being indivisible. This sentiment has been expressed by the saying, "*kenzen ichinyo* (*ken* and Zen are as one)." However, reconciling the contradiction between the fact that *ken* is for killing and Zen is a path for living is not a simple matter. In *JouseishiKendan*, swordsman and essayist Jouseishi writes, "If anyone reflects upon the mystery of *kenjutsu*, it is that one draws the sword he usually keeps sheathed on his side and gets into position, while the enemy also does the same. This is something to consider earnestly." The kenjutsu Jouseishi refers to is not a win or lose competition that involves bamboo shinai and protective gear with striking and stabbing according to set rules, but rather the way of life or death fighting in which one's life is determined in a very brief instant. Or as the Chozan Shissai writes in his *TenguGeijutsuRon*, "Kenjutsu are the techniques used in life or death situations."

As we can see, martial techniques determined the outcome life and death fights. The higher these techniques were developed, the more they became "rules for human life." While martial techniques were originally for killing in self-defense, they were elevated into precepts for living as *budo*. This must be understood to determine the difference between *bujutsu* (martial techniques) and *budo*. When etiquette is added to martial technique, the result is in a "way of living" that emphasizes a high degree of spiritual practice.

I will describe the Shinto, Buddhist, and Confucian norms that became part of budo in the next sections.

Japanese Shinto

Shinto is Japan's folk religion with origins 2,600 years ago that links the *kami* (gods or deities) and nature with people. It is a polytheistic religion that believes in 8 million *kami*. The *kami* that are worship at Shinto shrines are those that appear in Japan's mythology. The first written references to these kami are found in the Kojiki (712 AD) and Nihon Shoki (720 AD). The Kojiki and Nihon Shoki are collectively referred to as the "Ki-ki" and were the first historical accounts compiled after Japan was unified into a nation state and the Japanese emperor system was being formed. The Kojiki or "An Account of Ancient Matters," was compiled by Ō no Yasumaro and the Nihon Shoki or "the Chronicles of Japan" by Prince Toneri and others. It was in this time period that "Nihon" was first used as the name of the country.

The first *kami* to appear in Japanese mythology was Ame-no-minakanushi-no-kami. The two kami that created the Japanese archipelago were Izanagi and Izanami. Over 260 *kami* appear in the Kojiki. These kami are worshiped at Shinto shrines.

The first Japanese emperor was Jinmu, who was six generations removed from the *kami* known as Amaterasu-o-mikami. Amaterasu-o-mikami had entrusted her grandson, who was Jinmu's great-grandfather, Ninigi-no-mikoto, with a jewel, mirror, and sword and told him to "Value these objects and conquer Nihon to build an ideal nation." Ninigi-no-mikoto descended from Heaven onto Takachiho Peak in Hyuga. From there he brought the whole region of Hyuga under his control, but he still had a long way to go before he subdued the rest of Japan.

Kamu-yamato-iwarehiko-no-mikoto, Ninigi-no-mikoto's great-grandson who later became Emperor Jinmu, then announced: "Here in this western region, generations of our forefathers have ruled well and their favor has spread. However, in faraway lands, there are still borders that are being fought over. It is heard that in the east there are good lands surrounded by green mountains. This is surely the center of the nation of Japan. Let us go there and make a capital from which we can rule the lands in peace." Kamu-yamato-iwarehiko-no-mikoto then proceeded to carry out the grand undertaking of building an ideal nation as Amaterasu-o-mikami had requested.

Jinmu set out by ship from Hyuga and went through Usa in Oita and up the northern shore of Kyushu. From there, he passed through the Seto Inland Sea to Naniwa (present day Osaka) and to Kumano on the Kii Peninsula and into Yamato. This undertaking is known as the Jinmu's Eastern Expedition. Along the way, Jinmu face numerous misfortunes, including the loss of his older brothers. In response, Jinmu said, "[These misfortunes] are because I, a descendant of the Sun Goddess Amaterasu-o-mikami have advanced my troops in the direction of the rising sun. Let us retreat and offer prayers to the kami and with their divine strength at our backs we shall go forward." Thereafter, Jinmu regrouped to Kumano in the southern part of the Kii Peninsula, which enabled him to have the sun at his back when he entered Yamato.

Just before he ascended to the the position of emperor, Jinmu is said to have expressed his wish to work for the well-being of his subjects and revere the kami and ancestors and repay their kindness. Moreover, he was also said to hope for the cultivation of the correct mind and to create a harmonious world where everyone lived in peace as one family. Jinmu's words were distilled in the idealized concept of Hakkō ichiu," or "all the world under one roof."

Amaterasu-o-mikami: The Sun Goddess

Ameterasu-o-mikami is a female kami that sits at the apex of the 8 million kami worshiped in the Shinto religion. The male kami Izanagi performed a cleansing rite after returning from the hellish underworld in an unsuccessful attempt to bring back his wife Izanami. In doing so, he begat Amaterasu-o-mikami from the light of his left eye. The name Amaterasu-o-mikami symbolizes her being the sun that sustains all life. Such sun worship can be found throughout the world. From ancient times in Japan, *"hi no kami* (sun deities)" had been worshiped. Amaterasu-o-mikami originated from such ancient sun worship. However, in the case of Japan, Amaterasu-o-mikami retains the ancient religious legacy of sun worship along with the belief that she is the ancestor of a particular race of people.

Associated with Amaterasu-o-mikami is the famous myth of Ama-no-iwato-kakure (The Cave of Amaterasu-o-mikami). Because Amaterasu-o-mikami hid in a cave, the world lost its light, resulting in the proliferation of evil spirits and disasters. This mythical account no doubt symbolizes crop failure and the weakening of life force that come about from the shortening of the duration of sunlight in a day. These things further result in malnutrition, sickness, and starvation. The "hiding of the sun" could also be related to the memory of past ice ages that ancient people carried with them. It is probable that humans and religious ceremonies to plead for the reappearance of the sun. Such ceremonies that were based on the idea of the sun's "death and rebirth" of agricultural people were reflected in Ama-no-iwato-kakure. Consequently, Amaterasu-o-mikami could be seen as a mother deity that personified the fertility of the earth.

However, Amaterasu-o-mikami also had a male aspect. A scene in the myth where Amaterasu-o-mikami gallantly carries arms symbolizes this. Susano-no-mikoto, who had been wreaking havoc on earth, visited Takamagahara (where the *kami* reside). Amaterasu-o-mikami sensed that Susano-no-mikoto was coming to usurp her rule over Takamagahara and quickly armed herself. She first arranged her hair in the *mizura* hairstyle that males wore at the time and wrapped 500 stringed *magatama* (comma-shaped beads) around her hands and hair. She then put a quiver of 1,000 arrows on her back and another quiver of 500 arrows on her waist and took a very strong bow in her hand. Dressed for battle, she stomped on the earth until her feet sank into the soil as a strong warning to Susano-no-mikoto. Bows and arrows were weapons that symbolized military strength in ancient times. One could also say that in her full armed regalia, Amaterasu-o-mikami was a *kami* that symbolized military strength. Military strength was equal to the ability to protect national territory. Consequently, in the context of Amaterasu-o-mikami being revered as ancestral kami of the imperial line is the strong reliance on military strength.

In summary, Amaterasu-o-mikami has overlapping characteristics as a female mother of the earth and sun goddess and a male representation of military strength. That is the reason why she was able to push aside the multitude of other male *kami* to emerge as the supreme *kami* in Japan as well as the embodiment of the Shinto value of *makoto*.

Buddhism

A proficient martial artist serious about personal development cannot ignore the spiritual training offered by the teaching of Buddhism in Japan. Buddhism is the teaching of Sakyamuni who was born a prince of the Sakya Clan near the border between India and Nepal sometime in 400 or 500 B.C. As a youth Sakyamuni developed a greatly moved by the innate human suffering of birth, aging, sickness, and death. As a consequence, he left his privileged lifestyle and spent six years as an ascetic. After six years, he became known as the Buddha or "Awakened One." Thereafter, he began teaching the path to enlightenment, which anyone could attain. At the time, Japan was still in the Jomon Period where people lived in pit-style houses and engaged in hunting and gathering. Sakyamuni taught for 45 years and died at the age of 80. After his death, his disciples spread Buddhism throughout India. Around 270 B.C., Buddhism spread rapidly with the support of Ashoka, who assumed the position of Emperor of the Mauryan Empire in India. Thereafter, Buddhism traveled the Silk Road and eventually reached Japan via Kudara (Baekje) on the Korean Peninsula in 538 A.D. (or 552 A.D. according to another theory).

Important in Buddhist philosophy is the concept of *mu* or "nothingness." A samurai leaving for the battlefield had to come to terms with his possible impending death. Just what was on the minds of people who were in such extreme situations? Warrior generals made themselves into "nothingness." That is, they faced battle with a sense of *muga* or "selflessness" or "an absence of self." *Muga* was a concept informed by Buddhist philosophy.

Muga is truly an intriguing concept. We normally think that our own happiness is dependent the relationship between others and ourselves. However, *muga* entails a seemingly counterintuitive logic that says that our own happiness comes from forgetting ourselves and seeking the happiness of others. This in turn is based on the logic of interdependence where the existence of "self" and that of "other" are codetermined.

There is the expression of *meikyoushisui* or "as clear as an unclouded mirror or absolutely still water." For example, if there was absolutely no wind disturbing the water in a pond, a pagoda would be clearly reflected on it. However, at the moment that even a gentle breeze blowing over the pond, ripples on the surface of the pond would distort the image of the pagoda. When we look at things with a *meikyoushisui* mind, we are able to perceive see those things accurately, but if we regretfully let our "self" into the act of looking at things, it is like letting a wind blow over the surface of a pond, rendering it impossible to see things as they actually are.

Buddhism emphasizes emptiness in such words as, "*shiki fu i ku, ku fu i shiki, shiki soku ze ku, ku soku ze shiki* (Form is not different than emptiness; Emptiness is not different from Form. Indeed, form is emptiness; Emptiness is form)." In other words, Buddhism teaches us to not have attachments to any phenomenon because all phenomena are interdependent in existence. It also went further with the development of the concept of *mu*, wherein one would not have an attachment to a thing if he or she did not believe it existed. Buddhism even teaches that we should not even have attachments to the concepts of existence and non-existence. In this way, if one is awakened to the face that everything is empty (*ku*) and nothingness (*mu*), then he or she can go to war without fear of death.

Buddha changed the contents of his teachings depending on whom he was teaching to. There are said to be 84,000 teachings in Buddhism and if one were asked what the fundamental core of those teachings was, it would be difficult to answer succinctly. Consequently, from ancient times, Buddhism teachings have been organized into three (or four precepts depending on the tradition).

The precept of impermanence means that all things do not remain the same. This is especially so for humans, who age, get sick, and die. This is a fact that we humans must confront whether or not we like it. It is because of impermanence that one must diligently apply his or her mind to the way of Buddha

The precept of no self refers to the absence of any fixed or real essence of all things. It is because we believe that there is an essence of ourselves that a consciousness of "I" or "my" emerges to captivate our thoughts.

The precept of suffering points to the fact that this world of reincarnation and life itself is full of suffering. The sufferings that we experience are referred to as the Eight Sufferings.

The Suffering of Birth & Living: We suffer from our human birth.

Suffering of Aging: We suffer because we cannot become younger.

Suffering of Sickness: We suffer when we get sick.

Suffering of Death: We suffer from the inevitability of death.

To the above sufferings are four more:

Suffering of Parting: We suffer from the inescapable truth of having to part from people that are dear to us.

Suffering of Encountering What We Dislike: We suffer from having to meet people we do not like.

Suffering of Not Getting What We Want: We suffer because we cannot always get what we want.

Suffering of Our Own Existence: Generally, this means that we suffer from the existence of our physical body (or the Five Aggregates of Body, Consciousness, Perception, Sensation, and Reaction)

When Buddha reached enlightenment, he discovered certain truths that he taught as the Four Noble Truths, which are:

The Truth of Suffering: This is described by The Eight Sufferings

The Truth of Causes and Conditions: All suffering has the proper causes and conditions. The causes and conditions of suffering are the attachment that sentient beings have to things in this world.

The Truth of Cessation: If attachments or ignorance are eliminated, then suffering ceases

The Truth of the Path: There is a path and way to get rid off the attachments and ignorance that cause suffering. This path is known as the Eightfold Noble Path which includes the following:

1 Right View

2 Right Intention

3 Right Speech

4 Right Actions

5 Right Livelihood

6 Right Effort

7 Right Mindfulness

8 Right Concentration

In each case, one takes the "middle path" that avoids extremes. If one takes this Eightfold Noble Path, one will without fail reach a point of freedom from suffering or what is known as *nirvana*. Samurai relied on the Buddhist teachings of seeking *nirvana (peace of mind)* as part of their martial arts spiritual training as they prepared for battle.

From ancient times, Buddhism emphasized training in the sutras or doctrinal teachings (経), reason (論), discipline (律), and meditation (禅). However, in terms of the order in which these aspects of training appear, meditation could come first, followed by sutras, reason, and discipline. In terms of karate, training parallels meditation, kata parallels the sutras, *kumite* parallels reason, and *dan* (degree) ranking parallels discipline. Meditation and order pertain to actions, while the sutras and reasoning pertain to the written word. Because etiquette and manners are actions that represent the order of one's mind, they can be included as part of meditation (禅)。

Confucianism

Another important spiritual pillar for samurai following the warrior path was Confucianism. The founder of Confucianism, Confucius (551-479 B.C.), inherited the ideology of reverence for Heaven and its mandate and of respect for the ways of righteous "past kings." He made his mark in history as a great philosopher who revived propriety and music in ancient Zhou China. The core of his teachings includes:

1. Reverence for Heaven: This aspect of Confucian thought is based on the belief that the origin of all things is Heaven and that Shangdi (天帝) or creator deity should be held in awe.
2. Mandate of Heaven: All people were created by Heaven and governance should be carried out by a virtuous Emperor who has inherited the Mandate of Heaven.
3. The Way of Past Kings: Rulers should follow a virtuous path of governance.

Confucius created an ethical perspective based on human subjectivity and saw "benevolence (仁) Chinese: *ren*/Japanese: *jin*" as conceptualization of the moral aspects of universal human emotions. While he believed that "proper rites (礼) Chinese: *ri*/Japanese: *rei*" were necessary for the purpose of regulating human behavior externally, Confucius simultaneously advocated for virtuous governance as his political philosophy. In insisting that a ruler be paragon of moral virtue, he combined ethics with governance. Confucius' scholarly goal was to create an ethically superior society by calling for the ethical perfection of one's self as well as for working on the ethical perfection of others. He called the highest goal of individual and societal ethical perfection "sageliness (聖) Chinese: *sheng*/Japanese: *sei*." He referred to people who reached virtuous perfection as a "sages (聖人) Chinese: *shengren*/Japanese: *seijin*." In order to reach such a stage, a person needed to also possess "knowledge(知) Chinese: *zhi*/Japanese: *chi*" and "bravery (勇) Chinese: *yong*/Japanese: *yū*" along with benevolence.

However, benevolence was the core of Confucius' philosophy. The concept referred to the familiarity or closeness between humans and to the warm feelings that a person had for others. Proper rites form the basic standards for benevolence: it is through carrying out of proper rites that benevolence is realized. Further, all things in the universe originate from "Heaven (天) Chinese: *tian*/Japanese: *ten*," which has a foundational existence and maintains constant law and order. It follows humans are given autonomy and souls by Heaven and given the blessings of "Earth (大地) Chinese: *dadi*/Japanese: *daichi*." Heaven is the father, while Earth is the mother. As humans, we should learn from ways of Heaven and Earth to maintain their principles while respecting benevolence, righteousness (義) Chinese: *yi*/Japanese: *gi*), loyalty (忠) Chinese: *zhong*/Japanese *chū*), and filial piety (孝) Chinese: *xiao*/Japanese: *kō*) through holding on to virtue (德) Chinese: *de*/Japanese: *toku*) and returning kindness (恩) Chinese: *en*/Japanese: *on*) to others. This was the path to developing and improving oneself as an individual. The actual practice of morals and ethics centered around the relation between Heaven and humans was seen as the way to achieve peace. Confucius taught that "Harmony attained, Heaven and Earth align, all things are refined."

Confucius took the existing shamanistic beliefs of his time and synthesized them into a single moral and religious system devoted to upholding "virtue" and founded solidly on "benevolence" and its various aspects. However, we cannot forget that traditional Chinese ancestor worship is also at the core of Confucian morals. As such, Confucianism is characterized by both its humanitarian emphasis on "benevolence" and a status system that is rooted in male patriarchy.

While Confucius hoped that his philosophies would be adopted in the actual practices of governance, he was never able to see that happen. It was only through the later work of Mencius and other followers that support for his ideas grew and managed to be adopted during the Han Dynasty. Confucianism was a philosophy and set of morals and was largely void of any religious nature or as Confucius himself asserted, "A man of high virtue speaks not of monsters, deities, and divine powers." In later ages, however, Confucianism took on religious aspects as Confucius and other sages were worshiped through ceremonies. In the present, Confucianism remains as a dominant belief system for Chinese that prescribes ideal morals and social structure.

With the spread of Confucian thought through the work of Mencius and others, it became popular in governance during the Han Period. It was around that time that reading and studying Confucian classics began. Interpretations of Confucian classics were unified during the Tang Period. In the Sung Period, Neo-Confucianism developed as Zhu Xi reformed Confucianism in resistance to the influence of Buddhist thought. Wang Yangming emphasized putting Confucianism into actual practice and his philosophy, the Yangming School, developed during the Ming Period.

Confucianism reached Japan around the 5th century and influenced governance and society after it did. It reached the peak of its influence in the Edo Period (1603-1868). Fujiwara Seika and his student Hayashi Razan, were important officials under Tokugawa Ieyasu and scholars of the Neo-Confucianism. Consequently, Neo-Confucianism became integral to Japan's feudal structure as it spread among officials in the Tokugawa *bakufu* (military government) and to various feudal domains throughout Japan. During the Edo Period, many Confucian scholars engaged in vigorous debate. For example, Yangming scholars such as Nakae Tōju and Kumazawa Banzan as well as Kogaku (Ancient Learning) scholars such as Itō Jinsai developed a critique of the prevailing Neo-Confucianism.

Zen Buddhism

Zen Buddhism was brought from India to China by Bodhidharma who was said to be the 28th Patriarch of Buddhism in a line that went back to Gautama Buddha. It also known as Busshinshū, Darumashū and Ryōgshū. The *zen* that Bodhidharma taught is part of Mahayana Buddhist tradition and is not connected to similar schools that were part the Early Buddhist schools. It has further been given such names as Nyorai *zen* and Nyorai Seijo *zen*. The Indian term "diyana" was Sinicized as "zenna" and "zen."

The two *zen* traditions that were established in Japan during the Kamakura Period were the Rinzai and Sōchools. The Rinzai school traces its roots to the Linji school in China which was founded by Linji Yixuan (Japanese: Rinzi Gigen). Eisai brought Rinzai teachings to Japan from Sung China (1141-1215). The Japanese term *"zen"* originates from the Chinese *"chan,"* which itself is a derivative of the Indian practice of "Dhyana" or meditation. The goal of sitting meditation was to clearly observe one's self and reach enlightenment. Enlightenment cannot be conveyed in words is transmitted from master to disciple directly through the mind. Further, from ancient times, *zen* monks who attained enlightenment left behind somewhat mysterious dialectic riddles. These riddles, known as *"koan,"* were later adopted by *zen* scholars as ways to deepen their own training.

The expressions of reverence to the *"kamidana"* altar at martial arts *dojo* as well as the various forms of etiquette that involve showing respect towards one's master and other students and to the dojo as one enters and leaves all have their origins in *zendojo*. In the *zendojo*, training included not only sitting meditation, but a variety of routines that were carried out from the moment that a practitioner woke up to the moment he went to bed.

Taoism

Taoism is one of the three major religions of China (Confucianism, Buddhism and Taoism). Taoism is also referred to as Tao-ka (Taoist) and Tao-gaku (study of Taoism). Tao is an aboriginal and traditional religion of the Han Chinese people of which ultimate purpose is to become an immortal hermit, who endeavor to become integral with the eternal world of truth of the universe and human life by performing alchemy to produce and consume elixir of life. It is mostly uncertain how this philosophic with its religious element came into being. However, belief of Taoism is deeply rooted among Chinese population in Taiwan and Southeastern Asia. The concept of Tao made a significant impact on the Western philosophers in the late 20th century.

Taoism originated based on the ancient Chinese shamanism or *kidō* (literally, ogre's way). Additionally, Taoism must have multilayeredly and complexly incorporated the Mohist creed of *jōtei-kishin* (God in the heaven and the ogres below judging the people); the philosophy of Shintoism and ceremonial rites of Confucianism; teachings of Laozi and Zhuangzi on metaphysics of *gen* (origin of all matters) and *shin* (truth); the beliefs of Chinese Buddhism such as *gyōhō-rinne* (transmigration of soul is decided upon one's doing in life) and the doctrines and rites for emancipation from worldly attachments and enlightenment of the masses; and so forth. Taoism was established during Sui, Tang and Godai periods as a religious organization with its rites and doctrines.

In the broad sense, Taoism was purported as "teachings of saint" in which description also included Confucianism and Buddhism. The narrower description is "the teachings of Laozi and Zhuangzi about the Way."

During the Song dynasty, *naitan-jutsu* (or Neiden, to generate life elixir by circulating *ki* energy throughout the body by certain breathing technique) and *rendo* (level of mastery of *naitan-jutsu*) were actively practiced, and Taoism underwent a drastic transformation.

Taoism was introduced in Ryukyu. During the year 1430, one year after overthrowing the Nanzan (the Southern state of Ryukyu), the king Shō Hashi sent official envoys four times to pay tribute to the Ming Dynasty and was conventionally responded with gifts; for this year, it was 21,760 silver money. Also, the Ryukyuan historical account *Kyūyō* mentions that this was the same year when Saizan, who was sent as an envoy, funded to build a Daian Zenji temple in Ryukyu. The location of the temple is no longer recorded, but it's made known that the king Shō Taikyū made and placed a temple bell at the temple. Also, an official report was made by Kashiyō, a senior envoy from the dynasty, around the end of the era including two sections about Saizen's stone inscriptional record.

In the first part of the Saizan's stone inscription, it writes that, in 1430, Saizan risked his life to come all the way to the far land of Ryukyu. After several days from departure into the journey, the party faced a storm, which stopped mysteriously after Saizan saw a spark with size of a star shined just above the mast. As a faithful worshipper, Saizan was deeply thankful to the bless of Gods and protection by heavenly beings for letting them arrive safely at Ryukyu, and he built a temple so that the people of Ryukyu that is in the vicinity of his home nation of Buddhism can also revere the heavenly light.

Described in the second part that, as Saizen felt indebted to Gods of land and heaven for being able to safely travel again to Ryukyu, he remediated the palace that was built in his previous stay and added a garden pond and newly built a shrine named Dainan Senbutsu Reikaku (or Daian Senbukkaku) in the south of the palace. The building is referred in the first section as a Buddhist temple and a palace in the second section, but they refer to the same building that was purported to enshrine the Gods and Buddha. This temple shouldn't be considered as a Zen Buddhist temple even though it is mentioned in *Kyūyō* as "Daian Zenji."

When the Gods are mentioned in the accounts, they mean Dragon Gods or Water/Sea Gods. It's the same Dragon Gods that was in a poem,

"Mighty eight Dragon Kings, please halt the rain." With this evidence, I can confirm that Saizen's religious belief was Taoism.

The history of Ryukyuan's religious beliefs and local education system can't be explained without taking Taoism into the consideration. And for that, I will talk more in details about the construction of the Daian Senbutsu Reikaku of Saizen.

Taoism was established around the 3rd century around the end of the Latter Han Dynasty as a collection of various beliefs and religious practices such as the ancient Chinese teachings of nature and animal worshiping, incantations, the supernatural arts of hermit, etc. with the ancient philosopher Laozi's teachings at its core. The teachings of Buddhism was later incorporated as it became more popular. In the beginning of the Northern Wei Dynasty, Kou Qianzhi organized Taoism as an established religion, and it was treated as the nation religion. The ultimate goal of its teachings was to cultivate one's mind in order to surpass covetousness, to be able to foresee calamity, and to become immortal. During the Tang Dynasty around the 7th and 8th centuries was when Buddhism became widely popular; Japanese ascetics Kūkai and Saichō visited the nation to learn the teachings of Buddhism during this period; however, Taoism was similarly popular among its population. Because the founder figure of Taoism Laozi's family name was from the Tang Dynasty, he was considered as an ancestor from the dynasty, and his Taoism was treated as the nation religion for some time. Taoism was so popular that Laozi's text, *Tao Te Ching*, was some point a subject of the promotion examination for public servants.

The text has been read until today by the Han people to engage in religious practices and to learn moral teachings, and Ryukyuan people also had been influenced by it for a long time. Dainan Senbutsu Reikaku must have made a significant impact in Ryukyu, which had been unified as one nation just recently, in Saizen's policy aiming to lead and educate the indigenous population by showing how to choose the location and decide the spatial arrangement and orientation of the building; architectural methods; and so forth. Now we should rewind back the history and talk about *Tenpigū* temple located in Naha city that is considered to be the first Taoist temple in Okinawa and is thought to be built on the third year of Shō Hashi's accession to the throne. There are two Tenpigū in Naha; one is *Ue-tenpigū* (upper tempigū temple) and another is *Shimo-tenpigū* (lower tempigū temple). It is conceived that Shimo-tenpigū was built before Ue-tenpigū. The year of construction for Shimo-tenpigū had been unknown for a long time until a marking "built in the Eiraku 22 (The Eiraku 22 of the emperor Seiso of the Ming Dynasty is the year of 1424)" was found on one of the inner plates of the altar in the building. I can trust that this is a trustworthy fact since it is written in the Ryukyuan regional geography account *Ryukyu-koku Yurai-ki* (edited by the Ryukyu Dynasty in 1713).

However, we are still left with some uncertainties whether this is the actual year of construction since the only evidence is the writing on an inner plate of an altar that can't be specified if it indicated the year of construction or the plate was added on a later year. Therefore, there is a possibility of the temple being built even further back.

As Tenpigū is located in the Kume village where descendants of Kume Sanjūrokusei (group of professionals from the current Fujian province who were bestowed to Ryukyu by the Ming Dynasty) resided, and as recorded in the geographical record *Tōei Kyūki Zenshū* (old records of Kume village), it is obvious that Tenpigū was first worshiped by the people of Kume village. For that reason, there is a possibility that Tenpigū was built by the Kume Sanjūrokusei who moved to Ryukyu in during the reign of the king Satto. Even if it wasn't built during that time, it must have been built by their descendants, so it can be concluded that Shimo-tenpigū was built between 1392 and 1424.

Ue-tenpigū being built after Shimo-tenpigū is evident from the record made by an envoy from the Ming Dynasty, saying "catching the tide to the East to an island, the new palace of *tempi* is located after some walk up the mountain," that Ue-tenpigū is called the new building and is distinguished from the Shimo-tenpigū. According to the *Ryukyu-koku Yurai-ki,* Ue-tempigū was built between the years 1426 and 1499.

The Bell of Bankokushinryou

Ryukyu Shinto

There is a belief that the land and people of Ryukyu were created by the Sun-God; it can be witnessed in a song titled "*Mukashi hajimekara no fushi* (story of the beginning in the ancient times)" as second poem in the tenth volume of the *Omoro Sōshi.*

> Far in the ancient time,
> In the beginning of land and heaven,
> The great Sun-God shining down beautifully,
> Far in the ancient time,
> In the beginning of land and heaven,
> The Sun-God,
> The Sun-God,

Looking down far below on the earth,

Looking down far below on the earth,

Telling Amamikiyo,

Telling Shinerikiyo,

To build islands,

To build nations.

Many islands were built,

Many nations were built.

Until the islands were built,

Until the nations were built,

The Sun-God waited impatiently,

The Sun-God waited impatiently.

When islands and nations were built,

Told Amamikiyo to give birth to children,

Told Shinerikiyo to give birth to children,

To give birth to children of the God.

"Ama" of *Amamikiyo* signifies heaven, *"mi"* means "of", and *"kiyo"* means human. Therefore, *amamikiyo* is a heavenly being that came from the heaven to the island of Okinawa. The oldest ancestor of Ryukyuans is *amamikiyo*, and its people are thought to be descendants of the heavenly being.

Shinerikiyo is also referred to as *Neriya-no-hito* (human being from *neriya*). *Neriya* is also referred as *Nirai-kanai*, which is the utopia that exists beyond sea horizon. This idea of the universe with three dimensions consisting of the heaven, the land and the utopia was established in Ryukyu. More specifically, it were the Sun-God; the land created by the Sun-God and its people (children of *Amamikiyo* and *Shinerikiyo* or descendants of the God), and the utopia *Nirai-kanai*.

Amamikiyo gave birth to five children of three males and two females. They were the five beginnings: the ruler, the feudal lord, the farmer, the priestess and the ceremony. The beginning of ruler was the Tenson clan, the first lineage of ruler in Ryukyu; the feudal lord was *aji*; the farmer was common people; the priestess was the priestess of the highest rank; and the ceremony was all other priestesses. Worshipping of *Amamikiyo* and *Shinerikiyo* and of *Āmanchū* was first rooted among commoners and became the foundation of Ryukyu Shinto, and it eventually became the religion of the Ryukyu nation.

The Tenson clan of the five beginnings established the Tensonshi Dynasty that lasted 25 generations from the 4th to 12th centuries.

It was approximately between 365 A.D. and 1186 A.D. The Tensonshi Dynasty was succeeded by three generations of Shunten Dynasty (1187-1259), five generations of Eiso Dynasty (1260-1349), two generations of Satto dynasty (1350-1405), seven generations of the first Shōshi dynasty (1406-1469), and nineteen generations of the second Shōshi dynasty (1470-1879). The Ryukyu Dynasty lasted for 1,500 years until it was dissolved by an edict issued by the Japanese government in 1879. After many generations, Ryukyu became Okinawa prefecture of Japan.

On the other hand, the mainland Japan has been continuing the emperor (tennō) system for 2,665 years since the first emperor Kanmu (660 B.C. to 585 B.C.) to the current emperor Kinjō (1989~).

I have talked about religions and beliefs that influenced the principles of budō, or martial arts: Japanese Shinto, Buddhism, Confucianism, Zen Buddhism, Taoism, and Ryukyu Shinto. The foundation of martial arts was influenced uniquely by such religious practices and beliefs. Now, when did the term "budō" first appear? The oldest document that indicated the term was in the historical account, *Azuma Kagami* (1195), saying "A monk Kumagai Jirō Naozane visited from Kyoto. Since he quit practicing budō and took tonsure to seek for enlightenment, he wholeheartedly seeded for the pure land of Amitabha, and eventually, he disappeared into the Tōsan region." This is to mention his parting from martial art and delving into the Way of Buddhism. In the Kamakura period, the term is mentioned in the treatise *Taiheiki* that "As I assumed the position as the Shogun, I shall follow the Way of budō." Here, "budō" is used to assert that budō is the Way for the ruler and for *bushi* to obey. Furthermore, the term can be seen in *Heike Monogatari* (*"Tale of Taira Clan"*) that "budō is for a man of bravery and righteousness."

During the Edo period, the term "budō" was mentioned in various martial art treatises. It can be seen in the text of Takenouchi-ryū from 1641, *Torite Koshi no Mawari no Koto* (the techniques of capturing and restraining), suggesting to devote to budō as "These techniques are 25 *kogusoku koshinomawari,* or dagger techniques, and 5 arrest techniques. My father devoted himself to various types of *budo* from his early childhood." However, the term "budō" wasn't yet commonly used to refer to war strategies and martial techniques/arts in the Edo period to; rather, it was used similarly with bushidō and *shidō* that meant the *bushi*'s Way, or the principles. It was the principles for disciples of martial techniques or the way of life for *bushi*. This type of "budō" was constituent of concepts like "to die without regret", "to act on sincerity," and "to live for loyalty." Namely, this was the "modern budō."

In contrary, for the Contemporary Budō, even though its core is the concept of the Ancient Budō that emphasized loyalty and sincerity, it doesn't focus on fighting in battles and wars but to build a mature personality and to strengthen body and mind through training. Kanō Jigorō of Kodokan Judo Institute was who purposefully converted the term *bujutsu* (martial techniques) to *budō* (martial arts). Incidentally, he was one of the pioneers who established the concept of the "Contemporary Budō." Kanō was born in 1860 in Hyogo prefecture. Losing his mother at the age of 11, he moved to Tokyo with his father. He started learning English, German and Dutch under private teachers when he was 11 years old, graduated from the English school when he was 16, graduated from Tokyo Imperial University at 22, and founded Kodokan at the age of 24. Kanō was employed by Department of Imperial Household at 25 and became an assistant to professor of Gakushuin University. He was a public officer and also a teacher at the school that was associated with the Ministry of Education. Kanō's innate talent and favorable surrounding environment created the Kodokan Judo Institute.

Kanō mentions in his book titled "Kanō Jigorō" that "I used to be very hotheaded, but as my physical health was improved through practicing jūdō, my mental state gradually became calm and I realized how I could better control my emotions." He felt that many logics learned from competition of jūdō was widely useful in life, and the intellectual learnings that was part of training were universal knowledge that could be applied to any matters. Then he firmly believed that jūdō was not only to learn martial techniques but entails important learnings in intellectual, physical and moral aspects. He started learning jūdō from Fukuda Hachinosuke and Iso Masatomo of Tenjin Shin'yō-ryu in 1877 at the age of 18, and from the age 22, he learned from Iikubo Tsunetoshi of Kitō-ryu. He mentions that "as I learned from two schools of jūdō, Tenjin Shin'yō-ryu and Kitō-ryu, I realized that I couldn't learn entirety of jūdō from one school. Rather I believe that one should learn from more schools and masters to strive achieving the ultimate purpose of martial techniques and to be initiatively familiar with intellectual, moral and physical learnings. I believe jūdō is a good way." He asserted the importance of learning from different schools and that jūdō was a good way to train the intellectual, moral and physical learnings. And he wasn't to keep such an important lessons to himself but was determined to spread the teachings to all over the country.

Kanō explained why he changed the term from *jūjutsu* to *jūdō*. "After a deep contemplation, I realized that there is an underlying Way for *jujutsu*, and *jutsu* (techniques) is application of its fundamental principle. Therefore, it should be appropriate to teach the Way first, then teach the techniques as application of the Way. Therefore, I wanted to change the name completely, but I was originally able to reach my level because I was taught from my masters under this martial technique, jūjutsu, so I thought changing the name completely will be against my true intention. So I kept the word *jū,* and named it jūdō." Kanō believed that it's better and important to learn first from theory, or the Way, to understand the fundamental mentality before learning the techniques.

From the Meiji period, the term "budō" came in the spotlight again as the nationalism was exalted after the victories of the Sino-Japanese War and the Russo-Japanese War. The strategy of close combat came to the fore supported by the idea that the war victory against Russia that had superior machines and manpower was attained by the strong mentality. Accordingly, cultivation of aggressive mentality through training of martial techniques was strongly encouraged. Abovementioned mentality of aggressiveness such as "*bu* (the art of war) is to advance forward unstoppably with a spear in hands" became the zeitgeist of the time.

In concert with such a situation, Nishikubo Hiromitsu, the superintendent general of the time, asserted that "there should be an appropriate name that is in conformity with the true purpose of martial arts. Training of martial arts should be treated as a sacred act and shouldn't be trespassed on. Training session should be treated as if attending a school lecture on ethics." He also asserted that the term must be *budō* (martial art) instead of *bujyutu* (martial technique) in order to make sure that courtesy isn't ignored during training. Training must contain more than mere learning of techniques.

In January 1919, Nishikubo, as he assumed the position as the vice-president of the Dai Nippon Butoku Association and the principal of its technical college, Bujutsu Senmon Gakkō, changed the school name to Budō Senmon Gakkō and put much effort into shifting the terms *būjyutu* (self-defense technique), *Gekigen* (sword technique), and *Kyūjutsu* (archery) into *Jūdō*, *Kendō* and *Kyudō*, respectively.

The problem was that "budō" was used as a mean to promulgate the imperial government's policy whereas the original purpose of budō was to cultivate one's personality and to inherit the techniques; and the techniques were the self-defense techniques. Training of budō was exploited to exalt the "Yamato spirit" and aggressive mentality. The Yamato spirit, which was to cultivate "the determined mind that stays exalted until one's purpose is accomplished," was linked with the fundamental war mentality of "dying gracefully with no regret," and the imperial government saw budō as a useful device to cultivate nationalistic personality in each individual citizen. Budō was used as such a device to develop human resources under the general mobilization order, and the Yamato spirit mentality was treated as the first principle of national defense.

Budō of which original purpose was to delve into and refine oneself was so easily associated with the nationalistic ideal; it was perhaps because the solitary nature of its practice made the sense of relationship with other people pale. Practice of budō should begin with delving into one's deep consciousness and should stay consistently throughout within "Self", and it should never be linked with any national identity.

Section 4. Bushidō

Mentality and morality of Japanese people are directly and indirectly a product of Bushidō. The Way of *bushi*, or samurai, became the proper way of being a Japanese. The folk song of "flower is cherry blossom and person is *bushi*" prevailed far and wide in the nation. Incidentally, Bushidō was the Way to be achieved by *bushi*, but what does the term *bushi* truly mean?

When you think of a *bushi*, you may imagine a manly samurai wearing a topknot and carrying swords at his side. However, the history of *bushi* dates back even further. In the olden times, the people that were originally called *bushi* lived on the countryside far away from large cities; they were unsophisticated and simple with austerity and fortitude. They lived from hand to mouth. Their world was contained within conflicts in and between small villages, and their battles were never any larger. However, it gradually expanded; militant groups, which were organized spontaneously for naturally occurring incidents in communities, were transformed into larger organizations with political authority. Such organizations were managed by their own chiefs. This happened in the same nature as *aji* (or *anji*) of Ryukyu Kingdom. Then those *bushi* organizations started serving the Courts, royal families, regents, temples, and so forth, and with that, they gained a higher political status. *Bushi*, who were fighting for a village against another village, changed their battle grounds to political disputes between nations. By then, the highest authority that employed *bushi* was not *bushi* chiefs; they were employed by court nobles or the shogunate. The situation for *bushi* evolved as the time progressed; for instance, there was *mononofu* and *masurao*, who were government officials serving the Court; groups of *bushi*, who protected court nobles and manors of large temples; *gokenin-bushi* (retainers), who swore their allegiance to the shogun of the Kamakura shogunate in exchange for territorial rights; *sengoku-bushi* (warlords), who, without their own land, strived to reign over the whole nation; and modern *bushi*, who pledged their loyalty to the nation order. Evidently, *bushi*'s position and ideals shifted from time to time. Similarly, Bushidō was transformed from "Ancient Bushidō," "Medieval Bushidō" to "Modern Bushidō".

Ancient Bushidō

If *bushi* existed in the ancient times, *mononofu* would be the equivalent. *"Mono"* of *mononofu* has the same meaning as *"mono"* of *mono-no-gu* (men equipped with weapons) and *mono-gashira* (a military commander); *mono* referred to a weapon. Also, *"fu"* of *mononofu* could be interpreted as "a man," so mononofu could mean a man with a weapon, or a warrior. The term *"takeo"* had a similar meaning. It meant a gallant warrior. Similarly, in a treatise *Kojiki, takeshi* is referred to as a warrior, evidently, those terms meant a *bushi*.

I suggest that it's correct that *mono* of *mononofu* meant objects such as tools, weapons or armors and also warriors. Also, another theory is that the term was derived from the clan Momonobe. It is subsumed that a noun *mononofu* was formed by converting the family name Mononobe. "Be" of

Mononobe meant "a group of people." There is a possibility that the family name Mononobe was also called mononofu-be; all the more, the term *mononofu* should be explained along with the Mononobe clan.

How could it be possible that the name of a clan, Mononobe, became the term to call warriors in general while there were other clans as powerful as the Mononobe clan such as the Ōtomo clan? If the term *mononofu* was derived from the Mononobe, what was the reason for Mononobe clan to be chosen to be respectively called *mononofu*? It was strongly associated with the fact that the Mononobe clan was the protector of Isonokami-jingū Shrine, an arsenal of the Yamato Dynasty. A sacred sword of the dynasty, *furu-no-mitama-no-tsurugi*, was treasured at the arsenal. One possibility is that the Mononobe clan became the representative of all *mononofu* as the protector of the sacred sword and eventually was called *mononofu-be*.

Written in the poetry treatise *Yakumo-misho* is that "Mononofu are men of bravely. They are people of a faraway land. There is a deep mountain in Mutsu and Deba areas. Walking through the mountain isn't an easy task. They break tree branches along the way. That is to mark their way back. They are from a unpopulated land in the direction of Deba region."

According to a theory, "*mono*" of *mononofu* meant an object, but instead of a mere object, it was an object residing a spirit of God. And "*fu*" of *mononofu* signified "man of" or "servant of," meaning a person. Therefore, *mononofu* signified "a person with an object with spirit of God," in other words, a brave warrior, a person or an officer with a job as a warrior. "People of a faraway land" means that, in the ancient times, the degree of civilization depended on the distance from the capital city; therefore, the farther it was from the capital, it was less civilized and rural. The far land was the Michinoku region, or the nation of Ezo. Here, "people from the far land" can be presumed to be the country *bushi* from the Michinoku region.

The history of ancient *mononofu* started with the *bushi* class from the far East of the capital in the countryside, who gradually became powerful and eventually reached the medieval *bushi* class. The process of the transformation into the medieval Japan entailed the shift of the locations where historical events took place; it shifted from the capital to the countryside. The transformation of social class from the ancient times to the medieval era was caused by the *bushi* from rural areas in the far East taking over the status of court nobles of the capital city. The Way of the ancient bushidō was born between the cultures of countryside as mother and the bravery of *mononofu* as father.

Another term that should be mentioned is *"masurao."* It meant a strong brave man, and it's conceived to be another way of referring to a *bushi*; in *Manyōshū*, *masurao* is mentioned along with *mononofu*.

However, does that mean the Way of masurao is interchangeable with the Way of mononofu? It's not so. These two Ways both represented the same mannish characteristics but from different angles. What I mean by the same mannish characteristics is that they both indicate brave and manly qualities; a masurao is a strong, brave and young man, and a mononofu is a brave soldier. However, masurao can become mononofu only when it reaches the level of takeo as it can be mentioned as masura takeo. Conclusively, it can be said that, before that certain level, masurao referred to general bravely that isn't yet at the level of mononofu.

Mononofu was the ideal form of a warrior that was escalated from *masurao*. As read in poems as "*mononofu yaso uchibito* (many brave soldiers)" and "*mononofu yaso tomonowo* (many brave men with weapons)," *mononofu* became the true representative of nationalistic and brave warrior with ideal qualities. The reason for the lineage of *bushi* clans related to *masurao* to be broad and the clans related *mononofu* to be limited can be explained with the above reason.

Despite their differences, there is a commonality between *masurao* and *mononofu*; they are both ethical perspectives founded on principles of ancient officials. The Way of *masurao* was principles for officers in general, and the Way of *mononofu* was principles for military officers; it can be surmised that it was just a difference in focal point. Either way, *masurao* emphasized to also have qualities of *mononofu*, and vice versa. They are in a relation to complement each other.

Mononofu was not the only "Way" of ancient bushidō; the Way of *masurao* was also a form of the ancient bushidō. It's not the question about which Way, either *mononofu* or *masurao,* was the proper Way of ancient bushidō. Further, the Way of *mononofu* can't be referred generally as "bushidō", it is the "Ancient Bushidō", and the Way of *masurao* has a significant meaning as it supported the foundation of the Way of *mononofu* that was eventually incorporated into the later "bushidō"; these two Ways were not completely apart.

The Way of *Tsuwamono*

The term *mononofu* originally referred to weapons but later became to mean warriors. The term *tsuwamono* was developed similarly. *Tsuwamono* is thought to be originated from words like *tsumiha-mono* (metal object), *utsuha-mono* (forged steel bladed object), or *toha-mono* (sharp bladed object), but the theory more popular is that *"to"* of *"toha-mono"* was converted to *"tsu"* and the term *tsuwamono* took root. Also, the term *hei* (literally, a soldier) originally meant weapons. In China, it was said that *"hei* (weapon) is handled by a person; therefore, the person with a weapon can be referred to as *hei.*" It was the same way in Japan; *hei* referred to an object first, but eventually it became to indicate a warrior who used the weapon. It was the same for the term *tsuwamono*; it was a term for a type of weapon and later it was developed to refer to warriors who use the weapon.

If so, *tsuwamono* as a warrior or warriors could possibly become a common term to refer to an ideal form of a warrior just like the term *mononofu*; however, there isn't any evidence that this ancient word was treated like *mononofu*. What was different for *tsuwamono*?

I suppose that this term has a very close association with the term *hei* (a soldier). I can't be certain whether the term *tsuwamono* originated in Japan first before it was associated with the Chinese term *hei* or the Chinese terms were introduced first and *tsuwamono* was an interpretation of *hei*. However, what's certain is that both *hei* and *tsuwamono* were originally the terms to refer to weapons and were evolved to signify warriors or soldiers.

In ancient historical accounts, the term *hei* is often used to refer to soldiers. Nevertheless, this use of *hei* always referred to *ikusa-bito*, or common soldiers, who were on the front line of battle fields and didn't include commander level soldiers. Even though the original meaning of *tsuwamono* and *ikusa-bito* of ancient Japanese language are believed to not distinguish ranks of soldiers, when the term *tsuwamono* was used to refer to soldiers, there was an obvious distinction of ranks; it only referred to common soldiers. This distinction was commonly used by the era of the Yamato Dynasty. And as the time progressed through periods like the Ritsuryo period (mid 7th to 10th centuries C.E.) when social classes were strictly organized, the honorable use of the term *tsuwamono* became less and less common.

Tsuwamono was at the lowest of social strata; the life of *tsuwamono* was nothing but for those who didn't have any opportunity to be in a better life situation. However, in the medieval era, the leaders of *bushi* clans were finding new opportunities outside of their old social tradition by serving the court nobles; those *bushi* were given the social class as military officers. The position of a military officer was not simply given by being a part of a clan; they risked their lives to win the positions as leaders. Therefore, when they served a court noble, they actually wore armor and swords to protect their lord at their side. There wasn't anyone else that the court nobles could trust to protect them other than those *bushi* clans and their men. It was then that court nobles re-acknowledged that *bushi* was the professionals of war affairs.

The term *bushi* is used in the imperial edict *Zoku-Nihon-Shoki* (721 CE) to refer to a cultured person, who learn medicine and various arts that are valued highly in the nation. Similarly, the same edict written in 771 CE indicates that a Prince bestowed gifts on individuals who have above a certain rank, and the gifts varied depending on their ranks. Total of 55 people including a politician, a writer, a musician, a jurist, a mathematician, a doctor, a yin-yang master (*onmyōji*), an astronomer, a historian, a wealthy, an entrepreneur, an artisan, a *bushi* and so forth each received gifts such as yarns or live stocks. In this case, "*bushi*" is used to signify an officer, or a military officer. There was a rebellion of Fujiwara no Nakamaro around the end of the Nara period. In the rebellion, there were two adepts of *Kisha* (archery on horseback): Sakanoue no Karitamaro (father of Sakanoue no Tamuramaro) and Michishima no Shimatari, who were at first low-ranking officials and became and rendered distinguished service as *shōsō* and *shōgen* (secretary and third grade official of the Ritsuryō system). This is an example of an ancient *bushi*; the Way of *bushi* during this era was the Way of a military officer.

There is a poem that is talking about *bushi* in Manyōshū, third book, number 443. This is the only poem in Manyōshū that is using the term "*bushi*."

In the nation where clouds stretch widely in the vast sky, the people called *bushi* guard the gate of the emperor and God, and in the palace, they are loyal servants. They speak to their parents, wives and children that their names given by their ancestors shall prosper for a long time like a beautiful vine.

This poem was written by Ōtomo Sannaka, a member of the Ōtomo clan. Relatedly, there is another *chōka,* or a long verse Japanese poem, in Manyōshū written by a member of Ōtomo clan, Ōtomo no Yakamochi, in eighteenth book, number 4094, titled "Umi Yukaba (literally, "going to the sea")". When Ōtomo Sannaka reads "in the nation where clouds stretch widely in the vast sky, the people called *bushi* guard the gate of the emperor and God, and in the palace, they are loyal servants," his use of "*bushi*" is equivalent to *masurao* in Yokamochi's poem. Further, the term *masurao* also shares the same recognition that "their names inherited from their ancestors shall prosper for a long time;" it is similar to the tradition of fishermen or fish merchants, who passed on their professional knowledge to their children for generations. This ancient reading about *bushi* is not well known. Keichū's *Manyō-daichōki* (a commentary on the Manyōshū) and Moto'ori Norinaga's *Kojiki-den* (a commentary on the *Kojiki*) referred it as *mononofu*, but *Manyōshū-kogi* used the term *masurao*. Either way, the term *bushi* signified the people, who bravely served an ancient traditional militant job, and in the world of Yamato language, *masurao* and *mononofu* are used to refer to the same.

Medieval Bushidō (Bushidō of the Kamakura period)

During the transition period from the ancient to the medieval era, *bushi* were referred to as *"Kyūba-no-shi"* or *"Kyūsen-no-shi"*, or warriors with bow and arrow. In the account *Mutsu Waki* ("Tale of Mutsu"), when Minamoto no Yoritomo left the capital city to Sagami to become the governor of the province, he "enjoyed various kinds of martial techniques" and "hosted many *kyūsen-no-shi* from East as guests." The term *Kyūsen-no-shi* is used to refer to *bushi*.

There is a letter written to Sasaki Sadatsuna from Minamoto no Yoritomo that indicates how medieval bushidō were rooted during the era.

It writes, "for *bushi*, there are codes like those of monks, but there isn't any in writing. Most of the codes are the common sense and are for the purpose of serving a lord. In today's world, it means to protect the nation land of the lord Minamoto no Yoritomo. One should keep the loyalty even after one succeeded in expanding one's wealth, always dedicate one's body and life to the lord, and think that his life is not his own."

The ultimate purpose of *bushi* was to stabilize the public order and to protect the lord and his nation land as public officers. Bushidō of the Kamakura period was formulated as the Way of *tsuwamono*, who served ancient authorities, and the Way of retainers, who served feudal lords, were intermingled.

After the terms "the Way of *Kyūba*" or "the Way of *Kyūsen*" gained a significance to illustrate "the Way of warriors," it was further developed to signify more specific characteristics and rules of an ideal warrior. Taira no Masakado asserted, in his declaration of *Shin-noh,* or the new emperor, which can be conceived as the declaration of independence of the Taira clan, that the

205

Way of Kyūsen was what made him the winner and promised him to become the ruler of the nation. He declared "I was born with talent for martial techniques," "and the bow and arrow techniques have been helping the Dynasty to achieve a long prosperity." He mentions that the martial art of bow and arrow was the key for him to defeat all enemies and conquer the nation. Masakado recognized the Way of *Kyūsen* as the Way of winner; it was the Way of the ruler.

During the Kamakura period, those *bushi*, who reached the summit of the nation hierarchy by following the Way of *Kyūsen*, delved deeper into the Way. This was the point in history when the Way of bushidō was firmly established. Those who followed the Way highly valued the reputation of their names. When they said "if you follow the Way of bow and arrow, whether living or dying, your reputation must be revered," the Way of *Kyūsen* was no longer a mere martial technique. It was conceived as the Way to be a proper *bushi*. As a family precept of Hōjō Shigetoki, "one should be faithful even when social status or wealth is lost and should be loyal and against any temptations to side on stronger. That is what it means to follow the Way." Evidently, the Way was the codes for a proper *bushi*'s behavior. Also a historical epic, *Taiheiki*, mentioned that bushidō grew into a political morality that replaced the traditional way of court nobles.

The Minamoto clan made a breakthrough with their military force in the society of the traditional court nobles. Therefore, their victory of denying the ancient way opened up a new world for the *bushi* class. In contrary, the Taira clan tried to strengthen their status while keeping the old relationship with court nobles. For that reason, the Taira clan was clearly isolated as a usurper of the dynasty, and at the same time, as a betrayer from *bushi* class because of Taira's intention to exalt themselves to a higher authority over *bushi* class. The tragedy depicted in the literature *Heike Monogatari* ("the Tale of Taira Clan") was caused because the Taira clan was at the core of the transition from the ancient traditions to the medieval era.

Some members of the Taira clan accepted it as an honorable solitary; they were Taira no Kiyomori, Taira no Shigehira, Taira no Tomomori, and so forth. However, there were others such as Taira no Koremori and Taira no Tokushi, who couldn't stand strong against the pressure. Even though members of the Taira clan, as illustrated in the *Heike Monogatari,* followed different path ways, they all equally lived through the turning point of the history as the ancient bushidō transforming into new form.

An example of the medieval bushidō can be witnessed in a story of the Battle of Yashima. The Minamoto army was closed in on by the Taira army as the imperial palace was being burnt down, and Taira no Noritsune of the Taira clan, a glorious commander with one of the most powerful army of the clan, discharged an arrow towards Yoshitsune, the general of Minamoto army, as if to set an example of a fine warrior. Satō Saburō, a retainer of Yoshitsune, who rushed in front of his lord to protect him, received the arrow on his left shoulder through under the right arm and fell from his horse. By the time he was carried back to the camp, he was already at death's door.

Yoshitsune asks: "Saburō, what's on your mind?"
Saburō replies under faint breath: "I think this is the end for me."
Yoshitsune: "are there any words that you want to leave in this world?"
Saburō: "I have nothing to regret in this world; however, I repent my dying that I won't be able to see my lord achieve the fame." As a warrior, it is honorable to die with enemy's arrow on the battlefield. Especially, if the story can be told to the future generations about this warrior named Satō Saburō Tsugunobu from the country of Mutsu honorably died for saving the life of his lord at the shore of Yashima in the country of Sanuki, what an honor I can carry to the heaven."
Yoshitsune ordered to reverently take care of Saburō until his last breath.

Modern bushidō and Hagakure bushidō

Nitobe Inazō mentioned in his treatise that "bushidō provides principles for *bushi* to obey and proprieties for people to be educated." For 700 years from the 12th to 19th centuries, bushidō was rooted so firmly as the most highly valued virtue in Japan; however, its principles were not prevailed in writing but conveyed through oral instructions and proverbs that were often used for calligraphy by prominent *bushi* or retainers. Further, these principles for *bushi* were often communicated without words or in writing; they were unsaid laws. For that very reason, bushidō assumed a strong authority over *bushi* and were deeply engraved in people's mind.

Yamato spirit, or Japanese spirit, ultimately evolved to represent the national spirit of this island nation. Cherry blossom is a symbol representing the Yamato spirit and gives a special sentiment commonly shared among its people. Bushidō shows principles and at the same it gives an impelling drive in people's mind. "I knew that it would end so if I acted accordingly, but I was compelled by Yamato spirit." This poem was read by Yoshida Shōin the night before his execution. I ask a question; did the surging wave of the western civilization completely wipe out all the trails of rigorous works of the ancient Japanese? Henry Norman, who conducted research on the Far East, asserted that the only difference between Japan and other autocratic countries in Asia was that in Japan, "the most rigorous, noble and precise laws of virtue that has ever been created in the human history has the dominant power amongst its people."

Development of bushidō was greatly influenced by beliefs of *Shinto*. Shinto, the traditional religious practice unique to Japan, is deeply rooted in people's behavior and philosophy. Originally, it was an animism or shamanism in the ancient times; the object of worship gradually shifted from local to national ancestral Gods, and it was institutionalized by Yamato Dynasty. Shinto was developed as nation's original religion in contrast to Buddhism that was imported from foreign country. Having influences from beliefs of Buddhism and Confucianism, various Shinto sects were established such as Ryōbu Shinto, Ise Shinto, Yoshida Shinto, Suika Shinto, Fukko Shinto and so forth. From the Meiji period, Shinto shrines were placed under nation's management, and state Shinto was formed with Ise-jingū at the top of its hierarchy. However, after the Second World War, the structure was dissolved by the Shinto Directive. The Shinto Directive was a memorandum stipulating the "Abolition of Governmental Sponsorship, Support Perpetuation, Control, and Dissemination of State Shinto (*Kokka Shinto, Jinja Shinto*)" issued by GHQ to the Japanese government in 1945. According to this directive, the structure of Shinto shrines were changed from the state managed entities to religious organizations.

As mentioned above, Shinto doctrine existed in Japan before Buddhism and Confucianism were introduced, but what was the Shinto's doctrine? First doctrine was the veneration of nature. Evolving from this, the people learned that Gods resided in all elements of nature; in other words, Gods existed everywhere. Even today, ceremonies to wish or thank for abundant harvest are held all over Japan in accordance with local traditions that have been passed down for several hundreds of years. The emotion towards the land and nature expressed in those ceremonies are beyond mere materialistic perspective of land where crops were grown and harvested; reverence and appreciation for ancestral Gods and spirits sacredly reside in the land and nature are expressed and prayed for. That is one of the reasons how Japanese people cultivated special sentiments towards the nature of the nation.

The second doctrine is the ancestor worship. Christianity, Buddhism and Islam are all monotheism for Jesus, Buddha, and Allah, respectively. There is a belief in Japan that people are to become part of Gods after death; all deceased parents, grandparents, great-grandparents, and several generations antecedent are worshiped as Gods. People send prayers to their ancestral Gods for good harvests and safety and health of family. Especially in Okinawa, the ancestor worship, or Ryukyu Shinto, is the main religion. Because the ancestor worship is rooted so firmly, other religions aren't prevailed widely. Japanese

Shinto and Ryukyu Shinto are both polytheism, and it's an important distinction from other monotheistic religions such as Christianity and Islam.

The third doctrine is the patriotism and loyalty. The modern bushidō is also known as *Hagakure* bushidō. Yamamoto Tsunetomo's collection of his prose "Hagakure" radically describes his ultimate theory about *bushi*'s commitment for death. His words, "bushidō is to find the moment for death," became one of the famous expression for bushidō. At the end of the same paragraph, it writes "if by setting one's heart right every morning and evening, one is able to live as though his body were already dead, he gains freedom in the Way. His whole life will be without blame, and he will succeed in his calling." In other words, you will live on safely all your life if you are always prepared for death; therefore, it is basically the same principle described in the "Budō Shoshin-shū" written by Daidōji Yūzan (1639-1730).

For instance, it writes, "bushidō is to find the moment for death," and it continues, "when it comes to decision of life or death, there is only the quick choice of death. It is not particularly difficult. Be determined and advance. To say that dying without reaching one's aim is to die a dog's death is the frivolous way of sophisticates." If you must choose to live or die, choose to die, so live on prepared. It is simple as that; it's not so complicated. To calculate and ponder upon what makes your plan succeeded or to say you may die in vain if you fail is the frivolous bushidō from the city side.

The treatise Gorin-no-sho by Miyamoto Musashi from the approximate period writes, "the way of *bushi* is to learn how to live while having willingness to die at any moment," and it continues to mention that the same can be said for the monks, women or farmers in the sense that one should recognize his/her social duty and disgrace and momentously make up one's mind to accept death. And as I mentioned earlier, making accomplishments in the battles and establishing one's status is "the Way of a *bushi* who aim to master the art of war." To be always prepared to sacrifice one's life for his lord was the virtue of *bushi* until the end of the medieval era. The ultimate purpose was to win in the battles and advance in life, and achieving the death itself was not the main purpose. However, Tsunetomo, who was being reminded of his ambition every time he dreamt of being cut down or performing *hara-kiri,* often focused on death itself and fantasized ideal ways of death. As he writes, "even when you are defeated, be determined to keep facing your dead body to the opponent." It can be interpreted as a tenacity for winning battles in any mean possible, but it was rather about how to express his ambition by death. He was expressing a virtue of death, and the death was the ultimate goal.

Actually, this particular principle of Hagakure bushidō was utilized for militarism during the war time after the Meiji period. It was interpreted that "a *bushi* has the mind that can willingly transcend his own life as it is the life of the lord." By promulgating this slogan, the emperor was symbolized as the lord of the nation and the people of the nation as his children; the children must keep their loyalty by sacrificing their lives to the lord, the emperor, or the nation of Japan. Hagakure principles were expelled after the loss in the war. A writer Mishima Yukio reintroduced the ideas of Hagakure to the public and depicted his interpretations that were applicable in his time; however, because Mishima acted exactly according to his words by strictly following the principles of Hagakure, his death, again, made Hagakure to be condemned from public.

There are elements that structured the modern bushidō such as justice, bravery, loyalty, honor, hara-kiri, katana, and so forth, but in this section, I will talk about hara-kiri and katana.

Harakiri/Seppuku

What does *"hara"* mean? *Hara-kiri* (ritual suicide) and *katakiuchi* (revenge) are two social systems that are already written in detail by many foreign writers. How absurd to slice one's stomach by himself. One may be disgusted by the idea, much more so to those from foreign culture. *Hara-kiri* was a part of legal system, and it was a ritual. *Hara-kiri,* which was started in the medieval era, was a way for *bushi* to repent for a crime, to make an apology for his past, to be discharged from dishonor, to save a friend or to attest one's integrity.

After bowing once more, Zenzaburō unclothed his *hakama,* or a divided skirt, made of hemp cloth down to his *obi* belt to expose his upper body. As conventionally done, he carefully tacked the sleeves of undressed clothes under his knees so that he will not fall backwards. Well trained warriors of Japan was not to fall forward when facing a death.

Zenzaburō in his own timing picked up with his steady hands a short sword that was placed in front of him. He then took a moment to gaze at the sword as if he adored it. And he looked as if he was taking the time to concentrate before the end of his life.

Then, Zenzaburō deeply stabbed the left side of his lower stomach with the sword, slowly sliced to the right, and as the sword turned, he sliced slightly upwards. During this act filled with unimaginable agony, he didn't even move a muscle on his face. As he pulled out the sword and leaned forward, he exposed back of his neck. That was the first instant that his face was filled with pain, but with no sound. In that moment, a *kaisyaku* (an individual who served to behead after *hara-kiri* is done), who was quietly sitting next to Zenzaburō and observing every details of his movements, stood up and paused in a position to strike down with a sword. Next instant, a noise that cut through the heavy ambient sounded, and the body fell to the ground. With a slice of a sword, the head was removed from its body.

Silence prevailed the place and not a person saying a word, and the only sound there was the blood gushing out of the body that is now a chunk of meat with no soul. A great man of bravery and honesty has now mercilessly turned into a dead body. It was a horrifying view. The *kaisyaku* bowed once and wiped his blood-dripping sword with white paper, then he withdrew from the spot. The short sword, which was used for *harakiri*, was solemnly carried out from the site as an evidence of the execution.

After then, two coroner of Mikado government stood up and walked up to where the coroner of foreign country sat and said that Taki Zenzaburō's punishment was executed without hindrance. The ritual was then over, and we left the temple.

Here is another story about hara-kiri. Sakon and Naiki, brothers with twenty four years and seventeen years of age respectively, tried to assassinate Tokugawa Ieyasu to avenge their father's death. But regretfully, they were captured before they could reach the encampment of Ieyasu. Ieyasu admired the bravery of the young assassins and ordered to give an honorable death for them. The sentence was ordered to include all male of the family, which meant that their eight-year-old Hachimaro was to follow the brothers. The three were then taken to the temple for the execution. A doctor saw the execution and he left all the details in his diary. It writes as follows.

"As brothers took a seat before the execution, Sakon said to his youngest brother, 'Hachimaro, you go first. We will make sure that you will not fail to slice your stomach.' Hachimaro answered, 'I have never seen a man slicing his stomach. I'd like to see my brothers first and follow afterwards.' The two brothers smiled with tears in their eyes and said, 'how admirable, you are truly the son of our father.' Then the two older brothers moved Hachimaro in between them. Sakon stabbed the sword sword into his left side stomach and said, 'look carefully, Hachimaro, do you understand? Don't dig too deep. Don't fall backwards. Fall forward and don't break your posture.'

Naiki also said as his sword was inserted to his stomach. 'Keep your eyes somewhat open, otherwise you will look like a dead woman. Even when you doubt your strength to keep your posture straight and complete it, gather yourself to pull it up.' Hachimaro looked at both brothers alternatingly. He then quietly exposed his upper body and composedly executed himself accordingly with the teachings from his brothers."

Katana/Sword

Why is *katana* sword revered as the soul of *bushi*? Katana is the symbol of loyalty and honor. Also, bushidō made katana the symbol of power and bravery. Children of *bushi* families learned to swing katana at very young age. At the age of five, those children are dressed in a formal clothing and made to stand on a *go* checkerboard. That is when their toy swords were replaced by a real sword to be worn at their sides, and they were formally permitted to be a *bushi*, a very special day for the children.

After this inaugural ceremony is successfully conducted, the child would never be seen outside of his house without wearing the symbol of *bushi*, katana. However, a wooden sword coated with silver was carried instead of a real sword. Soon the child would wear a dull but a real sword. With the joy of wearing a real sword, the child would rush out of his house and try out the new sword on trees and stones. The child would eventually reach the age for the *genpuku* ceremony, or the ceremony of coming of age, and be allowed to be independent. He then would feel honored to wear such a keen weapon that can be used at any situation. Wearing a dangerous weapon would make him have pride and responsibility.

As it's said that "katana is not worn without profound determination," katana is the symbol of the loyalty and honor that are held deeply in *bushi*'s mind. Two katana were always worn at his side: long and short swords. At home, swords were placed at a study or a guest room where easily be visible and next to pillow within hands reach at night. Katana was adored as the owner's friend, and at some shrines and temples or prestigious families, some katana worthy of veneration were safely preserved. Even for a common short sword was regarded with deference. Therefore, any disrespect toward a sword meant an insult to its owner. Katana, that was the weapon to take opponent's life on battle fields, was also the instrument to look after its owner's life in hara-kiri ritual; katana was also a demon that takes lives even its owner's.

Forging of katana was an important ceremonial act. Katana makers were not merely blacksmiths but they were artisan who materialize God's intention. And even their workplace was a sacred place. They worshiped Gods and performed purification ceremony every day before work. Namely, "he poured all his energy to cast wrought iron." He beat the iron with a forging hammer, quenched it, and sharpened it on a whetstone. Those were all important ceremonial acts. It may be the noble spirit of the sword artisan, which give mysterious fascination and awe to Japanese swords.

The term "bushidō" was popularized in the Meiji period, but it doesn't mean bushidō was born in the period. Principles of bushidō was handed down since the ancient times until the modern time, and the name has been changing throughout the history like "the Way of Mononofu," "the Way of Masurao," "the Way of Takeo," "the Way of Tsuwamono," "the Way of Kyūsen," "the Way of Kyūba," "Budō," "Shidō," and "Bushidō." Despite the name change, the fundamental philosophy has been unchanged. Similarly, the term "karate" was first used in 1920s' but it doesn't mean that karate was founded in 1920s'; the name was changed from *tiy*, karate (唐手), to karate (空手). Karate was used in the ancient time during the *gusuku* period through medieval and the modern times. In the Ryukyu kingdom, *bushi* was referred variously like *touyunmya, toyumya, sedakako, ikusaseji, tatamikiyo, sejitaka, aji, bushigah, bushi, wakatukasa, yunu-nusu, hakara, gesu*, and so forth.

Bushidō was associated with nationalism that resulted with *son'noh-joh'i* ideology (advocating reverence for emperor and expulsion of foreigners). When *son'noh-joh'i* was exalted amongst the people in Japan in order to protect the nation from the Western powers that were sending troops to all over the world, placing colonies in South Eastern Asia, and trying to conquer China, Yoshida Shōin concertedly exhorted the spirit of bushidō. *Son'noh-joh'i* principle was then associated with imperialistic ideals and converted into the national ideology that prioritized the militaristic power.

Author: Koei Nohara （野原耕栄）Hanshi 9th Dan

1948	Born in Miyakojima Okinawa Japan
1973	B/A of Law Ryukyu University, Okinawa
1973-2008	Okinawa Prefectural Government Officer
2009~2014	PhD/Doctor of Sports Anthropology, Waseda University Tokyo
2008	Karate Hanshi 9th Dan

President Okinawa Karatedo Shorinryu Ryukyukan Karate Kobudo Federation

President All Ryukyus Full Contact Karate Association

President NPO Uchinahdiy Association

Translator: Wesley Ueunten
Professor of San Francisco State University
Wesley Ueunten was born and raised in Hawai'i and now teaches Asian American Studies at San Francisco State University. His grandparents on both sides of his family immigrated to Hawai'i from Okinawa. Because of his interest in his roots, he has worked and studied in Okinawa and Japan for many years. From 2014-2017 he was the president of the San Francisco Okinawa Kenjinkai.

Translator: Naoki Namihira
Translator/Interpreter
Born and raised in Okinawa, Naoki Namihira traveled and lived in America and Latin America for a decade. He is currently a translator/interpreter based in Okinawa, where he enjoys reading, cooking, eating, drinking, playing cello, building furniture, and running.

Copy editor: Susanne Beal
Former University of Chicago Press staff
Susanne is a former editor who worked at the University of Chicago Press. Her mother hails from Okinawa, and Susanne has visited many times. She loves Okinawan food, although being a vegetarian makes it very challenging. She lives near Chicago with her husband and son.